Where to Stay

In Northern Ireland

Hotels, Guesthouses, Bed & Breakfast
Self-Catering Accommodation
Hostels, Camping & Caravan Parks

Northern Ireland
Tourist Board

If you have any comments on listed establishments please write to: Director of Visitor & Industry Services, Northern Ireland Tourist Board, 59 North Street, Belfast BT1 1NB.

Pour tout commentaire relatif aux établissements répertoriés, écrire à: Director of Visitor & Industry Services, Northern Ireland Tourist Board, 59 North Street, Belfast BT1 1NB.

Wenn Sie Anmerkungen zu den aufgeführten Häusern haben, schreiben Sie bitte an: Director of Visitor & Industry Services, Northern Ireland Tourist Board, 59 North Street, Belfast BT1 1NB.

ISBN 0 946871 61 2

Printed by The Universities Press (Belfast) Ltd. 12m/11/93

1994

Stay Where to In Northern Ireland

CONTENTS

'Welcome to Northern Ireland'

Foreword by
Hugh O'Neill
Chairman, Northern Ireland Tourist Board.

The success of any trip relies to a large extent on the quality of the accommodation you have chosen. *Where to Stay in Northern Ireland 1994* is packed with the best. Budget or top-flight, all hotels, guesthouses, B&Bs, self-catering establishments and hostels listed here are carefully and regularly inspected by the Northern Ireland Tourist Board to ensure that all our visitors will be comfortable and enjoy their stay with us.

Thanks to the demands of a competitive industry, the standard of facilities and services is improving year by year and visitors can expect quality accommodation in all the price ranges available.

Many of our tourist information centres are now part of the GULLIVER network - a computerised system which can book a room for you immediately at any one of over 270 establishments throughout Northern Ireland.

If you have any comment, queries or complaints, please write to us at the Board. It will assist us to maintain the high standards and good value which you deserve. We want you to come back.

Enjoy your holiday!

Hugh O'Neill

How to use the guide

The wide range, good quality and convenient location of accommodation for visitors to Northern Ireland is reflected in this guide. Prices and details of facilities are given for over 1,000 places to stay, in four main sections:

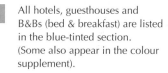

All hotels, guesthouses and B&Bs (bed & breakfast) are listed in the blue-tinted section. (Some also appear in the colour supplement).

Hostels - youth hostels, independent hostels and other low-cost accommodation (grey pages).

Self-catering accommodation (red pages).

Camping and caravan parks (green).

Hotels, guesthouses, B&Bs, hostels and self-catering accommodation are inspected regularly by the Northern Ireland Tourist Board (NITB) and meet minimum standards. Hotels are classified by a star system and guesthouses are graded - explained on page 8. The section on camping and caravan parks, which are not subject to NITB inspection, has been compiled from information supplied by the operators.

PRICES
Always confirm prices when you book. Accommodation rates in the main listings are the *maximum* for 1994 and include VAT. There may be seasonal reductions or lower-priced rooms. Many places offer special rates for weekend or midweek guests and for families. The prices given for dinner relate to a typical 3-course meal with starter, main course, dessert, VAT and service. High tea is usually a lighter meal.

Prices in the colour supplement are the *lowest* room rates per person sharing, plus breakfast. Entries in this supplement have been placed by proprietors who wish to highlight their establishments.

ACCESS FOR WHEELCHAIR USERS
If you use a wheelchair or have limited mobility, look for entries with one of the new, national 'accessible' symbols indicating those hotels, guesthouses and B&Bs where the standard of access is suitable for wheelchair users:

accessible to a wheelchair user travelling independently.

accessible to a wheelchair user travelling with assistance.

accessible to a person with limited mobility, but able to walk a few paces and up to a maximum of 3 steps.

The same information for self-catering accommodation will not be available until next year. In the meantime self-catering units which may be suitable for wheelchair users are indicated - see page 137. However, check essential details with the proprietor before you book the accommodation.

WALKING THE ULSTER WAY? 𝕜
Convenient places to stay, including campsites, are shown (𝕜). In areas where accommodation is less plentiful addresses may be off-route - check before you set off, and plan your schedule to take account of the availability of overnight accommodation.

Utilisation du guide

Ce guide reflète la variété et la qualité des possibilités d'hébergement proposées aux visiteurs en Irlande du Nord, ainsi que leur emplacement pratique. Il donne le prix et les détails des installations disponibles dans plus de 1 000 établissements en les divisant en quatre sections :

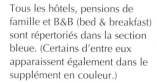

Tous les hôtels, pensions de famille et B&B (bed & breakfast) sont répertoriés dans la section bleue. (Certains d'entre eux apparaissent également dans le supplément en couleur.)

Auberges - auberges de jeunesse, auberges indépendantes et autres possibilités d'hébergement à moindre coût (pages grises).

Location de logements équipés (pages rouges)

Terrains de camping et de caravanes (pages vertes).

Les hôtels, pensions de famille, B&B et locations sont inspectés régulièrement par le Northern Ireland Tourist Board (NITB) et doivent se conformer à des normes minimum. Les hôtels sont classés selon un système d'étoiles et les pensions de famille reçoivent une classification - comme indiqué à la page 8. La section sur les terrains de camping et de caravanes, qui ne sont pas inspectés par le NITB, a été compilée à partir des informations fournies par leurs propriétaires.

PRIX
Demandez toujours confirmation du prix à la réservation. Les prix cités dans les listes représentent les tarifs *maximum* pour 1994 et comprennent la TVA. Les établissements pratiquent parfois des réductions saisonnières ou possèdent des chambres moins chères. De nombreux établissements proposent un tarif spécial pour les séjours individuels ou familiaux le week-end ou en milieu de

semaine. Les prix indiqués pour le dîner comprennent généralement un repas typique de trois plats avec hors-d'oeuvre, plat de résistance et dessert, ainsi que le service et la TVA. Le 'high tea' est généralement un repas plus léger.

Les prix dans le supplément en couleur représentent le tarif *minimum* de la chambre par personne, plus le petit-déjeuner. Les entrées figurant dans ce supplément ont été demandées par les propriétaires qui souhaitent attirer l'attention sur leur établissement.

ACCÈS POUR FAUTEUILS ROULANTS
Si vous utilisez un fauteuil roulant, ou si vous ne disposez que d'une mobilité limitée, recherchez les entrées qui comprennent les nouveaux symboles nationaux 'accessible'. Ils indiquent les hôtels, les pensions de famille et les B&B accessibles en fauteuil roulant :

Accessible aux personnes non accompagnées qui utilisent un fauteuil roulant.

Accessible aux personnes accompagnées qui utilisent un fauteuil roulant.

Accessible aux personnes ayant une mobilité limitée, mais qui sont en mesure de faire quelques pas et de monter jusqu'à trois marches.

Ces informations ne seront pas disponibles avant l'an prochain pour les locations de logements équipés. Entre temps, les locations permettant l'usage d'un fauteuil roulant sont signalées - voir la page 137. Il est toutefois nécessaire de vérifier les détails avec le propriétaire avant de réserver la location.

RANDONNÉES SUR
LE SENTIER ULSTER WAY
Ce guide vous indique (🚶) des endroits pratiques où vous pourrez vous arrêter en chemin, y compris des terrains de camping. Dans les espaces où les possibilités d'hébergement sont plus limitées, il se peut que les établissements spécifiés ne se trouvent pas directement sur le chemin. Vérifiez avant de partir et planifiez vos étapes en fonction des possibilités d'hébergement.

Dieser Führer spiegelt die große Auswahl, die gehobene Qualität und günstige Lage der Unterkünfte für Besucher von Nordirland wider. Er enthält Preise und Angaben über die Einrichtungen von über 1000 Unterkünften in vier Abschnitten:

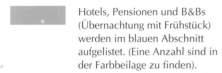 Hotels, Pensionen und B&Bs (Übernachtung mit Frühstück) werden im blauen Abschnitt aufgelistet. (Eine Anzahl sind in der Farbbeilage zu finden).

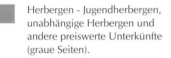 Herbergen - Jugendherbergen, unabhängige Herbergen und andere preiswerte Unterkünfte (graue Seiten).

 Unterkunft für Selbstversorger (rote Seiten).

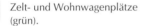 Zelt- und Wohnwagenplätze (grün).

Hotels, Pensionen, B&Bs, Herbergen und Unterkünfte für Selbstversorger werden regelmäßig vom Northern Ireland Tourist Board (NITB) inspiziert und entsprechen dessen Mindestanforderungen. Die Klasse der Hotels wird mit Sternen angegeben und Pensionen werden eingestuft - siehe Seite 8. Der Abschnitt über Zelt- und Wohnwagenplätze - diese werden nicht vom NITB inspiziert - wurde anhand der Angaben zusammengestellt, die von den Betrieben zur Verfügung gestellt wurden.

PRIX

Lassen Sie sich die Preise stets bei der Buchung bestätigen. Die Unterkunftspreise der aufgeführten Betriebe stellen die *Höchstpreise* für 1994 dar und gelten inklusive Mehrwertsteuer. Es werden unter Umständen saisonbedingte Preisermäßigungen oder verbilligte Zimmer angeboten. Zahlreiche Betriebe bieten Gästen während des Wochenendes oder der Woche Sonderangebote. Die Preise für das Abendessen

gelten für eine Mahlzeit mit drei Gängen mit einer Vorspeise, einem Hauptgericht und einer Nachspeise inklusive Mehrwertsteuer und Bedienung. 'High tea' ist gewöhnlich ein leichtere Mahlzeit.

Die Preise in der Farbbeilage stellen die *tiefsten* Zimmerpreise pro Person für zwei Personen, die ein Zimmer teilen, plus Frühstück dar. Eintragungen in diesem Abschnitt werden von Betrieben gemacht, die besonders auf sich aufmerksam machen möchten.

ZUGÄNGLICHKEIT FÜR ROLLSTUHLBENUTZER

Falls Sie einen Rollstuhl benutzen oder gehbehindert sind, halten Sie Ausschau nach Eintragungen mit einem der neuen, landesweiten 'Zugänglichkeits'-Symbole, die Hotels, Pensionen und B&Bs kennzeichnen, die für Rollstuhlbenutzer zugänglich sind.

& Zugänglich für Rollstuhlbenutzer ohne Begleitung.

& Zugänglich für Rollstuhlbenutzer mit Begleitung.

& Zugänglich für gehbehinderte Personen, die ein paar Schritte gehen und bis zu drei Stufen hochsteigen können.

Zweckdienliche Information steht nächstes Jahr auch für Unterkünfte für Selbstversorger zur Verfügung. In der Zwischenzeit wird auf Unterkünfte für Selbstversorger, die für Rollstuhlbenutzer zugänglich sind, besonders hingewiesen - siehe Seite 137. Lassen Sie sich sachdienliche Angaben jedoch vor dem Buchen vom Besitzer bestätigen.

UNTERWEGS ENTLANG DEM ULSTER WAY! &

Günstig gelegene Unterkünfte, einschließlich Zeltplätze, werden aufgeführt (&). In Gegenden, wo das Angebot beschränkt ist, werden unter Umständen Adressen abseits der Route angegeben - vergewissern Sie sich daher vor dem Aufbruch und planen Sie Ihr Programm je nach Verfügbarkeit von Übernachtungsmöglichkeiten.

Types of accommodation

The Northern Ireland Tourist Board has a statutory duty to inspect all accommodation units appearing in this guide. This ensures that they meet the minimum standards which apply to their category. The categories are hotels, guesthouses, bed & breakfast establishments, self-catering establishments and hostels.

Hotels are classified by a star system

Four stars **

Large hotels with high standards of comfort and service, in well appointed premises, run by a professional team. All bedrooms have a private bathroom, and some also have a private lounge. Food and beverage services meet exacting standards and there is good room service.

Three stars *

Hotels offering good facilities and a wide range of services in comfortable surroundings. Food, wines and refreshments are available during the day and all bedrooms have ensuite facilities.

Two stars **

Hotels offering good facilities with a satisfactory standard of accommodation, food and services. The majority of bedrooms have ensuite facilities.

One star *

Hotels with acceptable standards of accommodation and food. Some bedrooms have ensuite facilities.

Hotels which did not satisfy the criteria of the classification scheme at the time of going to press are listed on page 131. The list includes hotels which, at the time of inspection, did not meet the requirements of the particular star rating for which they had applied.

Guesthouses are divided into grades A and B

Grade (A)

Comfortable establishments offering a range of facilities, including lounge and dining room for the exclusive use of guests. A choice of main course for evening meal is usually available. Washbasins are provided in all bedrooms and many have private bathrooms.

Grade (B)

Well furnished houses offering comfortable accommodation with a satisfactory standard of food and service. Most bedrooms have washbasins and some have ensuite facilities.

Some guesthouses, indicated by (U) after the name, are ones which have not been in operation long enough for their grading to be assessed, or they are establishments where the grading is being reviewed.

Bed & breakfast establishments

This category covers a variety of houses in both town and country areas, ranging from large period residences to modern bungalows. Evening meals are available in many of them.

Self-catering establishments

Self-catering establishments listed in this guide offer comfortable accommodation and catering facilities and are professionally managed.

Hostels

Hostels, which include youth hostels and boarding schools, provide clean, simple accommodation at a budget price.

Accommodation plus ... leisure facilities

Hotels with comprehensive leisure facilities

Bayview Hotel, Portballintrae
indoor pool, sauna, solarium, tennis.

Bohill Hotel & Country Club, Coleraine
gym, indoor pool, jacuzzi, sauna, steam room, putting green.

Burrendale Hotel, Newcastle
gym, indoor pool, jacuzzi, sauna, steam room, sunbeds, hair/beauty salon.

Culloden Hotel, Belfast
gym, indoor pool, jacuzzi, steam room, squash, sunbeds, tennis, hair/beauty salon.

Dunadry Inn, Dunadry
gym, indoor pool, jacuzzi, sauna, steam room, sunbed, croquet lawn.

Glenavon House Hotel, Cookstown
indoor pool, jacuzzi, fitness suite, games room, beauty salon, horse riding.

La Mon House Hotel, Belfast
gym, jacuzzi, indoor pool, sauna, sunbeds, hair salon, horse riding.

Slieve Donard Hotel, Newcastle
gym, indoor pool, jacuzzi, tennis, steam room, sunbeds, putting green.

Other places with leisure facilities

Belfast and area

Malone Lodge Hotel, Belfast
sauna.

Queen's University, Belfast
indoor pool, squash, tennis, gym.

Stranmillis College, Belfast
gym, tennis.

County Antrim

Auberge de Seneirl, Bushmills
sauna, indoor pool.

Ballygally Castle Hotel, Ballygalley
tennis, putting green.

Ben Neagh House, Crumlin
tennis.

Chimney Corner Hotel, Newtownabbey
sauna, golf, gym, tennis.

Country House Hotel, Kells
sauna, games room, indoor pool.

Eglinton Hotel, Portrush
sauna.

Galgorm Manor, Ballymena
tennis, pony trekking, sauna.

Highways Hotel, Larne
tennis.

Maddybenny Farm, Portrush
horse riding, show jumping arena.

Magherabuoy House Hotel, Portrush
sauna.

Marathon House, Carrickfergus
tennis.

Newmills, Carrickfergus
sauna.

Seacon Hall, Ballymoney
tennis.

Tullyglass House Hotel, Ballymena
putting green.

University of Ulster, Newtownabbey
gym, indoor pool, sauna, tennis.

West Strand, Portrush
sauna.

County Armagh

Bannview Squash Club, Portadown
squash, sauna.

Silverwood Hotel, Craigavon
driving range.

County Down

Ardshane Country House, Holywood
croquet lawn.

Barnageeha, Killinchy
tennis.

Beechill, Newtownards
outdoor pool.

Accommodation plus ... leisure facilities

The Cottage, Bryansford
tennis, putting green.

Enniskeen Hotel, Newcastle
tennis.

Ernsdale, Newtownards
sauna.

Glassdrumman Lodge, Annalong
tennis.

Glen House, Crawfordsburn
sauna.

O'Hara's Royal Hotel, Bangor
sauna, solarium.

Pear Tree Farm, Ballynahinch
sauna.

Sandeel Lodge, Groomsport
indoor pool, sun lounge.

Tullynacrew, Portaferry
riding school, fishing.

County Fermanagh

Jamestown House, Ballinamallard
tennis.

Lough Melvin Holiday Centre, Garrison
water-based activities.

Manor House Hotel, Killadeas, Enniskillen
marina, tennis.

Mullynaval Lodge, Kesh
sauna, snooker room.

Share Centre, Lisnaskea
tennis, football, water-based activities.

Wil-mer Lodge, Lisbellaw
spabath, jacuzzi.

County Londonderry

Beech Hill Country House Hotel, Londonderry
tennis.

Bohill Hotel, Coleraine
indoor pool, sauna, gym, putting green.

Broomhill House Hotel, Londonderry
sauna.

Bushtown House Country Hotel, Coleraine
sauna, indoor pool, fitness room.

Drenagh, Limavady
tennis.

Edgewater Hotel, Portstewart
sauna, jacuzzi, sunbeds.

Everglades Hotel, Londonderry
sauna.

Greenhill House, Coleraine
tennis.

Haven, Londonderry
sauna.

Magee College, Londonderry
tennis.

Oregon, Portstewart
sauna.

Raspberry Hill Health Farm, Londonderry
sauna, indoor pool, tennis.

Tullyverry House, Eglinton
tennis.

University of Ulster, Coleraine
sauna, squash, tennis.

Waterfoot Hotel, Londonderry
sauna.

Wild Geese Centre, Garvagh
adventure sports.

County Tyrone

Blessingbourne, Fivemiletown
tennis.

Grange Hotel, Dungannon
tennis.

Inn on the Park, Dungannon
tennis.

Silverbirch Hotel, Omagh
mini gym, sauna, sunbed.

Many establishments have a games room
– please look for ♣ in the main listings.

Accommodation plus...conference facilities

Northern Ireland is increasingly popular as a conference venue. The hotels, guesthouses and other centres mentioned below offer a range of conference facilities and they all have at least 25 bedrooms. In addition, many smaller establishments can host non-residential conferences. These are indicated in the main listings by the conference symbol ☎. Please contact the establishments direct for full details.

Belfast and area

Beechlawn Hotel, Dunmurry
Culloden Hotel, Holywood
Europa Hotel, Belfast
Glenavna House Hotel, Newtownabbey
La Mon House Hotel, Comber
Malone Lodge, Belfast
Park Avenue Hotel, Belfast
Plaza Hotel, Belfast
Queen's Elms, Queen's University, Belfast
Queen's University Common Room, Belfast
Renshaw's Hotel, Belfast
Stormont Hotel, Belfast
Stranmillis College, Belfast
Wellington Park Hotel, Belfast
Ulster People's College, Belfast
University of Ulster, Jordanstown

County Antrim

Adair Arms Hotel, Ballymena
Ballygally Castle Hotel, Ballygalley
Beach House Hotel, Portballintrae
Castle Erin Guesthouse, Portrush
Chimney Corner Hotel, Newtownabbey
Country House Hotel, Ballymena
Dunadry Inn, Dunadry
Eglinton Hotel, Portrush
Galgorm Manor, Ballymena
Magherabuoy House Hotel, Portrush
Marine Hotel, Ballycastle
Novotel, Belfast International Airport

County Armagh

Carngrove Hotel, Portadown
Seagoe Hotel, Portadown
Silverwood Hotel, Craigavon

County Down

Burrendale Hotel, Newcastle
Castlewellan Christian Conference Centre, Castlewellan
Glenada House, Newcastle
Kilmorey Arms Hotel, Kilkeel
Mourne Country Hotel, Newry
O'Hara's Royal Hotel, Bangor
Old Inn, Crawfordsburn
Slieve Donard Hotel, Newcastle
Strangford Arms Hotel, Newtownards
Tedworth Hotel, Bangor
White Gables Hotel, Hillsborough
Winston Hotel, Bangor

County Fermanagh

Killyhevlin Hotel, Enniskillen *(see also self-catering section)*
Fort Lodge Hotel, Enniskillen

County Londonderry

Bohill Hotel and Country Club, Coleraine
Broomhill House Hotel, Londonderry
Bushtown House Country Hotel, Coleraine
Edgewater Hotel, Portstewart
Everglades Hotel, Londonderry
Gorteen House Hotel, Limavady
Magee College, Londonderry
University of Ulster, Coleraine
Waterfoot Hotel, Londonderry
White Horse Hotel, Londonderry
Wild Geese Centre, Omagh

County Tyrone

Benburb Centre, Benburb
Fir Trees Lodge Hotel, Strabane
Glenavon House Hotel, Cookstown
Silverbirch Hotel, Omagh

Special mentions - from the guidebooks

Northern Ireland hotels and guesthouses are winning more and more recognition in well known guides to tourist accommodation. Here is a list of places to stay which have been recommended in the most recent editions of the following well known guides: *Ackerman, Bridgestone Irish Food Guide, Egon Ronay, Good Food Guide, Good Hotel Guide* and *Michelin.*

Hotels and guesthouses which have been commended for culinary excellence in one or more of these guides are marked [†]. Hotels and guesthouses which have attained 'A Taste of Ulster' membership are also indicated [†].

Belfast and area

	page
Ash-Rowan Guesthouse Michelin	19
The Cottage Michelin	25
Culloden Hotel [†] Ackerman, Egon Ronay, Michelin, 'A Taste of Ulster' member	17
Dukes Hotel [†] Ackerman, Egon Ronay, 'A Taste of Ulster' member	17
La Mon House Hotel Egon Ronay	19
Malone Guesthouse Michelin	21
Plaza Hotel Egon Ronay, Michelin	19
Somerton Guesthouse Michelin	21
Stormont Hotel [†] Michelin, 'A Taste of Ulster' member	17

	page
Wellington Park Hotel Egon Ronay	17

County Antrim

	page
Adair Arms, Ballymena Michelin	32
Auberge de Seneirl [†]*, Bushmills* Bridgestone, Good Food Guide, Good Hotel Guide	36
Bayview Hotel, Portballintrae Egon Ronay, Michelin	50
The Beeches Guesthouse [†]*, Antrim* 'A Taste of Ulster' member	29
Bushmills Inn [†]*, Bushmills* Egon Ronay, Michelin, 'A Taste of Ulster' member	36
Causeway Hotel, Giant's Causeway Michelin	44
Country House Hotel, Ballymena Michelin	32
Derrin House, Larne Michelin	47
Dunadry Inn [†]*, Dunadry* Ackerman, Egon Ronay, Good Hotel Guide, Michelin	44
Londonderry Arms [†]*, Carnlough* 'A Taste of Ulster' member	37
Magherabuoy House Hotel [†]*, Portrush* Michelin, 'A Taste of Ulster' member	51
Magheramorne House Hotel, Larne Egon Ronay	47
Templeton Hotel [†]*, Templepatrick* Egon Ronay, Michelin, 'A Taste of Ulster' member	58
White Gables Country House [†]*,* *Portballintrae* 'A Taste of Ulster' member	50

Special mentions - from the guidebooks

County Down

	page
Burrendale Hotel [†], Newcastle Michelin, 'A Taste of Ulster' member	82
Glassdrumman Lodge [†], Annalong Good Hotel Guide, Michelin	65
Greenacres [†], Newtownards 'A Taste of Ulster' member	87
O'Hara's Royal Hotel [†], Bangor 'A Taste of Ulster' member	68
Old Inn [†], Crawfordsburn Ackerman, Egon Ronay, Michelin	74
The Old Schoolhouse [†], Comber 'A Taste of Ulster' member	74
Portaferry Hotel [†], Portaferry Ackerman, Bridgestone, Michelin, 'A Taste of Ulster' member	89
Strangford Arms Hotel, Newtownards Egon Ronay, Michelin	87
White Gables Hotel [†], Hillsborough Michelin, 'A Taste of Ulster' member	77
Wyncrest Guesthouse [†], Kilkeel 'A Taste of Ulster' member	80

County Fermanagh

	page
Jamestown House [†], Ballinamallard 'A Taste of Ulster' member	91
Killyhevlin Hotel, Enniskillen Michelin	92
Mahon's Hotel, Irvinestown Michelin	97
Tullyhona House [†], Florencecourt 'A Taste of Ulster' member	93

County Londonderry

	page
Beech Hill House [†], Londonderry Bridgestone, Good Food Guide, Good Hotel Guide, 'A Taste of Ulster' member	113
Blackheath House [†], Coleraine Ackerman, Bridgestone, Egon Ronay, Good Food Guide, Good Hotel Guide, Michelin, 'A Taste of Ulster' member	107
Camus House, Coleraine Michelin	107
Edgewater Hotel, Portstewart Michelin	117
Everglades Hotel [†], Londonderry Egon Ronay, Michelin, 'A Taste of Ulster' member	113
Greenhill House [†], Coleraine Michelin, 'A Taste of Ulster' member	107
Maritima House, Castlerock Michelin	106
Waterfoot Hotel [†], Londonderry Michelin, 'A Taste of Ulster' member	113
White Horse Hotel, Londonderry Michelin	113

County Tyrone

	page
Fir Trees Lodge Hotel, Strabane Michelin	129
Grange Lodge [†], Dungannon 'A Taste of Ulster' member	123
Greenmount Lodge [†], Omagh 'A Taste of Ulster' member	127
Greenvale Hotel [†], Cookstown 'A Taste of Ulster' member	120
Inn on The Park [†], Dungannon 'A Taste of Ulster' member	123

How to get to Northern Ireland - by air

Direct from	To	Airline	Reservations ☎
LONDON Heathrow	Belfast Int.	British Airways	081-897 4000
LONDON Heathrow	Belfast Int.	British Midland	(0345) 554554
LONDON Heathrow	Belfast City	Manx Airlines	(0345) 256256
LONDON Gatwick	Belfast City	Jersey European	(0345) 676676
LONDON Luton	Belfast Int.	Britannia	Travel agents
LONDON Luton	Belfast City	Manx Airlines	(0345) 256256
NEW YORK	Belfast Int.	American Trans Air	(800) 382-5892
AMSTERDAM	Belfast Int.	KLM	(020) 6495070
Aberdeen	Belfast City	Manx Airlines	(0345) 256256
Birmingham	Belfast Int.	British Airways	(0345) 222111
Birmingham	Belfast City	Jersey European	(0345) 676676
Blackpool	Belfast City	Jersey European	(0345) 676676
Bristol	Belfast City	Jersey European	(0345) 676676
Cardiff	Belfast City	Manx Airlines	(0345) 256256
East Midlands	Belfast Int.	British Midland	(0345) 554554
Edinburgh	Belfast City	Loganair	031-333 3338
Exeter	Belfast City	Jersey European	(0345) 676676
Glasgow	Belfast Int.	British Airways	(0345) 222111
Glasgow	Belfast City	Loganair	041-889 3181
Glasgow	Londonderry	Loganair	041-889 3181
Guernsey	Belfast City	Jersey European	(0345) 676676
Humberside	Belfast Int.	British Airways	(0345) 222111
Isle of Man	Belfast City	Jersey European	(0345) 676676
Jersey	Belfast City	Jersey European	(0345) 676676
Leeds/Bradford	Belfast Int.	Air UK	(0345) 666777
Leeds/Bradford	Belfast City	Jersey European	(0345) 676676
Liverpool	Belfast City	Manx Airlines	(0345) 256256
Manchester	Belfast Int.	British Airways	(0345) 222111
Manchester	Belfast City	Jersey European	(0345) 676676
Manchester	Belfast City	Loganair	061-832 9922
Manchester	Londonderry	Loganair	061-832 9922
Newcastle-upon-Tyne	Belfast City	Gill Air	091-286 2222
Southampton	Belfast City	Yorkshire European	(0345) 626217
Teesside	Belfast City	Yorkshire European	(0345) 626217

- and sea

Ferry services from Britain and Europe to Ireland - North and South

Depart	To	Carrier	Reservations ☎
SCOTLAND			
Stranraer	Belfast	SeaCat	(041) 204 2266 9 sailings per day, 1½ hrs
Stranraer	Larne	Stena Sealink	(0776) 2262 8-9 sailings per day, 2½ hrs
Cairnryan	Larne	P&O European Ferries	(058 12) 276 6 sailings per day, 2¼ hrs
WALES			
Fishguard	Rosslare	Stena Sealink	(0233) 647047 2 sailings per day, 3½ hrs
Holyhead	Dublin	B+I Line	051-227 3131 2 sailings per day, 3½ hrs
Holyhead	Dun Laoghaire	Stena Sealink	(0233) 647047 8 sailings per day, 3½ hrs (2 hrs catamaran)
ENGLAND			
Liverpool	Belfast	Norse Irish Ferries	(0232) 779090 1 sailing per day, 11 hrs
ISLE OF MAN			
Douglas	Belfast	Isle of Man Steam Packet Company	(0624) 661661 2-4 sailings per week May-Sept only, 4½ hrs
FRANCE			
Le Havre	Rosslare	Irish Ferries	Le Havre 35 53 28 83 2-4 sailings per week, 22 hrs
Le Havre	Cork	Irish Ferries	Le Havre 35 53 28 83 1 weekly sailing
Cherbourg	Rosslare	Irish Ferries	Cherbourg 33 44 28 96 1-3 sailings per week, 17 hrs
Roscoff	Cork	Brittany Ferries	Roscoff 98 29 28 28 2 sailings per week, March-Oct only, 15 hrs
St Malo	Cork	Brittany Ferries	St Malo 99 40 64 41 1 weekly sailing, June-Sept only, 18 hrs

Note: hours of sailing are approximate

Rail and coach services from Dublin to Belfast: there are 6 trains each day (3 on Sunday) from Connolly St Station to Belfast. The Dublin-Belfast express train takes 2 hours. Stops for ordinary trains include Newry, Portadown and Lisburn. Rail information: ☎ Dublin 366222/Belfast 230310. The Dublin-Belfast express coach service runs 4 times a day (3 times on Sunday) and takes 3 hours. Set-down points include Newry, Banbridge, Dromore, Hillsborough and Dublin airport. Information: ☎ Dublin 366111/Belfast 333000.

Useful addresses and publications

 **Northern Ireland
Tourist Board**

Northern Ireland Tourist Board Offices

Head Office
59 North Street, Belfast BT1 1NB.
☎ (0232) 231221 (administration),
fax (0232) 240960.

Great Britain
11 Berkeley Street, London W1X 5AD.
Freefone 0800 282662.
☎ 071-493 0601, fax 071-499 3731.

135 Buchanan Street, 1st Floor,
Glasgow G1 2JA.

Republic of Ireland
16 Nassau Street, Dublin 2.
☎ Dublin 6791977, fax Dublin 6791863.

North America
551 Fifth Avenue, 7th Floor, New York,
NY 10176.
☎ (212) 922 0101 or (800) 326-0036,
fax (212) 922 0099.

Canada
111 Avenue Road, Suite 450,
Toronto M5R 3J8.
☎ (416) 925 6368, fax (416) 961 2175.

France
3 rue de Pontoise, 78100 St Germain-en-Laye.
☎ (1) 39 21 93 80 (trade enquiries only),
fax (1) 39 21 93 90.
Minitel 3615 Nord Irlande.

Germany
60329 Frankfurt/Main, Taunusstrasse 52-60.
☎ (069) 23 45 04, fax (069) 238 07 17.

Extra copies of this book are available
from all Northern Ireland Tourist Board
offices, price £3.50. Or you can order it -
and any of the publications listed below -
direct by post from:

Tourist Information Centre
59 North Street
Belfast BT1 1NB
☎ (0232) 246609

Most publications are free of charge.
Where prices (sterling) are given, postage
is included.

Northern Ireland - an introduction in
English, French, German, Spanish, Italian
or Dutch - *specify language.*

Heritage of Northern Ireland - map folder
locates 70 important historic monuments.

Where to Eat 1994 - pocket guide to over
1,600 restaurants, teashops, pubs. £2.50.

Ireland North - holiday map,
scale 1:250 000 ($^1/_4$ inch to 1 mile). £3.

Ulster-American Heritage Trail
- illustrated map. 50p.

Land of Cuchulain and St Patrick
- map folder with accommodation and
prices, includes Monaghan, Louth, South-
East Down and Armagh. In English,
French, German, Italian or Irish.

Events 1994 - illustrated.

Holidays Afloat - cruising on Lough Erne.

Stop and Visit 1994 - information bulletin
listing museums, castles, forests, stately
homes, ancient monuments, with current
opening times and admission charges.

In London tourist information on Northern
Ireland is available 7 days a week from the
All Ireland desk at:

British Travel Centre
12 Regent Street
Piccadilly Circus SW1

Other information guides on a wide range of
subjects and activities, from genealogy and golf
to steam trains and walking, are available. If
you have a special interest and would like
further information please write to the Tourist
Information Centre at the address above.

People Travel…

…by Mail!

A Royal Mail Postbus is serving the Enniskillen, Maguiresbridge and Tempo areas of Co. Fermanagh. A return evening service from Enniskillen to Belfast International Airport is also available.

Further details of routes and fares can be found in the postbus guide available at Tourist Information Offices or by contacting The Customer Service Centre Tel: (0232) 892000

1994 COLOUR SUPPLEMENT

Belfast

B & B from £47.50
Open all year

Europa Hotel **
Great Victoria St
Belfast BT2 7AP
☎ (0232) 327000 Fax (0232) 327800

Situated in the heart of Belfast's Golden Mile, beside the Grand Opera House. This 200-bedroom hotel offers the choice of an award-winning gourmet restaurant or a bistro, with nightly entertainment in Harpers Bar. Paradise Lost nightclub. Now a member of Hastings Hotels.

B & B from £22.50
Open all year

Beechlawn House Hotel **
4 Dunmurry Lane, Dunmurry
Belfast BT17 9RR
☎ (0232) 612974 Fax (0232) 623601

Beechlawn House was the Metcalfe family home until its conversion to a hotel in 1965. Still owned and managed by the family, the hotel has been extended and renovated to provide modern facilities while retaining its homely atmosphere.

Dukes Hotel ***
65 University St
Belfast BT7 1HL
☎ **(0232) 236666 Fax (0232) 237177**

Beautiful new hotel located beside Ulster Museum and Botanic Gardens, and less than a mile from the city centre. 21 luxury ensuite bedrooms, hi-tech gymnasium and saunas. Golf nearby. Elegant restaurant serving international cuisine. Popular bar for the smart set.

B & B from £22.50

Open all year

Lansdowne Court Hotel **
657 Antrim Rd, Belfast
BT15 4EF ☎ **(0232) 773317**
Fax (0232) 370125

Refurbished and modernised in 1992, this hotel is designed with guest comfort in mind. Five minutes from the city centre, with Cave Hill and Belfast lough in view. Shopping and leisure centres, golf course, Belfast Castle and Zoo nearby.

B & B from £22.50

Open all year

Park Avenue Hotel **
158 Holywood Rd
Belfast BT4 1PA
☎ **(0232) 656271 Fax (0232) 471417**

The Park Avenue Hotel complex offers comfort and convenience for business or pleasure. Luxury and standard accommodation at very competitive rates. Our popular restaurant offers a wide range of catering with extensive à la carte and bistro menus.

B & B from £30

Open all year

Plaza Hotel **
15 Brunswick St
Belfast BT2 7GE
☎ **(0232) 333555 Fax (0232) 232999**

Peaceful but central location, near sea, bus and rail links. 10 minutes from Belfast City Airport. Close to all shopping, sporting and leisure facilities. Excellent à la carte restaurant in beautiful conservatory area, bar snacks also available. 70 ensuite rooms with modern facilities.

B & B from £35

Open all year

Regency Hotel **
8 Lower Crescent
Belfast BT7 1RN
☎ **(0232) 323349 Fax (0232) 320646**

The Regency Hotel is situated in Belfast's tree-lined Botanic Avenue, only minutes from the city centre and convenient for shopping and entertainment. The hotel has been tastefully refurbished, and the family management ensures a friendly atmosphere.

Miss Valerie Hamill,
General Manager

B & B from £50

Open all year

La Mon House Hotel *
41 Gransha Rd
Castlereagh BT23 5RF
☎ **(0232) 448631 Fax (0232) 448026**

Situated in the countryside, within easy reach of Belfast City Airport (four miles), Belfast International Airport (15 miles) and the city centre. 38 ensuite bedrooms with TV, telephone and coffee service. Enjoy our health spa, swimming pool, sauna and jacuzzi.

Mrs Isobel Huddleson,
Proprietor

B & B from £25

Open all year

Renshaw's Hotel *
75 University St
Belfast BT7 1HL
☎ (0232) 333366 Fax (0232) 333399

Once Renshaw's Tutorial College, this splendid hotel offers quality and comfort. Close to Queen's University and Golden Mile. Spacious bedrooms with ensuite facilities and luxury amenities. Delicious 'Rice & Spice' restaurant and traditional bar. Function and banqueting facilities.

B & B from £25

Open all year

Stranmillis Lodge Guesthouse (A)
14 Chlorine Gardens
Belfast BT9 5DJ
☎ (0232) 682009 Fax (0232) 682009

Stranmillis Lodge is an elegant town house situated in the fashionable Stranmillis/ Malone area of south Belfast. Close to Queen's University. Within walking distance of Belfast city centre, Ulster Museum and many restaurants and theatres.

B & B from £28

Open all year

Helga Lodge
7 Cromwell Rd
Belfast BT7 1JW
☎ (0232) 324820 Fax (0232) 320653

Belfast's best value. Quiet, friendly, homely atmosphere. A short walk from city centre, Queen's University, Botanic Gardens, hospital and rail station. All rooms have colour TV, telephone and constant hot water. 16 rooms ensuite. Authentic Irish breakfast.

B & B from £15

Open all year

The Beeches (A)
10 Dunadry Rd, Muckamore
Antrim BT41 2RR
☎ (0849) 433161 Fax (0849) 433161

Situated on the A6 at Dunadry, near the International Airport. This secluded guesthouse, in landscaped grounds, offers quiet rural accommodation with a friendly atmosphere. 'A Taste of Ulster' member. Home-made soups a speciality. Golf, fishing and watersports nearby. No smoking.

Mrs Marigold Allen, Proprietor

| B & B from £25 |
| Open all year |

Marine Hotel ***
1 North St
Ballycastle BT54 6BN
☎ (026 57) 62222 Fax (026 57) 69507

Situated on the seafront at Ballycastle, two minutes walk from the beach and other amenities such as grass tennis courts, a bowling green and an 18 hole golf course. All 32 ensuite rooms have panoramic sea views of Rathlin Island, Fair Head and the Mull of Kintyre.

| B & B from £25 |
| Open all year |

Holestone House
23 Deer Park, Doagh
Ballyclare BT39 0RH
☎ (0960) 352306

This family-owned Georgian residence is set in quiet woodland, only 13 miles from Belfast. The house retains all its original character, with high ceilings and bright spacious bedrooms, three of which are ensuite. Convenient to Belfast International Airport.

| B & B from £15 |
| Open all year |

Country House Hotel ***
20 Doagh Rd
Ballymena BT42 3LZ
☎ **(0266) 891663 Fax (0266) 891477**

Situated in the heart of county Antrim, 30 minutes drive from Belfast, the International Airport, Larne harbour and the north coast. All rooms ensuite. International cuisine by award-winning chefs. Leisure complex and new conservatory lounge.

Marie Boyle & Bob Isles, Managers

B & B from £40

Open all year

Tullymore House (B)
2 Carnlough Rd, Broughshane
Ballymena BT43 7HF
☎ **(0266) 861233 Fax (0266) 862238**

A comfortable family inn situated in eight acres of gardens below Slemish mountain. Gateway to the glens of Antrim and coast road. Famous for our gourmet carvery open seven days for lunch and dinner.

B & B from £30

Open all year

Beechfield
81 Galgorm Rd
Ballymena BT42 1AA
☎ **(0266) 659709**

Beechfield is a listed building, set in mature grounds. Five minutes from town centre, and convenient to Belfast International Airport and Larne harbour. Three ensuite rooms. Excellent home cooking. Ideal base for visiting the glens of Antrim and the Giant's Causeway.

B & B from £25

Open all year

Bushmills Inn ***
25 Main St
Bushmills BT57 8QN
☎ (026 57) 32339 Fax (026 57) 32048

At the home of the world's oldest distillery, between the Giant's Causeway and Royal Portrush Golf Club, this award winning hotel has faithfully recreated its origins as an old coaching inn - open peat fires, gas lights, cottage-style ensuite bedrooms and secret room. Egon Ronay recommended.

B & B from £29

Open all year

Londonderry Arms Hotel **
20 Harbour Rd, Carnlough
BT44 0EU ☎ (0574) 885255/885458
Fax (0574) 885263

Historic hotel in the glens of Antrim. Holds AA Courtesy & Care award. Family-owned and managed. Open all year for morning coffee, lunch, bar lunch, afternoon tea, high tea and à la carte. Ideal venue for conferences, weddings and activity holidays.

Mr Frank O'Neill,
Proprietor

B & B from £32.50

Open all year

Caldhame Lodge (B)
102 Moira Rd
Crumlin BT29 4HG
☎ (0849) 423099

Situated on a large dairy farm, this newly built guesthouse is central to Belfast, Lisburn, Antrim and the M1, and is only five minutes from Belfast International Airport. All ensuite rooms. A warm welcome is always guaranteed, home cooking a speciality.

B & B from £14.50

Open all year

Keef Halla Country House (U)
20 Tully Rd, Nutt's Corner
Crumlin BT29 4AH
☎ (0232) 825491

A recently opened guesthouse, five minutes from Belfast International Airport. All rooms have TV, tea/coffee facilities and some are ensuite. Convenient to Belfast, Antrim, Lisburn and the M1 motorway. Fishing, golf, shooting and leisure complex nearby.

| B & B from £13.50 |
| Open all year |

Causeway Hotel **
40 Causeway Rd, Giant's Causeway
BT57 8SU ☎ (026 57) 31226/31210
Fax (026 57) 32552

Situated on the north Antrim coast at the entrance to the world famous Giant's Causeway, this old family hotel has been tastefully renovated to provide modern facilities while retaining its old grandeur and charm. The 16 ensuite bedrooms have TV and tea-making facilities.

| B & B from £25 |
| Open all year |

Drumnagreagh Hotel **
Coast Rd
Glenarm BT44 0BB
☎ (0574) 841651 Fax (0574) 841651

At the entrance to the glens of Antrim, with panoramic views of the Scottish coast. 16 luxury rooms with ensuite facilities. Challenging golf course nearby. Sunday carvery, grill bar and à la carte restaurant. Ideal for conferences, weddings and activity breaks.

| B & B from £27.50 |
| Open all year |

Magheramorne House Hotel **
59 Shore Rd
Larne BT40 3HW
☎ **(0574) 279444 Fax (0574) 260138**

Set in 43 acres of woodland
and manicured gardens,
overlooking Larne lough, the
Magheramorne House Hotel
can offer a relaxing
atmosphere for business or
pleasure with easy access to
Belfast, the International
Airport and Antrim coast.

B & B from £25
Open all year

Derrin House (A)
2 Prince's Gardens
Larne BT40 1RQ
☎ **(0574) 273269/273762**

Beautifully appointed
guesthouse, family-run since
1964. Ideally situated for
touring the Antrim coast and
glens of Antrim, yet close to
Larne harbour and only 30
minutes from Belfast. All
rooms have colour TV and
most are ensuite. Friendly,
welcoming atmosphere.

B & B from £12.50
Open all year

Cairnview
13 Croft Heights, Ballygalley
Larne BT40 2QS
☎ **(0574) 583269**

Large, modern house with
luxury rooms, four miles
north of Larne on the famous
Antrim coast road. Convenient
to Larne harbour, Cairndhu
Golf Club and the Ulster
Way, and just a short walk
from the beach. All rooms
have tea-making facilities
and some are ensuite.

B & B from £15
Open all year

Chimney Corner Hotel ***
630 Antrim Rd, Newtownabbey
BT36 8RH ☎ (0232) 844925/844851
Fax (0232) 844352/842058

The hotel is built around the old Belfast/Antrim Halfway House. Situated in a rural setting 10 mins from Belfast city centre and the International Airport, and on the main route to Larne harbour terminal. All 63 ensuite bedrooms have telephone, radio and TV. Belfast Castle and Zoo nearby.

B & B from £22.50
Open all year

Bayview Hotel **
2 Bayhead Rd
Portballintrae BT57 8RZ
☎ (026 57) 31453 Fax (026 57) 32360

Renowned hotel overlooking the bay, ideal for both activity and family holidays. All rooms are ensuite with sea views and have TV with satellite reception. Indoor heated pool, sauna and games room. Hotel's own boat offers sightseeing trips along the Causeway coast.

B & B from £35
Open all year

Magherabuoy House Hotel ***
41 Magheraboy Rd
Portrush BT56 8NX
☎ (0265) 823507 Fax (0265) 824687

Atlantic views, luxurious, elegant surroundings, friendly, efficient staff and professionalism at all times combine to make the Magherabuoy the ideal venue for short breaks, conferences, tour groups and golf parties. Excellent entertainment and leisure facilities.

B & B from £37.50
Open all year

Templeton Hotel **
882 Antrim Rd
Templepatrick BT39 0AH
☎ (084 94) 32984 Fax (084 94) 33406

This tranquil lakeside hotel is in the easily accessible Antrim countryside. Rich in architectural detail, the prestigious Templeton has 20 luxurious bedrooms, an elegant à la carte restaurant, Upton grill room, function suite, and Sam's public lounge.

| B & B from £35 |
| Open all year |

County Down

Millbrook Lodge Hotel *
5 Drumaness Rd
Ballynahinch BT24 8LS
☎ (0238) 562828 Fax (0238) 565402

Country manor set in the heart of Down, on the doorstep of Newcastle where the mountains of Mourne sweep down to the sea. The hotel caters for weddings, conferences and functions. 16 luxury ensuite bedrooms. Weekly dinner dance and famous Club Nova Nite Club.

| B & B from £47 |
| Open all year |

White Horse Hotel *
17 High St
Ballynahinch BT24 8AB
☎ (0238) 562225

This well maintained family hotel has been run by the Poland family for almost 50 years. Recently refurbished with 12 rooms, most ensuite, with direct dial telephone and satellite TV. Guests can enjoy the lounge, coffee shop, games room, function room and popular night club.

| B & B from £25 |
| Open all year |

Winston Hotel *
19 Queen's Parade
Bangor BT20 3BJ
☎ **(0247) 454575 Fax (0247) 454575**

Overlooking Bangor marina and seafront gardens. 28 comfortable rooms, mostly ensuite with colour TV and direct dial telephone. Convenient to local shopping and leisure facilities. Only 15 minutes drive from Belfast. Central for day trips to all parts of Northern Ireland.

Mr Alastair Good,
Director

B & B from £22.50

Open all year

Tara Guesthouse (B)
51 Princetown Rd
Bangor BT20 3TA
☎ **(0247) 468924/(0850) 422067**

Tara guesthouse is in a quiet area, minutes from the new marina, beaches and other amenities. Parking for guests. All rooms are comfortably furnished with colour TV, and six are ensuite. Tea/coffee-making facilities. A friendly atmosphere and warm welcome assured.

B & B from £13

Open all year

Old Inn **
15 Main St
Crawfordsburn BT19 1JH
☎ **(0247) 853255 Fax (0247) 852775**

Coaching inn dating back to 1614. Ideal for both business and leisure pursuits. Three miles from Bangor and 11 miles from Belfast. All bedrooms are ensuite and the restaurant and bistro offer a variety of locally produced foods of a high standard. Award-winning garden.

B & B from £29

Open all year

Glen House (U)
212 Crawfordsburn Rd
Crawfordsburn BT19 1HY
☎ **(0247) 852610 Fax (0247) 852229**

Quietly situated, with character and charm, in large grounds. Excellent for business trips, golfing and family holidays. Short walk to restaurant, pub, beach, bus and train. Rooms ensuite, with hospitality tray, TV and clock radio. Private parking. National award for Best Breakfast.

Mrs Noreen Harte,
Proprietor

B & B from £20

Open all year

Abbey Lodge Hotel *
38 Belfast Rd
Downpatrick BT30 9AU
☎ **(0396) 614511 Fax (0396) 616415**

Situated in the heart of Down, only 35 minutes from Belfast, you will find yourself among the famous drumlins, picturesque Quoile river, historical Inch Abbey and only minutes from St Patrick's burial ground. Excellent cuisine at competitive prices with friendly and courteous staff.

B & B from £22.50

Open all year

Sylvan Hill House
76 Kilntown Rd
Dromore BT25 1HS
☎ **(0846) 692321**

Listed Georgian 'one and a half' storey house built in 1781. Beautiful setting with mature trees and panoramic views of the Mourne and Dromara mountains. Log fires, home baking. Off main Dublin road, 30 minutes from Belfast and four miles from Hillsborough.

B & B from £18

Open all year

Carrig-Gorm
27 Bridge Rd
Helen's Bay BT19 1TS
☎ (0247) 853680

Part-Victorian 18th-century country house, half a mile from the sea. Lovely coastal walks. Places of interest nearby include the Ulster Folk & Transport Museum. Restaurants, golf courses and Belfast City Airport easily accessible. Log fires in lounge hall. Family room ensuite.

B & B from £18

Open all year

Rayanne House (A)
60 Demesne Rd, Holywood
BT18 9EX ☎ (0232) 425859/423364
Fax (0232) 425859

The McClelland family, renowned for their award winning restaurant, Schooner, now offer first-class ensuite accommodation in their elegant Victorian home. Excellent food and service with all the added facilities required by today's tourist or business executive.

Mr & Mrs McClelland, Proprietors

B & B from £35

Open all year

Morne Abbey Guesthouse (B)
16 Greencastle Rd
Kilkeel BT34 4DE
☎ (069 37) 62426

Country house on mixed farm in magnificent setting, half a mile from Kilkeel. Fishing, horse riding, tennis, bowls and golf nearby. One mile from the sea, four miles from the Silent Valley. A warm welcome assured. Home cooking a speciality. Five rooms, two ensuite.

B & B from £13.50

Open April-Sept

Lough View
31 Rowreagh Rd
Kircubbin BT22 1AS
☎ **(024 77) 38324 Fax (024 77) 38708**

Lough View Bed and Breakfast is set on the shores of Strangford lough with spacious gardens and walks down to the beach. Two miles from Kirkistown race course and golf club. Convenient to Lough Cowey Fishery and Northern Ireland Aquarium in Portaferry.

| B & B from £15 |
| Open all year |

Burrendale Hotel & Country Club *
51 Castlewellan Rd
Newcastle BT33 0JY
☎ **(039 67) 22599 Fax (039 67) 22328**

Nestling between the Mourne mountains and the Irish Sea, the Burrendale is the ideal centre for your holiday. Extensive leisure facilities include swimming pool, jacuzzis, saunas and gym. The Burrendale has a well founded reputation for good food, fine wines and a very relaxing atmosphere.

| B & B from £40 |
| Open all year |

Enniskeen House Hotel *
98 Bryansford Rd
Newcastle BT33 0LF
☎ **(039 67) 22392 Fax (039 67) 24084**

Delightfully situated in mature private gardens with stunning mountain views, this country house is an ideal base for a tranquil break. Comfortable accommodation with ensuite facilities and delicious cuisine entice you to relax and savour life's finer moments.

| B & B from £32 |
| Open March-Nov |

The Briers (U)
39 Middle Tollymore Rd
Newcastle BT33 0JJ
☎ (039 67) 24347

Restored 18th-century home set at the foot of the Mournes. Featured by Judith Chalmers in 'High Days and Holidays'. Favoured by international visitors. Restaurant and gardens. Included in publication 'Best of Bed & Breakfast in Ireland' by Elsie Dillard.

B & B from £16
Open all year

The Cottage (U)
81 Burrenreagh Rd, Bryansford
Newcastle BT33 0PU
☎ (039 67) 24698 Fax (039 67) 24698

Charming 19th-century country guesthouse in tranquil village of Bryansford, three miles from Newcastle, opposite Tollymore Forest Park. Secluded landscaped gardens with tennis and golf facilities, and all contemporary conveniences. International reputation for hospitality and fine food.

B & B from £22.50
Open Feb-Nov

Glenada
29 South Promenade
Newcastle BT33 0EX
☎ (039 67) 22402 Fax (039 67) 26229

Situated at the foot of the Mournes, overlooking Dundrum Bay. Nine ensuite rooms with colour TV, telephone and tea/coffee facilities. Eight family and eight standard rooms. Excellent facilities throughout with high standard cuisine and friendly service.

B & B from £13.50
Open all year

Hillside Guesthouse (U)
1 Rock Rd
Newry BT34 1PL
☎ (0693) 65484/61430

Overlooking Slieve Gullion and Carlingford mountains, this country guesthouse is ideal for a family break. Five minutes from Newry town, ¾ mile off main Newry-Belfast road. All three rooms have ensuite facilities. Fishing nearby, seaside 15 minutes.

B & B from £14
Open all year

Greenacres (A)
5 Manse Rd
Newtownards BT23 4TP
☎ (0247) 816193

Spacious country guesthouse set in one acre of beautiful gardens. Central for fishing, golf, National Trust properties and leisure centre. Belfast nine miles. 'Taste of Ulster' member. Excellent home cooking and warm hospitality assured.

B & B from £15
Open all year

Edenvale Country House
130 Portaferry Rd
Newtownards BT22 2AH
☎ (0247) 814881

Beautifully restored Georgian country house, just two miles from Newtownards in a delightfully secluded area. Extensive views over Strangford lough and the National Trust Wildfowl Refuge to the Mournes. Sailboarding, birdwatching, golf and horse riding within easy reach. Stabling for horses or dogs.

B & B from £15
Open all year

Portaferry Hotel ***
10 The Strand
Portaferry BT22 1PE
☎ (024 77) 28231 Fax (024 77) 28999

The Portaferry Hotel is a charming waterside village inn with well appointed ensuite bedrooms. Award winning seafood restaurant. Local places of interest include Castleward, Mount Stewart, Castle Espie, St Patrick's Vale and the renowned Royal County Down Golf Course.

| B & B from £32.50 |
| Open all year |

Forestbrook House
11 Forestbrook Rd
Rostrevor BT34 3BT
☎ (069 37) 38105

Situated at the foot of Slieve Martin and at the top of the Fairy Glen. This detached, listed property, built in 1700, is set in a healthy atmosphere of pine, mountain and sea air. Nearby is a yacht club, golf club, tennis courts, children's playground and excellent fishing facilities.

| B & B from £13 |
| Open all year |

Riverside House
601 Loughshore Rd
Belleek BT93 3FT
☎ (036 56) 58649

Modern bungalow in quiet rural setting. Selection of bedrooms, some ensuite. Situated half a mile from Belleek on A46 shore road. Convenient to Belleek Pottery and the beautiful beaches of Donegal.

| B & B from £15 |
| Open March-Sept |

Killyhevlin Hotel ***
Dublin Rd
Enniskillen BT74 4AU
☎ (0365) 323481   Fax (0365) 324726

The Killyhevlin hotel and chalets are situated on the shores of Lough Erne, in the heart of beautiful Fermanagh. Luxury rooms with ensuite facilities. Close to fishing and watersports. Ideal spot for conferences, weekend breaks and family holidays.

| B & B from £30 |
| Open all year |

Manor House Hotel ***
Killadeas
Enniskillen BT94 1NY
☎ (036 56) 21561   Fax (036 56) 21545

This grand Victorian country mansion has been tastefully restored to provide present day luxury in splendid stately surroundings. The hotel lies on the shores of Lough Erne in an area of outstanding beauty. A new health and country club is scheduled to open in April 1994.

Miss Brona Donnelly
& Mrs Mary McKenna

| B & B from £30 |
| Open all year |

B & B from £19

Open Jan-Nov

Belmore Court Motel
Tempo Rd
Enniskillen BT74 6HR
☎ **(0365) 326633 Fax (0365) 326362**

Enniskillen's newest motel. 35 luxury apartments, 31 with kitchens, four with tea-making facilities. All are ensuite, with satellite TV, telephone and car parking. Five minutes walk from town centre. Ideal for touring Fermanagh Lakeland and Donegal.

B & B from £15

Open all year

Tullyhona House (A)
59 Marble Arch Rd
Florencecourt BT92 1DE
☎ **(0365) 348452**

This award-winning beef and sheep farm guesthouse is near Marble Arch Caves. Ensuite rooms with colour TV and hairdryer. A la carte menu. Children welcome, play area. Pony trekking and golf nearby. Calving tours in season. All home cooking and baking. Buffet style breakfast, barbecue evenings.

Mr & Mrs Armstrong, Proprietors

B & B from £10

Open Feb-Dec

Lough Melvin Holiday Centre
Garrison BT93 4FG
☎ **(036 56) 58142**
Fax (036 56) 58719

A superb residential centre comprising 11 bedrooms and small dormitory. Situated in the heart of Ireland's Lake District. Quality restaurant, games room, tourist information, caravan and camping, children's play area. Activities include fishing, canoeing and pony-trekking.

Greenwood Lodge (B)
Erne Drive, Ederney
Kesh BT93 0EF
☎ (036 56) 31366

Situated near Castle Archdale and Kesh. This comfortable guesthouse has ensuite rooms which are centrally heated with tea-making facilities and TV. Convenient for boating, fishing, golf, pony trekking and touring the Fermanagh Lakeland, Donegal and Omagh areas.

B & B from £13.50
Open all year

Drumshane Hotel **
Lisnarick BT94 1PS
☎ (036 56) 21146
Fax (036 56) 21311

New first-class, high standard hotel with 10 rooms. A striking focal point in Lisnarick. Spacious interior with lots of character. A la carte menu in the 'Wedgewood' restaurant with emphasis on fresh local produce. Our motto is 'small in stature - gigantic in quality'.

Mr Noel Smyth,
Manager

B & B from £30
Open all year

Ortine Hotel *
Main St
Lisnaskea BT92 0JD
☎ (036 57) 21206 Fax (036 57) 21206

Formerly a coaching inn, the hotel is perfectly located for business, conference or weekend breaks. Ensuite rooms with TV, radio, and direct dial telephone. Entertainment, coffee shop. Special offers for groups, senior citizens and activity breaks.

Mr Walter Jordan,
Proprietor

B & B from £24
Open all year

Bohill Hotel & Country Club **
69 Cloyfin Rd
Coleraine BT52 2NY
☎ (0265) 44406/7 Fax (0265) 52424

Breathtaking style and
unique warmth of welcome
ensure your stay is very
special. The hotel, on the
famous Causeway coast,
has 36 ensuite rooms, and
an unrivalled culinary
reputation. Excellent leisure
complex with heated
swimming pool.

B & B from £33

Open all year

Lodge Hotel **
Lodge Rd
Coleraine BT52 1NF
☎ (0265) 44848 Fax (0265) 54555

A family-run hotel in private
grounds, on the outskirts of
Coleraine. Parking for 200
cars. All rooms ensuite. Live
entertainment at weekends.
Near Giant's Causeway,
Portrush and Portstewart.
Several first-class golf courses
within a five-mile radius.

Mr Andy Stephens,
Proprietor

B & B from £26

Open all year

Blackheath House (A)
112 Killeague Rd, Blackhill
Coleraine BT51 4HH
☎ (0265) 868433 Fax (0265) 868433

Georgian rectory set in two
acres of landscaped gardens
with five luxurious ensuite
rooms. In the cellars is the
highly acclaimed restaurant
'MacDuff's'. Ideal location
from which to explore the
Causeway coast or play golf
on one of the eight local
courses.

B & B from £30

Open all year

Coolbeg
2e Grange Rd
Coleraine BT52 1NG
☎ **(0265) 44961**

Modern bungalow set in a pleasant garden on the edge of town. All rooms have TV and tea/coffee making facilities, and three are ensuite. Coolbeg is a Category One house suitable for wheelchair users. Ideal for touring north Antrim coast.

B & B from £15
Open all year

Drenagh House
17 Dowland Rd
Limavady BT49 0HP
☎ **(050 47) 22649 Fax (050 47) 22061**

Classical 1835 Lanyon mansion with beautiful interior, fine gardens and mature woodland. Well placed for Magilligan Strand and the beauty spots of Downhill, Giant's Causeway and Donegal. Tennis and riding available. Superb cuisine.

B & B from £50
Open Feb-Nov

The Poplars
352 Seacoast Rd
Limavady BT49 0LA
☎ **(050 47) 50360**

Six miles from Limavady, The Poplars is convenient to Benone Strand, a 9-hole golf course, and Ulster Gliding Club. All rooms hot & cold with tea/coffee-making facilities. Ramp to house for wheelchair use. Home cooking a speciality.

B & B from £15
Open all year

B & B from £24

Open all year

Waterfoot Hotel ***
14 Clooney Rd, Caw
Londonderry BT47 1TB
☎ **(0504) 45500 Fax (0504) 311006**

The Waterfoot Hotel is of unique design. Its main public areas are circular and on several levels affording excellent views of the Foyle river and Donegal mountains. All ensuite rooms have colour TV and telephone. New leisure facilities scheduled for 1994.

B & B from £14

Open all year

No 10
10 Crawford Square, Northland Rd
Londonderry BT48 7HR
☎ **(0504) 265000**

Spacious modernised Victorian house in unspoilt Victorian square. Five minutes walk from city centre. All rooms have hot & cold, central heating, TV and tea-making facilities. Ample parking available. Friendly and comfortable atmosphere with personal attention at all times.

6-day stay £180

Open Jan-Nov

Raspberry Hill Health Farm
29 Bond's Glen Rd
Londonderry BT47 3ST
☎ **(0504) 398000 Fax (0504) 398000**

Set in beautiful countryside of the scenic Bond's Glen at the foot of the Sperrins, Raspberry Hill is rapidly becoming a haunt of the discerning visitor. The 'Raspberry Hill experience' is one of complete relaxation and enjoyment where the visitor feels completely rejuvenated.

Mrs Claire Danton,
Proprietor

Robin Hill
103 Chapel Rd, Waterside
Londonderry BT47 2BG
☎ (0504) 42776

The peace of the countryside in the middle of town - a period residence set in 1½ acres of its own grounds. An oasis of charm and family-run hospitality with good food and accommodation. Close to bus and train stations and a short drive from Eglinton Airport.

B & B from £13
Open all year

Oregon Guesthouse (A)
168 Station Rd
Portstewart BT55 7PU
☎ (0265) 832826

Half a mile from Portstewart in a quiet rural setting, on the B185. This award-winning guesthouse has nine modern bedrooms, eight ensuite, one with a sauna. Tea/coffee, TV and hairdryers available and ample private parking. Within easy reach of golf, fishing and horse-riding.

Mrs Vi Anderson, Proprietor

B & B from £17.50
Open Feb-Nov

Ashleigh House
164 Station Rd
Portstewart BT55 7PU
☎ (0265) 834452

Ashleigh House offers first class accommodation. All rooms are ensuite and on the ground floor, with tea-making facilities, central heating and colour TV. Car parking available. Easy access to golf, boating, fishing and pony trekking.

B & B from £15
Open all year

Strandeen
63 Strand Rd
Portstewart BT55 7LU
☎ (026 583) 3159

Strandeen offers panoramic ocean views from comfortable ensuite rooms. Scenic five minute walk to miles of beach cared for by the National Trust or to the promenade and harbour. Enjoy a very warm welcome and high standard of housekeeping. No smoking.

B & B from £17.50

Open all year

County Tyrone

Glenavon House Hotel *
52 Drum Rd
Cookstown BT80 8JQ
☎ (064 87) 64949 Fax (064 87) 64396

Situated in the centre of the province - the ideal base for your visit to Northern Ireland. Recently extended to include a leisure centre with swimming pool, jacuzzi, steam room, fitness suite and gym plus conference centre. The hotel can provide you with all the comforts of home.

B & B from £30

Open all year

Greenvale Hotel *
57 Drum Rd, Cookstown
BT80 8QS ☎ (064 87) 62243/65196
Fax (064 87) 65539

Formerly an early 19th-century residence, situated in its own private grounds on the outskirts of Cookstown. Just one mile from an 18-hole golf course. Grill, à la carte, Sunday carvery and bar snack menus available. The hotel also caters for weddings, conferences and entertainment.

B & B from £25

Open all year

Inn on the Park Hotel **
Moy Rd
Dungannon BT71 6BS
☎ **(086 87) 25151 Fax (086 87) 4953**

This is a country-style hotel set in seven acres of landscaped gardens. All bedrooms are ensuite with colour TV. There are unlimited sporting facilities, parklands, architectural and historic sites. Horse riding and in-house entertainment.

B & B from £20
Open all year

Valley Hotel **
60 Main St
Fivemiletown BT75 0PW
☎ **(036 55) 21505 Fax (036 55) 21688**

This family-run hotel is situated on the Tyrone/ Fermanagh border, which is perfect for touring the Sperrins, the banks of Lough Erne and Donegal. The hotel offers a special rate for weekend breaks and has entertainment to suit everyone.

B & B from £30
Open all year

Royal Arms Hotel **
51 High St
Omagh BT78 1BA
☎ **(0662) 243262/3 Fax (0662) 45011**

Family-owned and managed, with 21 ensuite rooms and modern facilities. A la carte restaurant and bistro. Local attractions include Ulster American Folk Park, Gortin Glen Forest Park, Sperrin Heritage Centre and Ulster History Park. Listed building, old world charm.

B & B from £32
Open all year

1994

Where to Eat

In Northern Ireland

14th year – best-selling guide!

Restaurants, Coffee Shops, Pubs & Hotels – *plus* 'A Taste of Ulster'

Pocket-sized paperback for glove compartment! Comprehensive listing by town and village for over 1,600 eating places including all 'Taste of Ulster' restaurants, pubs and coffee shops. Opening times, price bands, brief description of food. Available from bookshops, newsagents, tourist information centres, airports, garage forecourts etc. throughout Britain and Ireland, price £2.50.

Visit the Tourist Information Centre

Situated in the heart of Belfast, the tourist information centre offers an extensive range of services, including a Bureau de Change and many locally produced gifts and souvenirs.

An advanced, computerised information and reservations system known as GULLIVER makes accommodation bookings, whether for business or holiday, much easier and faster.

The centre has a wealth of leaflets and brochures packed with holiday ideas, and the friendly, professional staff will be delighted to help you with suggestions and reservations.

Tourist Information Centre
59 North Street, Belfast BT1 1NB.
Tel: (0232) 246609.

**Accommodation reservations
by credit card: Freephone 0800-317153**

Northern Ireland
Tourist Board

The Festive Season.

In Northern Ireland it lasts all year round.

Whether it's the pageant of history or the latest street players, Northern Ireland is a living theatre of entertainment - buskers, folk culture, humour, festivals of music, art and drama, film and dance. All on a backdrop of fine hotels, restaurants, architecture and superb landscapes.

So, if there's a special interest in your life, then Northern Ireland is the place to be, where you can enjoy some of the most spontaneous pleasures you'll ever remember.

Northern Ireland Tourist Board

59 North Street, Belfast BT1 1NB.
Tel: (0232) 246609.

Belfast

Hotels

CULLODEN HOTEL ****
142 Bangor Rd, Holywood, BT18 0EX.
☎ (0232) 425223. Fax 426777.
B&B s£106 d£140. BB&M s£122
d£172. Rooms 91, ensuite 91.
Dinner £16. Last orders 2145 hrs.
Open all year ex 24 & 25 Dec.

EUROPA HOTEL ****
Great Victoria St, BT2 7AP.
☎ (0232) 327000. Fax 327800.
B&B s £100 d£130. BB&M s£115 d£160.
Rooms 198 , ensuite 198.
High tea £6.95 Dinner £18.95. Last
orders 2330 hrs. Open all year.

BEECHLAWN HOUSE HOTEL ***
4 Dunmurry Lane, Dunmurry, BT17 9RR.
☎ (0232) 612974. Fax 623601.
B&B s£60 d£72. BB&M s£72 d£96.
Rooms 34, ensuite 34. High tea £6.50.
Dinner £12. Last orders 2130 hrs.
Open all year.

DUKES HOTEL ***
65 University St, BT7 1HL.
☎ (0232) 236666. Fax 237177.
B&B s£76.50 d£92. BB&M s£91 d£122.
Rooms 21, ensuite 21. Dinner £20. Last
orders 2230 hrs. Open all year.

GLENAVNA HOUSE HOTEL ***
588 Shore Rd, Newtownabbey, BT37 0SN.
☎ (0232) 864461. Fax 862531.
B&B s£65 d£80. Rooms 33, ensuite 33.
High tea £12. Dinner £16.50. Last orders
2200 hrs. Open all year.

**NOVOTEL BELFAST INTERNATIONAL
AIRPORT** ***
BT29 4AB
☎ (0849) 422033. Fax (0849) 423500.
B&B s£64.50 d£72.50. Rooms 108, ensuite
108. High tea £7. Dinner £10. Last orders
2400 hrs. Open all year.

STORMONT HOTEL ***
587 Upper Newtownards Rd, BT4 3LP.
☎ (0232) 658621. Fax 480240.
B&B s£90 d£140. BB&M s£110 d£180.
Rooms 106, ensuite 106. High tea £8.50.
Dinner £20. Last orders 2130 hrs.
Open all year.

WELLINGTON PARK HOTEL ***
21 Malone Rd, BT9 6RU.
☎ (0232) 381111. Fax 665410.
B&B s£75 d£90. BB&M s£90 d£120.
Rooms 50, ensuite 50. High tea £5.95.
Dinner £15. Last orders 2145 hrs.
Open all year.

Facilities are liable to change. Check prices when you book. Key to symbols is on the back flap.

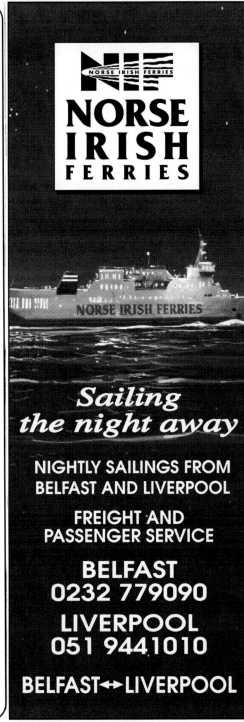

BALMORAL HOTEL **
Black's Rd, BT10 0NF.
☎ (0232) 301234. Fax 601455.
B&B s£25 d£40. BB&M s£35 d£60.
Rooms 44, ensuite 44. High tea £8.
Dinner £10. Last orders 2300 hrs.
Open all year.

LANSDOWNE COURT HOTEL **
657 Antrim Rd, BT15 4EF.
☎ (0232) 773317. Fax 370125
B&B s£66 d£80. BB&M s£81 d£110.
Rooms 25, ensuite 25. High tea £12.50.
Dinner £15. Last orders 2130 hrs.
Open all year.

MALONE LODGE **
(Mr & Mrs B Macklin), 60 Eglantine Avenue
BT9 6DY, ☎ (0232) 382409. Fax 382706
B&B s£50 d£70. Rooms 33, ensuite 33.
High tea £7.95. Dinner £14.95. Last orders
2130 hrs. Open all year.

PARK AVENUE HOTEL **
158 Holywood Rd, BT4 1PA.
☎ (0232) 656271. Fax 471417.
B&B s£65 d£80. BB&M s£77 d£104.
Rooms 70, ensuite 35. High tea £10.
Dinner £15. Last orders 2030 hrs.
Open all year.

PLAZA HOTEL **
15 Brunswick St, BT2 7GE.
☎ (0232) 333555. Fax 232999.
B&B s£59 d£69. BB&M s£70.59 d£80.10.
Rooms 73, ensuite 73. Dinner £10.95.
Last orders 2230 hrs. Open all year.

REGENCY HOTEL **
8 Lower Crescent, BT7 1RN.
☎ (0232) 323349. Fax 320646.
B&B s£50 d£60. Rooms 14, ensuite 14.
High tea £9. Dinner £15. Last orders
2200 hrs. Open all year.

LA MON HOUSE HOTEL *
41 Gransha Rd, Castlereagh, BT23 5RF.
☎ (0232) 448631. Fax 448026.
B&B s£60 d£95. BB&M s£70.50
d£105.50. Rooms 38, ensuite 38. High
tea £7. Dinner £10.50. Last orders 2145
hrs. Open all year.

RENSHAWS HOTEL *
75 University St, BT7 1HL. ☎ (0232)
333366. Fax 333399.
B&B s£55.95 d£66.95. BB&M s£65.95
d£86.95. Rooms 20, ensuite 20. High tea
£6.95. Dinner £11.95.
Last orders 2300 hrs. Open all year.

Guesthouses

ASH-ROWAN GUEST HOUSE (A)
(Mrs E Hazlett), 12 Windsor Avenue,
BT9 6EE. ☎ (0232) 661758/661983.
Fax 663227.
B&B s£38 d£56. BB&M s£55 d£90.
Rooms 4, ensuite 4. Dinner £17.
Last orders 1900 hrs. Open all year.

B&B = bed and breakfast   s = single   d = double   BB&M = bed, breakfast & evening meal

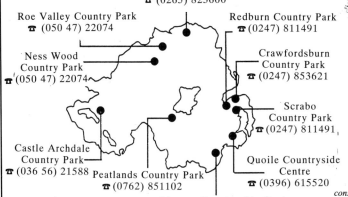

CAMERA GUEST HOUSE (A)
(Miss A Drumm), 44 Wellington Park,
BT9 6DP. ☎ (0232) 660026.
B&B s£27.50 d£37.50. Rooms 11,
ensuite 7. Open all year.

✻ ᴥ ⋔ ▥. ⛶ ⎀ ⌿ ⒠

MALONE GUEST HOUSE (A)
(Mrs E McClure), 79 Malone Rd, BT9 6SH.
☎ (0232) 669565.
B&B s£29 d£45. Rooms 7, ensuite 7.
Open all year.

Ⓣ Ⓟ ⓞᴀᴘ ▥. ⛶ ⌿

SOMERTON GUEST HOUSE (A)
(Mr & Mrs E Lynch), 22 Lansdowne Rd,
BT15 4DB. ☎ (0232) 370717.
B&B s£18 d£32. BB&M s£25 d£46.
Rooms 8. Dinner £7. Last orders
1800 hrs. Open all year.

Ⓣ Ⓟ ♠ ✻ ⛇ ᴥ ⓞᴀᴘ ▥. ⛶ ⋌ ⌿ ⒠

STRANMILLIS LODGE (A)
(Messrs Barton/Sinnamon),
14 Chlorine Gardens, BT9 5DJ.
☎ (0232) 682009. Fax 682009.
B&B s£40 d£56 . BB&M s£52.50 d£81.
Rooms 6, ensuite 6. High tea £8.50.
Dinner £12.50. Last orders 1900 hrs.
Open all year.

Ⓣ Ⓟ ᴥ ▥. ⛶ ⎀ ⋌ ⌿ ⒠

WINDERMERE HOUSE (A)
(Misses M&A Murray) 60 Wellington Park,
BT9 6DP. ☎ (0232) 662693/665165.
B&B s£16.50 d£40. BB&M s£28.50 d£64.
Rooms 8, ensuite 2. High tea £7.50.
Dinner £12. Last orders 1830 hrs. Open
all year.

Ⓣ Ⓟ ᴥ ⓞᴀᴘ ▥. ⋌ ⒠

EGLANTINE GUEST HOUSE (B)
(Mr & Mrs K Cargill), 21 Eglantine Avenue,
BT9 6DW. ☎ (0232) 667585.
B&B s£17 d£32. Rooms 6. Open all year.

ᴥ ▥. ⋌

LISERIN GUEST HOUSE (B)
(Mr & Mrs S Smith), 17 Eglantine Avenue,
BT9 6DW. ☎ (0232) 660769.
B&B s£17 d£32. Rooms 6. Open all year.

⏆ ♠ ᴥ ▥. ⋌

PEARL COURT HOUSE (B)
(Mrs P Blakely), 11 Malone Rd, BT9 6RT.
☎ (0232) 666145.
B&B s£17 d£34. Rooms 9, ensuite 2.
Open all year.

Ⓟ ᴥ ▥. ⛶ ⋌

BIENVENUE (U)
(Mrs S Henderson & Mr G Senninger),
8 Sans Souci Park, Malone Rd, BT9 5BZ.
☎ (0232) 681731. Fax 663021.
B&B s£35 d£45. BB&M s£ 42.50, d£50.
Rooms 4, ensuite 4. High tea £4.50.
Dinner £7.50. Last orders 2200 hrs.
Open all year.

Ⓟ ⏆ ✻ ᴥ ⓞᴀᴘ ▥. ⛶ ⎀ ⋌ ⌿ ⒠

KILNAMAR (U)
(Mrs E Lunn), 174 Finaghy Rd South, Upper
Malone, BT10 0DH. ☎ (0232) 611564.
B&B s£25 d£45. BB&M s£34 d£63.
Rooms 3, ensuite 1. High tea £9.50.
Dinner £10.50. Open all year.

Ⓟ ✻ ᴥ ⓞᴀᴘ ▥. ⛶ ⌿ ⎀ ∪

Facilities are liable to change. Check prices when you book. Key to symbols is on the back flap.

Where to Play in Northern Ireland

Castle Entertainment Centre

OPEN 9AM TO 2AM DAILY

Raceview, Factory Road, Enniskillen
Telephone (0365) 324172

Something for all the family, including

Bowlervision

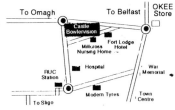

The most advanced Tenpin Bowling system in the world
An entertaining sport which can be enjoyed by all ages

Cineworld

Three of Ireland's most luxurious and modern Cinema
Theatres, guaranteed to show all the latest releases

Adventureworld

One of the UK's largest and most exciting soft-play
indoor adventure park for children from 3 to 14

To complete your visit we also offer the following
A superb Hot Food Bar serving everything from coffee to dinner
A delightful Candy Bar to cater for even the sweetest tooth!
A spacious pool and amusement area for the young (and not-so-young!)

OPEN EVERY DAY 10AM UNTIL VERY LATE
FOR BOOKINGS AND ENQUIRIES
TELEPHONE: (0247) 454729

NORTHERN IRELANDS LEADING
ADVENTURE PLAYGROUND FOR CHILDREN

TENPIN BOWLING

The biggest and best jungle for kids,
Pitfalls and Traps, Freefall Slide,
Snake Forest, Bouncey Castle,
Spookey Caves, Toddlers Section
Trained Staff in Attendance

4 Screen Cinema,
7 days a week,
Double Seats!,
Latest Selections
Cinema Shop.

16 Lanes, 7 days a week,
10 am - midnight,
Coaching available,
Computerised score

All facilities fully bookable for private parties, schools, birthdays, conference etc.

Battle adventure in the futuristic combat zone

The greatest leisure, pleasure,
fitness, entertainment,
family fun centre in the
country!

- *18 Lane Bowlervision*
  - *Amazon Adventure Park*
    - *Quasar Laser*
      - *4-Screen Cineplex*
        - *Jet snacks*

All under one roof!

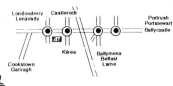

Riverside Park, Coleraine. Tel. (0265) 58011

LISMORE LODGE   (U)
(Mr & Mrs J Devlin), 410 Ormeau Rd,
BT7 3HY. ☎ (0232) 641205.
B&B s£18 d£38. Rooms 7, ensuite 4.
Open all year.

OAKHILL HOUSE   (U)
(Mrs M Noble), 59 Dunmurry Lane,
BT17 9JR. ☎ (0232) 610658. Fax 621566.
B&B s£50 d£70. BB&M s£65 d£100.
Rooms 3, ensuite 3. Dinner £15.
Last orders 1600 hrs. Open all year ex
Christmas.

ROSELEIGH HOUSE   (U)
(Mr & Mrs P McKay), 19 Rosetta Park,
BT6 0DL. ☎ (0232) 644414.
B&B s£29 d£41. Rooms 7, ensuite 7.
Dinner £14. Last orders 2000 hrs.
Open all year.

Bed & Breakfast

AISLING HOUSE
(Mrs D Devenny), 7 Taunton Avenue,
Antrim Rd, BT15 4AD. ☎ (0232) 771529.
B&B s£15 d£29. Rooms 3.
Open all year.

ARDLEA
(Mrs G Lee), 38 Ashley Gardens,
BT15 4DN. ☎ (0232) 770896.
B&B s£15 d£28. Rooms 2. Open all year.

ASHBERRY COTTAGE
(Mr S Mitchell), 19 Rosepark Central,
Dundonald, BT5 7RN. ☎ (0232) 482441.
B&B s£15 d£29.
BB&M s£20 d£40. Rooms 3.
High tea £6. Dinner £7.50. Open all year.

BEAUMONT LODGE
(Mrs V Kidd) 237 Stranmillis Rd, BT9 5EE.
☎ (0232) 667965.
B&B s£20 d£40. BB&M s£26, d£50.
Rooms 4, ensuite 1. High tea £6. Dinner
£9. Last orders 1900 hrs. Open all year.

BEN EADAN
(C Rooney), 9 Thorburn Rd, Antrim Rd,
BT36 7HZ. ☎ (0232) 777764.
B&B s£15 d£28. Rooms 2, ensuite 1.
Open all year.

BOTANIC LODGE
(Mrs S Moore), 87 Botanic Avenue, BT7
1JN. ☎ (0232) 327682/247439.
B&B s£18 d£34. BB&M s£28 d£54.
Rooms 16, ensuite 1. Dinner £10.
Last orders 2100 hrs. Open all year.

BOWDENS
(Mrs C Bowden), 17 Sandford Avenue,
BT5 5NW. ☎ (0232) 652213.
B&B s£14 d£28. Rooms 2. Open all year.

B&B = bed and breakfast   s = single   d = double   BB&M = bed, breakfast & evening meal

THE COTTAGE
(Mrs E Muldoon), 377 Comber Rd,
Dundonald, BT16 0XB. ☎ (0247) 878189.
B&B s£16 d£30. Rooms 2.
Open all year.

CRECORA
(Mrs J Moore), 114 Upper Newtownards
Rd, BT4 3EN. ☎ (0232) 658257.
B&B s£15 d£30. Rooms 5, ensuite 1.
Open all year.

DRUMRAGH
(Mrs S Cooper), 647 Antrim Rd, BT15 3EA.
☎ (0232) 773063.
B&B s£15 d£30. Rooms 4.
Open all year.

DUN-ROAMIN
(Mr D Smyth), 172 Upper Newtownards
Rd, BT4 3ES. ☎ (0232) 659902.
B&B s£16 d£27. Rooms 7. Open all year.

THE EAGLES
(Mrs L McMichael),
131 Upper Newtownards Rd, BT4 3HW.
☎ (0232) 673607.
B&B s£15 d£30. Rooms 4. Open all year.

EAST SHEEN HOUSE
(Mrs R Davidson), 81 Eglantine Avenue,
BT9 6EW. ☎ (0232) 667149.
B&B s£14 d£28. Rooms 3 , ensuite 1.
Open all year.

THE GEORGE
(Mrs C McGuinness), 9 Eglantine Avenue,
BT9 6DW. ☎ (0232) 683212.
B&B s£15 d£30. Rooms 4. Open all year.

Mrs E GILLESPIE
No 23, 23 Derryvolgie Ave, BT9 6FN.
☎ (0232) 681549.
B&B s£25 d£40. Rooms 2. Open all year.

HELGA LODGE
(Mr N Will), 7 Cromwell Road, BT7,1JW
☎ (0232) 324820. Fax 320653.
B&B s£17 d£32. BB&M s£32 d£62. Rooms
32, ensuite 16. Dinner £15. Last orders
1700 hrs. Open all year.

JAMES HOUSE
(Mrs S Fleming), 55 Oakland Avenue,
BT4 3BW. ☎ (0232) 650374.
B&B s£12.50 d£25. Rooms 3. Dinner £6.
Last orders 1100 hrs. Open all year.

LUCY'S LODGE
(Mrs F McLean), 72 Salisbury Avenue,
BT15 5EB. ☎ (0232) 776036.
B&B s£15 d£30. Rooms 4. Open all year.

MANOR HOUSE
(Mrs P Tully), 12 The Manor, Blacks Rd,
BT10 0HD. ☎ (0232) 600807.
B&B s£17.50 d£35. Rooms 1, ensuite 1.
Open all year.

Facilities are liable to change. Check prices when you book. Key to symbols is on the back flap.

AD
VENTURE

Olympic Ice Rink   10 Pin Bowling

Indianaland   Laserquest

DUNDONALD
INTERNATIONAL
Ice Bowl

111 Old Dundonald Road, Belfast Tel : (0232) 482611

MARANTHA
(Mrs E McCrea), 398 Ravenhill Rd,
BT6 0BA. ☎ (0232) 645814.
B&B s£15 d£28. BB&M s£18, d£35.
Rooms 5. High tea £5. Dinner £6. Last
orders 1500 hrs. Open all year.

P ❀ ⛄ ᴮᴬᴾ ▥ ▢ ⚒ ↾

MARINE HOUSE
(Mrs M Corrigan), 30 Eglantine Avenue,
BT9 6DX. ☎ (0232) 662828/381922.
B&B s£15 d£28. BB&M s£25 d£48. Rooms
9, ensuite 2. High tea £8. Dinner £10. Last
orders 2000 hrs. Open all year.

P ❀ ⛄ ▥

Mrs E McNAMARA
7 Fortwilliam Park, BT15 4AL.
☎ (0232) 779904.
B&B s£14 d£28. Rooms 4, ensuite 1.
Open all year.

P ❀ ⚡ ⛄ ▥ ▢ ⛏ ⚒ ↾

QUEEN'S ELMS
Queen's University, 78 Malone Rd,
BT9 5BW. ☎ (0232) 381608. Fax 666680.
Bed only s£10 d£15. Rooms 300.
Open Jul-Sept.

P ❀ ⛄ ⊡ ▥ ⚒ ⚓

QUEEN'S UNIVERSITY COMMON ROOM
1 College Gardens, University Rd,
BT9 6BQ. ☎ (0232) 665938. Fax 681209.
B&B s£35 d£50. Rooms 25, ensuite 17.
Open all year.

⚑ ⛄ ▥ ▢ ⛏ ⚒ ✱ ↾ ⚓ ⊞

STRANMILLIS COLLEGE
Stranmillis Rd, BT9 5DY.
☎ (0232) 381271.
Groups only.
Rooms 450. Open Mar/April & Jun-Aug.

P ❀ ♣ ⛄ ▥ ⚒ ✱ ⚲ ⚓

YWCA HOSTEL
Queen Mary's Hall, 70 Fitzwilliam St,
Lisburn Rd, BT9 6AX. ☎ (0232) 240439.
B&B s£13 d£26. BB&M s£18.50 d£37.
Rooms 17. Dinner £5.50.
Last orders 1500 hrs.
Open all year (ex Easter & Christmas).

⌂ ❀ ⛄ ▥ ⚒ ✱

B&B = bed and breakfast   s = single   d = double   BB&M = bed, breakfast & evening meal

County Antrim

ANTRIM

Hotels

DEERPARK HOTEL *
71 Dublin Rd, BT41 4PN.
☎ (0849) 462480. Fax 467126.
B&B s£40 d£60. Rooms 19, ensuite 15.
Open all year.

🅃 🅿 🏠 ❄ ♣ ⛷ ❗ ⛄ 🐎 🏚 💻 ❑ 📞 ✂ 🎵 ⌂ ∪
✓ ⛴ ⚓ ♨ ⊞

Guesthouses

THE BEECHES (A)
(Mrs M Allen), 10 Dunadry Rd,
Muckamore, BT41 2RR.
☎ (0849) 433161. Fax 433161.
B&B s£30 d£50. BB&M s£41 d£72.
Rooms 5, ensuite 4. Dinner £11.
Last orders 2000 hrs. Open all year.

🅿 🏠 ❄ ♣ ⛷ ⛄ OAP 💻 ❑ ✂ 🎵 ⌂ ∪ ⛴ ⚓ ⊞

Bed & Breakfast

BALLYARNOTT HOUSE
(Mrs H McMinn), 7 Oldstone Hill,
Muckamore, BT41 4SB.
☎ (0849) 463292.
B&B s£13 d£26. Rooms 3. High tea
£5.50. Dinner £6.50. Open all year.

🅿 ❄ ♣ ⛄ 💻 ✂

Mr & Mrs J M DENNISON
23 Thornhill Rd, BT41 2LH.
☎ (0849) 462964.
B&B s£13 d£26. Rooms 3. Open all year.

🅿 ♣ ⛄ 💻 ✂ ⌂ ♨

SPRINGHILL
(Mrs Rosemary McKeown), 37 Thornhill
Rd, BT41 2LH. ☎ (0849) 469117.
B&B s£13 d£26. Rooms 2. High tea £5.
Dinner £8. Open all year.

🅿 ❄ ♣ ⛷ ⛄ 💻 ✂ ⌂ ∪ ⚓

BALLINTOY

Bed & Breakfast

WHITEPARK HOUSE
(Mr & Mrs R Isles), Whitepark Bay,
BT54 6NH. ☎ (026 57) 31482.
B&B s£20 d£35. Rooms 3. Open all year.

🅃 🅿 🏠 ❄ ♣ ⛷ 💻 ✂ ⚘

BALLYCASTLE

Hotels

MARINE HOTEL   ***
1 North St, BT54 6BN. ☎ (026 57) 62222.
Fax 69507.
B&B s£37.50 d£52.50. BB&M s£50
d£77.50. Rooms 32, ensuite 32. High tea
£9.50. Dinner £15. Last orders 2130 hrs.
Open all year.

🅃 🅿 🏠 ⛷ ❗ ⛄ 🎲 OAP 🐎 💻 ❑ 📞 ✂ 🎵 ∪
⛴ 🍽 🌐 ⚘ ⊞

Guesthouses

GLENLUCE (B)
(Marian Brady), 42 Quay Rd,
BT54 6BH. ☎ (026 57) 62914.
B&B s£18 d£20. Rooms 14, ensuite 6.
High tea £6. Open all year.

🅿 ❄ ⛄ 💻 ❑ ✂ 🎵 ⌂ ∪ ⚘

Facilities are liable to change. Check prices when you book. Key to symbols is on the back flap.

HILSEA (B)
(Mr M Jameson), 28 Quay Hill, BT54 6BW.
☎ (026 57) 62385/63624.
B&B s£14 d£28. BB&M s£20 d£40.
Rooms 21, ensuite 1. High tea £6. Dinner
£6. Last orders 2000 hrs. Open Mar-Oct.

COLLIERS HALL (U)
(Mrs M McCarry), 50 Cushendall Rd,
BT54 6QR. ☎ (026 57) 62531.
B&B s£15 d£33. BB&M s£25 d£53.
Rooms 3, ensuite 2. High tea £5. Dinner
£10. Last orders 1200 hrs. Open Apr-Sept.
On A2, 2m E of Ballycastle

FRAGRENS (U)
(Mr & Mrs Frayne), 34 Quay Rd,
BT54 6BH. ☎ (026 57) 62168.
B&B s£14.50 d£29. BB&M s£22.50 d£58.
Rooms 8, ensuite 3. Dinner £8.
Last orders 2200 hrs. Open all year.

Bed & Breakfast

AMMIROY HOUSE
(Mrs M Crawford), 24 Quay Rd, BT54 6BH.
☎ (026 57) 62621.
B&B s£13 d£26. Rooms 2. Open all year.

ARDMARA
(Mr & Mrs H Herron), 34 Whitepark Rd,
BT54 6LJ. ☎ (026 57) 69533.
B&B s£17 d£28. Rooms 3, ensuite 1.
Open Apr-Sept.

DRUMAWILLAN HOUSE
(Mr & Mrs J Todd), 1 Whitepark Rd,
BT54 6HH. ☎ (026 57) 62539.
B&B s£14 d£28. Rooms 3.
Open all year.

FAIR HEAD VIEW
(Mrs K Delargy), 26 North St, BT54 6BW.
☎ (026 57) 62822.
B&B s£11 d£22. Rooms 3. Open all year.

GLENHAVEN
(Mrs A Gormley), 10 Beechwood Avenue,
BT54 6BL. ☎ (026 57) 63612.
B&B s£15 d£26. Rooms 3. Open all year.

GORTCONNEY FARM
(Mrs H Smyth), Gortconney, 52 Whitepark
Rd, BT54 6LP. ☎ (026 57) 62283.
B&B s£14 d£27. Rooms 3. Open Apr-Oct.

KENMARA HOUSE
(Mr E Shannon), 45 North St, BT54 6BP.
☎ (026 57) 62600.
B&B s£16 d£35. Rooms 3, ensuite 2.
Open Feb-Nov.

KILMEAN FARM
(Mr & Mrs Kane), 4 Glenstaughey Rd,
BT54 6NE. ☎ (026 57) 63305.
B&B s£12.50 d£25. Rooms 2.
Open Mar-Sept.

B&B = bed and breakfast   s = single   d = double   BB&M = bed, breakfast & evening meal

RATHUSHARD
(Mrs J Lynn), 3 Rathlin Rd, BT54 6DD.
☎ (026 57) 62237.
B&B s£13 d£26. Rooms 2. Open all year.

🅿 ❄ 🌿 🐴 🖾 ⅍ ♪ ⌐ ∪ ✓ ⚲

SILVERSPRINGS
(Mrs M Mulholland), 20 Quay Rd,
BT54 0BH. ☎ (026 57) 62080.
B&B s£15 d£30. Rooms 2, ensuite 2.
Open Easter-Oct.

🅿 ❄ ♣ 🌿 🐴 🖾 ♪ ⌐ ∪ ◭ ⚲

Miss B WINTER
1 Knocklayde View, BT54 6DY.
☎ (026 57) 62703.
B&B s£12.50 d£25. Rooms 2.
Open Apr-Oct.

🅿 ❄ 🌿 🐴 🖾 ⅍ ⚲

BALLYCLARE

Bed & Breakfast

BEECHCROFT
(Mrs B McKay), 43 Belfast Rd, Ballynure,
BT39 9TZ. ☎ (0960) 352334.
B&B s£14 d£28. BB&M s£20 d£40.
Rooms 2. Open all year.

🅿 ❄ ♣ 🌿 🐴 🖾 🖾 ⅍ ♪ ⌐ ∪ ✓ ⚲ 🎔

FAIRWAYS
(Mrs A Berry), 30 Orpinsmill Rd, BT39 0SX.
☎ (0960) 342419.
B&B s£16. BB&M s£25. Rooms 3, ensuite 1.
Dinner £9. Open all year.

🆃 🅿 ❄ ♣ 🌿 🐴 🖾 ⌐ ⅍ ♪ ⌐

HOLESTONE HOUSE
(Mrs AV Hamilton), 23 Deer Park, Doagh,
BT39 0RH. ☎ (0960) 352306.
B&B s£20 d£30. Rooms 4, ensuite 3.
Open all year.

🅿 🏠 ❄ ♣ 🌿 🐴 🖾 ⌐

ROCKBANK
(Mrs H Park), 40 Belfast Rd, Ballynure,
BT39 9TZ. ☎ (0960) 352261.
B&B s£12 d£24. Rooms 2. Open all year.

🅿 ❄ ♣ 🌿 🐴 🖾 🐎 🖾 ⅍ ⚲

RUA-WAI FARM
(Mrs A Hunter), 149 Templepatrick Rd,
BT39 9RW. ☎ (0960) 352417.
B&B s£12 d£24. Rooms 3. Open all year.
On A57, 8m E of Airport

🅿 ❄ ♣ 🌿 🐴 🖾 🖾 ⌐ ⅍ ♪ ⌐ ∪ ✓ ⚲

TILDARG HOUSE
(Mrs J Thompson), 50 Collin Rd, BT39 9JS.
☎ (0960) 322367.
B&B s£18 d£35. Rooms 4, ensuite 1.
Open all year.

🅿 🏠 ❄ ♣ 🌿 🐴 🖾 ⅍ ♪ ⌐

VALLEYVIEW HOUSE
(Mrs P Mitchell), 52a Templepatrick Rd,
BT39 9TX. ☎ (0960) 342254.
B&B s£17 d£32. BB&M s£26.50 d£51.
Rooms 2, ensuite 1. High tea £7.50.
Dinner £9.50. Last orders 2000 hrs.
Open all year.

🆃 🅿 ❄ ♣ 🌿 🐴 🖾 🖾 ⌐ ⅍ ♪ ⌐ ∪ ✓ ◭ ⚲

Facilities are liable to change. Check prices when you book. Key to symbols is on the back flap.

WOODBINE COTTAGE
(Mrs M Crawford), 98 Carrickfergus Rd,
Ballynure, BT39 9QP. ☎ (0960) 352092.
B&B s£13.50 d£27. BB&M s£22.50 d£45.
Rooms 3, ensuite 1. High tea £7. Dinner
£9. Last orders 2000 hrs. Open all year.
Off A2, 4m E of Ballyclare

Hotels

BALLYGALLY CASTLE HOTEL ***
274 Coast Rd, BT40 2RA. ☎ (0574)
583212. Fax 583681.
B&B s£45 d£68. BB&M s£59 d£82.
Rooms 30, ensuite 30. High tea £8.50.
Dinner £14. Last orders 2130 hrs.
Open all year.

Bed & Breakfast

CAIRNVIEW
(Mrs J Lough), 13 Croft Heights, BT40 2QS.
☎ (0574) 583269.
B&B s£15 d£30. Rooms 4, ensuite 3.
Open all year.
4m N of Larne

GLENCAIRN
(Mrs I Moore), 2 Drumnagreagh Rd,
Cairncastle, BT40 2RL.
☎ (0574) 583502/583252.
B&B s£16 d£30. Rooms 2, ensuite 2.
Open all year.

TE EN TEASA
(Mrs G Davis), 4 Coastguard Cottages,
BT40 2QX. ☎ (0574) 583591.
B&B s£12.50 d£25. Rooms 2, ensuite 2.
Open all year.

Hotels

GALGORM MANOR ****
Ballymena BT42 1EA. ☎ (0266) 881001.
Fax 88080.
B&B s£79 d£99. Rooms 23, ensuite 23.
Last orders 2130 hrs. Open all year.

ADAIR ARMS HOTEL ***
Ballymoney Rd, BT43 5BS. ☎ (0266)
653674. Fax 40436.
B&B s£53 d£72. BB&M s£65 d£98.
Rooms 40, ensuite 40. High tea £8.50.
Dinner £12. Last orders 2130 hrs.
Open all year.

COUNTRY HOUSE HOTEL ***
20 Doagh Rd, Kells, BT42 3LZ. ☎ (0266)
891663. Fax 891477.
B&B s£70 d£80. Rooms 40, ensuite 40.
High tea £11. Dinner £17. Last orders
2115 hrs. Open all year.

B&B = bed and breakfast   s = single   d = double   BB&M = bed, breakfast & evening meal

TULLYGLASS HOUSE HOTEL *
178 Galgorm Rd, BT42 1HJ .
☎ (0266) 652639/652315. Fax 46938.
B&B s£27.50 d£50. BB&M s£38.50 d£72.
Rooms 14, ensuite 14. High tea £6.50.
Dinner £11. Last orders 2145 hrs. Open
all year.

🅿 🏨 ✿ ♣ 🍽 🐎 [OAP] 🛏 📞 ✂ 🎵 ▶ 🎯 £

Guesthouses

TULLYMORE HOUSE   (B)
(Mr J Hill), 2 Carnlough Rd, Broughshane,
BT43 7HF. ☎ (0266) 861233. Fax 862238.
B&B s£40 d£55. BB&M s£49 d£73.
Rooms 10, ensuite 10. High tea £9.
Dinner £9.50. Last orders 2130 hrs.
Open all year.

🆃 🅿 🏨 ✿ ♣ 🎿 🍽 🐎 🛢 🛏 📞 ✂ 🎵 ▶ U ⚓
⛵ ⚓ 🎯 £

Bed & Breakfast

ARDMORE HOUSE
(Mrs A Bamber), 51 Thomas St, BT43 6AZ.
☎ (0266) 47772.
B&B s£16 d£30. BB&M s£21 d£42.
Rooms 14. Dinner £6. Open all year.

🆃 🅿 🏨 ✿ 🐎 [OAP] 🛢 ✂ 🎵 ▶ ⛵ ⚓ 🎯

ASHDENE
(Mrs J Tennant), 60 Ballymacvea Rd,
Shankbridge, BT42 2LT. ☎ (0266) 898100.
B&B s£16 d£28. Rooms 3. Open Jun-Sept.
Off A26, 4m S of Ballymena

🅿 🏨 ✿ 🐎 🦌 🛢 ✂ ▶

BEECHFIELD
(Mr & Mrs R Logan), 81 Galgorm Rd,
BT42 1AA. ☎ (0266) 659709.
B&B s£15 d£25. BB&M s£22
d£39. Rooms 6, ensuite 3. High tea £5.
Dinner £7. Last orders 2000 hrs.
Open all year.

🅿 🏨 ✿ ♣ 🐎 🛢 🛏 ✂ 🎵 ▶ U ⚓

CARNVIEW
(Mr & Mrs McKeown), 5 Drumfin Rd,
BT34 6TT. ☎ (0266) 685340.
B&B s£14 d£28. Rooms 3. Open all year.

🅿 ✿ ♣ 🎿 🐎 [OAP] 🛢 ✂ 🎵

CROSSVIEW
(Mrs D Hanna), 146 Crankill Rd,
Glarryford, BT44 9EY. ☎ (0266) 685360.
B&B s£14 d£28. BB&M s£20 d£40.
Rooms 2. High tea £6. Dinner £6. Last
orders 2030 hrs. Open all year.

🅿 ✿ ♣ 🎿 🐎 [OAP] 🛢 ✂ 🎵 ▶

DIAMOND BAR
(Mrs M Logan), 17 The Diamond, Ahoghill,
BT42 1JZ. ☎ (0266) 871251.
B&B s£15 d£25. Rooms 3. Open all year.

🅿 🍽 🐎 [OAP] 🛢 ✂ 🎵 ▶ U ⛵ ⚓

ELM TREE HOUSE
(Mrs H Edmondson), 62 Old Tullygarley
Rd, BT42 2JD. ☎ (0266) 48461.
B&B s£15 d£28. Rooms 2, ensuite 2.
Open all year.
Off B18, 2m SW of Ballymena

🆃 🅿 ✿ ♣ 🐎 🛢 🛏 ✂ 🎵 ▶ ⚓

Facilities are liable to change. Check prices when you book. Key to symbols is on the back flap.

33

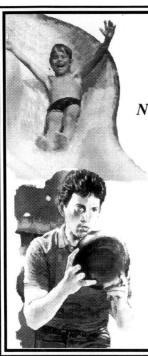

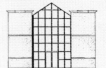

NEELSGROVE FARM
(Mrs M Neely), 51 Carnearney Rd,
Ahoghill, BT42 2PL. ☎ (0266) 871225.
B&B s£14 d£28. BB&M s£21 d£42. Rooms
3, ensuite 1. High tea £6.50. Dinner £7.
Last orders 1400 hrs. Open all year.

QUARRYTOWN LODGE
(Mrs M Drennan), 15 Quarrytown Rd,
Broughshane, BT43 7LB. ☎ (0266) 862027.
B&B s£17 d£30. BB&M s£25 d£46. Rooms
4, ensuite 3. High tea £6. Dinner £8.
Last orders 2030 hrs. Open all year.

SHANLEIGH HOUSE
(Mrs M Hunter), 8 Shandon Park,
Grange Rd, Galgorm Rd, BT42 2ED.
☎ (0266) 44851.
B&B s£14 d£26. Rooms 5, ensuite 1.
Open all year.

SLEMISH HOUSE
(Miss B Shaw), 51 Albert Place, BT43 6DY.
☎ (0266) 47383.
B&B s£16 d£26. Rooms 2. Open all year.

SLEMISH VIEW
(Mr & Mrs W Millar), 75 Cromkill Rd,
BT42 2JR. ☎ (0266) 40355.
B&B s£10 d£20. BB&M s£15 d£30.
Rooms 3. High tea £5. Dinner £7.
Last orders 2230 hrs. Open all year.

SPRINGMOUNT
(Mrs R Bell), 31 Ballygowan Rd, Kells,
BT42 3PD. ☎ (0266) 891275.
B&B s£12 d£24 . Rooms 3.
Open all year.

WILMAUR
(Mrs M Caves), 83 Galgorm Rd, BT42 6AA.
☎ (0266) 41878.
B&B s£16.50 d£32. Rooms 4, ensuite 3.
Open all year.

BALLYMONEY

Guesthouses

COOLEEN   (A)
(Mrs E Hammond), 15 Coleraine Rd, BT53
6BP. ☎ (026 56) 63037.
B&B s£20 d£35. BB&M s£27.50 d£50.
Rooms 6, ensuite 6. High tea £6. Dinner
£7.50. Open all year.
On B62, 1/2m N of Ballymoney

COUNTRY GUEST HOUSE   (B)
(Mr & Mrs F Brown), 41 Kirk Rd, BT53
8HB. ☎ (026 56) 62620.
B&B s£15 d£30. BB&M s£23 d£46.
Rooms 4, ensuite 4. High tea £8.
Open all year.

Facilities are liable to change. Check prices when you book. Key to symbols is on the back flap.

35

SEACON HALL (U)
(Alice Christie), 40 Seacon Park, BT53,
6QB. ☎ (026 56) 62754.
B&B s£17 d£34 BB&M s£25 d£50. Rooms
4, ensuite 4. High tea £6. Dinner £8. Last
orders 1900 hrs. Open all year.

Bed & Breakfast

CONISTON
(Mrs M Gowland), 87 Balnamore Rd,
BT53 7PU. ☎ (026 56) 64752.
B&B s£14 d£28. BB&M s£19.50 d£37.
Rooms 3, ensuite 3. High tea £5.50. Last
orders 1700 hrs. Open all year.

Mrs M McCONAGHIE
293 Moyarget Rd, Mosside, BT53 8EG.
☎ (026 57) 41471.
B&B s£11 d£22. BB&M s£15 d£30.
Rooms 2. High tea £3.50. Dinner £4.50.
Open all year.

MILLVIEW
(Mr & Mrs J Wilson), 16 Kilmoyle Rd,
BT53 6NR. ☎ (026 57) 41070.
B&B s£12 d£24. Rooms 2. Open all year.

MOORE LODGE
(Sir Wm & Lady Moore). ☎ (026 65) 41043.
B&B s£40 d£65. Rooms 3, ensuite 3.
Open May-Aug.

PINEVIEW
(Mrs M Simpson), 111 Castlecatt Rd,
BT53 8AP. ☎ (026 57) 41527.
B&B s£13.50 d£27. Rooms 1.
Open Mar-Sept.

SANDELWOOD
(Mrs S Brown), 98 Knock Rd, BT53 6NQ.
☎ (02656) 62621.
B&B s£12 d£24. Rooms 2. Open Mar-Oct.

BUSHMILLS

Hotels

BUSHMILLS INN   ***
25 Main St, BT57 8QN. ☎ (026 57) 32339.
Fax 32048.
B&B s£48 d£74. Rooms 11, ensuite 11.
High tea £9. Dinner £15.
Last orders 2130 hrs. Open all year.

Bed & Breakfast

ARDEEVIN
(Mrs J Montgomery), 145 Main St,
BT57 8QE. ☎ (026 57) 31661.
B&B s£14 d£28. Rooms 3, ensuite 1.
Open Feb-Dec.

B&B = bed and breakfast   s = single   d = double   BB&M = bed, breakfast & evening meal

AUBERGE DE SENEIRL
(Messrs J & B Defres), 28 Ballyclogh Rd,
BT57 8UZ. ☎ (026 57) 41536.
B&B d£74. Rooms 5, ensuite 5.
Dinner £17. Last orders 2130 hrs.
Open all year.

DANESCROFT
(Mrs O Rutherford), 171 Whitepark Rd,
Portbraddan, BT57 8SS.
☎ (026 57) 31586.
B&B s£19 d£35. Rooms 3, ensuite 3.
Open all year (ex Christmas).
On A2, 5m NE of Bushmills

Mrs JANE GREGG
167 Causeway Rd BT57. ☎ (026 57)
31846.
B&B s£13 d£26. Rooms 2. Open Apr-Oct.

KNOCKLAYDE VIEW
(Mrs J Wylie), 90 Causeway Rd, BT57 8SX.
☎ (026 57) 32099.
B&B s£13 d£26. Rooms 2. Open all year.

Mrs McMULLAN
4 Castlenagree Rd, BT57 8SW.
☎ (026 57) 31154.
B&B s£12.50 d£25. Rooms 3. Open Apr-Sept.

MONTALTO HOUSE
(Mrs D Taggart), 5 Craigaboney Rd, BT57
8XD. ☎ (026 57) 31257.
B&B s£17 d£32. Rooms 5. Open Mar-Oct.
Off B17, W of Bushmills

Mrs E RANKIN
198 Ballybogey Rd, BT57 8UH.
☎ (026 57) 31793.
B&B s£12.50 d£25. Rooms 2.
Open Apr -Sept.

THE SYCAMORES
(Mrs V Sharpe), 56 Priestland Rd, BT57
8UR. ☎ (026 57) 31145.
B&B s£12.50 d£25. Rooms 3. Open all
year.

VALLEY VIEW
(Mrs V McFall), 6a Ballyclough Rd, BT57
8TU. ☎ (026 57) 41608/41319.
B&B s£12 d£23. Rooms 2. Open all year.
On B67, 4m N of Ballymoney

Hotels

LONDONDERRY ARMS HOTEL **
20 Harbour Rd, BT44 0EU.
☎ (0574) 885255/885458. Fax 885263.
B&B s£45 d£65. BB&M s£56.50 d£86.
Rooms 21, ensuite 21. High tea £10.
Dinner £14.95. Last orders 2100 hrs.
Open all year.

Facilities are liable to change. Check prices when you book. Key to symbols is on the back flap.

Guesthouses

BETHANY   (A)
(Mrs M Aiken), 5 Bay Rd, BT44 0HQ.
☎ (0574) 885667.
B&B s£13.50 d£27. Rooms 7, ensuite 7.
Open all year.

BRIDGE INN   (B)
(Mr & Mrs J Davison), 2 Bridge St,
BT44 0EH. ☎ (0574) 885669.
B&B s£15 d£28. BB&M s£20 d£38.
Rooms 5. High tea £5. Dinner £6.
Last orders 2030 hrs. Open all year.

Bed & Breakfast

GLENVIEW
(Mrs T McKay), 124 Ballymena Rd,
BT44 0LA. ☎ (0574) 885546.
B&B s£13.50 d£27. Rooms 3.
High tea £6. Open all year.

CARRICKFERGUS

Hotels

COAST ROAD HOTEL   *
28 Scotch Quarter, BT38 7DP.
☎ (0960) 351021. Fax 351021.
B&B s£40 d£60. Rooms 20, ensuite 14.
High tea £9. Dinner £12. Last orders
2100 hrs. Open all year.

DOBBINS INN HOTEL   *
6 High St, BT38 9HE. ☎ (0960) 351905.
B&B s£40 d£62. BB&M s£49 d£78. Rooms
13, ensuite 13. High tea £6. Dinner £9.
Last orders 2100 hrs. Open all year.

Bed & Breakfast

BEECHGROVE
(Mr & Mrs J Barron), 412 Upper Rd,
Trooperslane, BT38 8PW.
☎ (0960) 363304.
B&B s£13.50 d£25. BB&M s£20.50
d£39. Rooms 6, ensuite 2. Dinner £5.
Last orders 1900 hrs. Open all year.
Off A2, 1m S of Carrickfergus

CRAIGS FARM
(Mrs J Craig), 90 Hillhead Rd, Ballycarry,
BT38 9JF. ☎ (0960) 353769.
B&B s£14.50 d£29. Rooms 3, ensuite 2.
Open all year.

DRUMGART
(Mrs E Loughridge), 48 Hillhead Rd,
Ballycarry, BT38 9HE. ☎ (0960) 353507.
B&B s£12 d£24. Rooms 1. Open Apr-Sept.

Mrs E GRAHAM
54 Liberty Rd.
BT38 9DJ. ☎ (0960) 366219.
B&B s£15 d£30. Rooms 3, ensuite 2.
Open all year.

HIGHLANDS
(Mrs S Hilditch), 34 Cairn Rd, BT38 9AP.
☎ (0960) 364773.
B&B s£15 d£30. Rooms 2, ensuite 1.
Open all year.

LANGSGARDEN
(Mrs C Begley), 70 Scotch Quarter, BT38
7DP. ☎ (0960) 366369/(0860) 910317.
B&B s£15.50 d£31. Rooms 11.
Open all year.

MARATHON HOUSE
(Mrs J Kernohan), 3 Upper Station Rd,
BT38 8RQ. ☎ (0232) 862475.
B&B s£15 d£30. Rooms 4, ensuite1.
Open all year.

MARINA HOUSE
(Mr & Mrs G Mulholland), 49 Irish Quarter
Sth, BT38 8BL. ☎ (0960) 364055.
B&B s£17.50 d£35. Rooms 9, ensuite 2.
Open all year.

NEWMILLS
(Mrs P Maguire), Ballycarry, BT38 9JW.
☎ (0960) 372699. Fax 353220.
B&B s£25 d£50. Rooms 1. Open Apr-Oct.

SEAVIEW
(Mr J P Sutherland), 33 Larne Rd, BT38 7EE.
☎ (0960) 363170.
B&B s£15 d£30. BB&M s£19 d£36.
Rooms 2, ensuite 1. High tea £3. Dinner
£4.
Last orders 2200 hrs. Open Apr-Oct.

CLOUGHMILLS

Bed & Breakfast

BREEZEMOUNT
(Mrs M O'Mullan), 27 Ballylig Rd, Dunloy,
BT44 9DS. ☎ (026 563) 468.
B&B s£14.50 d£29. Rooms 2. Open all
year.

CRUMLIN

Guesthouses

CALDHAME LODGE   (B)
(Mr & Mrs McKavanagh), 102 Moira Rd,
BT29 4HG. ☎ (0849) 423099.
B&B s£15 d£29. BB&M s£23.50
d£45. Rooms 4, ensuite 4. High tea £8.50.
Dinner £9.50. Last orders 2200 hrs.
Open all year.
5m from Airport

CROSSROADS COUNTRY
  GUEST HOUSE   (B)
(Mr W Lorimer), 1 Largy Rd, BT29 4AH.
☎ (0849) 452491.
B&B s£14 d£28. BB&M s£20
d£40. Rooms 3. Dinner £6.
Last orders 2100 hrs. Open all year.
3m S of Airport

Facilities are liable to change. Check prices when you book. Key to symbols is on the back flap.

KEEF HALLA   (U)
(Mr & Mrs C Kelly), 20 Tully Rd, Nutts
Corner, BT29 4AH. ☎ (0232) 825491.
B&B s£15 d£27. BB&M s£23.50 d£44.
Rooms 4, ensuite 1. High tea £8. Dinner
£8.50. Last orders 1930 hrs. Open all year.

🅣 🅟 ✿ ♠ ⅍ ☜ 🛏 ☐ ⚥ ♪ ↾ ∪ ⚓ ◬ ⚡

Bed & Breakfast

ASHMORE
(Mrs M McClure), 64 Main St, Glenavy,
BT29 4LP. ☎ (0849) 422773.
B&B s£12 d£24. Rooms 2, ensuite 1.
Open all year.
On A26, S of Airport

🅟 ✿ ♠ ⅍ ☜ 🛏 ⚥

BEN NEAGH HOUSE
(Mr & Mrs A Peel), 11 Crumlin Rd,
BT29 4AD. ☎ (0849) 422271.
B&B s£15 d£30.
Rooms 5. Open all year.

🅟 🏠 ✿ ♠ ☜ 🛏 ⚥

CLEARSPRINGS FARM
(Mrs E Duncan), 9 Belfast Rd. BT29 4FA.
☎ (0232) 825275.
B&B s£13 d£26. BB&M s£18, d£36.
Rooms 3, ensuite 1. High tea £5. Dinner
£7. Open all year.
4m from Airport

🅣 🅟 ✿ ♠ ☜ 🛏 ⚥ ♪ ↾ ⚓ ⚡

DUNORE HOUSE
(Mrs A Hyde), 8 Crookedstone Rd,
Aldergrove, BT29 4EH. ☎ (0849) 452291.
B&B s£12 d£24. Rooms 3. Open all year.
¹/₂ m from Airport

🅟 🏠 ✿ ♠ ⅍ ☜ 🛏 ⚥

HILLVALE FARM
(Janet E Duncan), 11 Largy Rd, BT29 4AH.
☎ (0849) 422768.
B&B s£13 d£26. Rooms 3. Open all year.
3m S of Airport

🅟 ✿ ♠ ⅍ ☜ 🛏 ⚥ ♦ ♪ ↾ ⚓ ⚡

MOUNT PLEASANT
(Mrs A Kennedy), 12a Carmavy Rd,
BT29 4TF. ☎ (0849) 452346.
B&B s£16 d£30. Rooms 2, ensuite 1.
Open all year.
2m from Airport

🅣 🅟 ✿ ♠ ⅍ ☜ 🛏 ☐ ⚥ ◉

PRIMROSE FARM
(Mrs R Minford) 30 Tully Rd, Nutts Corner,
BT29 4SW. ☎ (0232) 825200.
B&B s£13.50 d£27. BB&M s£18 d£36.
Rooms 2. High tea £4.50. Last orders 2100
hrs. Open all year.

🅟 ✿ ♠ ☜ OAP 🛏 ☐ ⚥

SEACASH HOUSE
(Mrs I McIlwaine), 21 Killead Rd,
BT29 4EL. ☎ (0849) 423207.
B&B s£12.50 d£25. Rooms 3.
Open all year.

🅟 ✿ ♠ ☜ 🛏 ⚥ ↾

Facilities are liable to change. Check prices when you book. Key to symbols is on the back flap.

CUSHENDALL

Hotels

THORNLEA HOTEL *
6 Coast Rd, BT44 0RU. ☎ (026 67)
71223/71403. Fax 71362.
B&B s£23.50 d£42. BB&M s£32 d£50.50.
Rooms 13, ensuite 12. High tea £6.50.
Dinner £12. Last orders 2115 hrs. Open all
year.

🅿️ ✳️ ♣ ⚡ ❗ 🐎 🌙 📻 🖥 📞 ✂️ ♪ ⌐ U ✓ 🔺
❗ 🎿 ♿

Bed & Breakfast

ARDCLINIS ACTIVITY CENTRE
11 High St, BT44 0NB. ☎ (026 67) 71340.
B&B d£26. BB&M d£40. Rooms 2. Dinner
£7. Last orders 2100 hrs. Open all year.

🆃 🅿️ 🏠 ⚡ 🐎 🄰🄿 🖥 ✂️ ♪ ⌐ U 🔺 🎿 ♿

ASHLEA
(Mrs M McCurry), 2 Tromra Rd, BT44 0SS.
☎ (026 67) 71651.
B&B s£13 d£26. BB&M s£20 d£40.
Rooms 3, ensuite 1. Open Apr-Sept.

🅿️ ✳️ ♣ ⚡ 🐎 🄰🄿 🖥 📞 ✂️ ♪ ⌐ U ✓ 🔺 🎿 ♿

THE BURN
(Mr & Mrs D McAuley), 63 Ballyeamon Rd,
BT44 0SN. ☎ (026 67) 71733.
B&B s£13 d£24. BB&M s£22 d£42. Rooms
2, ensuite 1. High tea £7. Dinner £9.
Last orders 2100 hrs. Open all year.

🅿️ ✳️ ♣ ⚡ 🐎 🖥 ✂️ ♪ ⌐ U 🔺 🌐 ♿

CULBIDAGH HOUSE
(Mrs R Hamill), 115 Red Bay Rd,
BT44 0SH. ☎ (026 67) 71312.
B&B s£13 d£26. Rooms 3, ensuite 1.
Open Apr-Sept.

🅿️ ✳️ ♣ ⚡ 🐎 🖥 📺 ✂️ ⌐ U ♿

CULLENTRA HOUSE
(Mrs O McAuley), 16 Cloghs Rd, BT44 0SP.
☎ (026 67) 71762.
B&B s£12.50 d£25. Rooms 3, ensuite 2.
Open all year.

🆃 🅿️ ✳️ ♣ ⚡ 🐎 🖥 📺 ✂️ ⌐ U 🌐 ♿

GLENDALE
(Mrs M O'Neill), 46 Coast Rd, BT44 0RX.
☎ (026 67) 71495.
B&B s£13 d£26. Rooms 3. Open all year.

🅿️ ✳️ ♣ ⚡ 🐎 🐎 📻 🖥 📺 ✂️ ♪ ⌐ U ✓ 🔺 🎿 ♿

FAIRY GLENN
87 Layde Rd, BT44 0NH.
☎ (026 67) 71128.
B&B s£10 d£18. BB&M s£16.50 d£33.
Rooms 2. Dinner £6.50. Last orders 2000
hrs. Open Mar-Sept.

🅿️ ✳️ ♣ ⚡ 🐎 🄰🄿 🖥 ✂️ ♪ ⌐ U 🔺 🎿 🌐 ♿

MOUNTAIN VIEW
(Mrs B O'Neill), 1 Kilnadore Rd, BT44 0SG.
☎ (026 67) 71246.
B&B s£12 d£24. Rooms 3. Open all year.

🆃 🅿️ 🏠 ✳️ ♣ 🐎 🄰🄿 🖥 ♪ ⌐ 🔺 🎿 ♿

MOYLE VIEW
(Mrs M Gaffney), 2 Ardmoyle Park,
BT44 0QL. ☎ (026 67) 71580.
B&B s£15 d£26. Rooms 3, ensuite 1.
Open all year.

🅿️ ✳️ ♣ ⚡ 🐎 🄰🄿 🖥 📺 ✂️ ♪ ⌐ U 🔺🎿🌐♿

B&B = bed and breakfast   s = single   d = double   BB&M = bed, breakfast & evening meal

REALT NA MARA
(Mrs K McManus), 85 Layde Rd,
BT44 0HN. ☎ (026 67) 71670.
B&B s£11 d£25. Rooms 2, ensuite 1.
Open all year.

RIVERSIDE
(Mr & Mrs P McKeegan), 14 Mill St,
BT44 0RR. ☎ (026 67) 71655.
B&B s£13 d£26. BB&M s£20 d£40.
Rooms 3. Open all year.

RYANS
(Mrs M Lawlor), 9 Shore St, BT44 0NA.
☎ (026 67) 71583.
B&B s£12 d£24. BB&M s£16
d£32. Rooms 2. Open all year.

SHRAMORE
Mrs K Quinn), 27 Chapel Rd, BT44 0RS.
☎ (026 67) 71610.
B&B s£12.50 d£25. Rooms 3.
Open Jun-Sept.

TROSBEN VILLA
(Mary Rowan), 8 Coast Rd, BT44 0RU.
☎ (026 67) 71130.
B&B s£15 d£30. Rooms 7, ensuite 3.
Open all year.

CUSHENDUN

Guesthouses

THE CUSHENDUN (B)
(Mr R McDonnell), 10 Strandview Park,
BT44 0PL. ☎ (026 674) 266.
B&B s£15 d£30. BB&M s£20 d£40.
Rooms 15. High tea £7. Dinner £7.
Last orders 1900 hrs. Open Jul & Aug.

Bed & Breakfast

SLEEPY HOLLOW
(Mrs W McKay) 107 Knocknacarry Rd,
BT44 0NT. ☎ (026 674) 513.
B&B s£15 d£26. Rooms 2, ensuite 2.
Open all year.

THE VILLA
(Mrs C Scally), 185 Torr Rd, BT44 0PU.
☎ (026 674) 252.
B&B s£15 d£30. BB&M s£24
d£48. Rooms 3. High tea £7. Dinner £8.50.
Last orders 1930 hrs. Open Apr-Oct.

Facilities are liable to change. Check prices when you book. Key to symbols is on the back flap.

DUNADRY

Hotels

DUNADRY HOTEL
 & COUNTRY CLUB ****
2 Islandreagh Drive, BT41 2HA.
☎ (0849) 432474. Fax 433389.
B&B s£85 d£100. Rooms 67, ensuite 67.
Last orders 2145 hrs. Open all year (ex 24-
26 Dec).

🆃 🅿 🏮 �֎ ✦ ⚶ ▮ ➙ 🕳 🖥 ⌧ ↰ ⟋ ▮ ∪ ⟋
◭ ⇄ ⫲ 🔄

GIANT'S CAUSEWAY

Hotels

CAUSEWAY HOTEL   **
40 Causeway Rd, BT57 8SU.
☎ (026 57) 31226/31210. Fax 32552.
B&B s£35 d£55. BB&M s£47 d£80. Rooms
16, ensuite 16. High tea £7.50. Dinner
£13.50. Last orders 2115 hrs. Open all
year.

🅿 🏮 ✖ ✦ ⚶ ▮ ➙ 🕳 🖥 ⌧ ↰ ⟋ ▮ ∪ ◭ ▮
🔄 🗒

Guesthouses

CARNSIDE GUEST HOUSE   (B)
(Mrs F Lynch), 23 Causeway Rd,
BT57 8SU. ☎ (026 57) 31337.
B&B s£15 d£30. BB&M s£20 d£48. Rooms
8, ensuite 2. High tea £8. Dinner £9.
Last orders 1900 hrs. Open Jan-Nov.
On B146, 2m N of Bushmills

🆃 🅿 ✖ ✦ ⚶ ➙ 🖥 ⟋ ↰ ▮ 🔄

Bed & Breakfast

HILLCREST COUNTRY HOUSE
(Mr & Mrs M McKeever), 306 Whitepark
Rd, BT57 8SN. ☎ (026 57) 31577.
B&B s£30 d£44. Rooms 3, ensuite 3. High
tea £8.50. Dinner £16. Last orders 2130
hrs. Open Feb-Dec (closed Christmas).

🆃 🅿 🏮 ✖ ✦ ⚶ ▮ ➙ 🖥 ⌧ ↰ ⟋ ▮ ∪ ⟋ ◭
⇄ ▮ 🗒

LOCHABER
(Mrs R Ramage), 107 Causeway Rd,
BT57 8SX. ☎ (026 57) 31385.
B&B s£12 d£24. Rooms 2.
Open all year.

🅿 ✖ ✦ ⚶ ➙ OAP 🖥 ▮ 🔄

GLENARIFF (or Waterfoot)

Guesthouses

GLENARIFF INN (B)
(Paul & Anne Delargy), Main St ,Waterfoot,
BT44 0RB.
☎ (026 67) 71339.
B&B s£12.50 d£25 BB&M s£18.50 d£37.
Rooms 4. High tea £7.95. Dinner £9.95.
Last orders 2100 hrs Open all year.

🅿 ✦ ⚶ ▮ ➙ OAP ✂ ✪ ⟋ ↰ ∪ ◭ ⇄ ▮ 🔄

Bed & Breakfast

THE BAY
(Mr & Mrs J Colligan), 204 Coast Rd,
BT44 0RB. ☎ (026 67) 71858.
B&B s£15 d£28. Rooms 3. Open Jun-Sept.

🅿 ✖ ✦ ⚶ ➙ 🖥 ⌧ ✂ 🔄

B&B = bed and breakfast   s = single   d = double   BB&M = bed, breakfast & evening meal

CARA
(Mrs C Graham), 14 Warren Park,
BT44 0RL. ☎ (026 67) 71013.
B&B s£13 d£26. Rooms 2. Open Apr-Oct.

P ✿ ♣ ⚶ ⛤ 👓 🏠 ✂ ● ♪ 🏌 U ⚓ 👤

DIESKIRT FARM
(Mrs K McHenry), 104 Glen Rd, BT44 0RG.
☎ (026 67) 71308/71796. Fax 71308.
B&B s£16 d£32. BB&M s£22 d£44. Rooms
3, ensuite 1. High tea £6. Last orders 2245
hrs. Open May-Oct.

P ✿ ♣ ⚶ ⛤ 🏠 ✂ ♪ 🏌 U ⚓ 👤 ⊞

GLEN VISTA
(Mrs S McAllister), 245 Garron Rd,
BT44 0RB. ☎ (026 67) 71439.
B&B s£12 d£24. Rooms 4. Open Jun-Sept.

P ✿ ♣ ⚶ ⛤ 👓 🏠 ✂ ♪ 🏌 U ⚓ 👤

LASATA
(Mrs B Leech), 72 Glen Rd, BT44 0RG.
☎ (026 67) 71578.
B8B s£16.50 d£33. Rooms 2, ensuite 2.
Open all year.

P ✿ ♣ ⚶ ⛤ 👓 🏠 ⬜ ✂ ♪ 🏌 U ⭕ ⚓ 👤

LURIG VIEW
4 Lurig View, Glenariff, BT44 0RD.
☎ (026 67) 71618.
B&B s£12, d£26. Rooms 2. Open Apr-Nov.

P ✿ ♣ ⚶ ⛤ 🏠 ✂ 👤

Hotels

DRUMNAGREAGH HOTEL **
Coast Rd, BT44 0BB. ☎ (0574) 841651.
Fax 841651.
B&B s£40 d£57. BB&M s£50 d£75.
Rooms 16, ensuite 16. High tea £7. Dinner
£12. Last orders 2100 hrs. Open all year.

T P 🏨 ✿ ♣ ⚶ ⚑ ⛤ 👓 🐕 🏠 ⬜ ☎ ✂ ♪ 🏌
U ✓ ⚓ 👤 🖂

Bed & Breakfast

BURNSIDE FARM
(Mr & Mrs T Palmer), 37 Dickeystown Rd,
BT44 0BA. ☎ (0574) 841331.
B&B s£15 d£25. Rooms 2. Open Apr-Oct.

P ✿ ♣ ⚶ ⛤ 👓 🏠 ✂ ♪ 🏌 ⚓ 👤

DUNLUCE
(Mrs M McAllister), 5 The Cloney,
BT44 0BB. ☎ (0574) 841279.
B&B s£12.50 d£25. Rooms 3.
Open Apr-Oct.

P ✿ ♣ ⚶ 🏠 ⬜ ✂ ♪ 👤

GLEN VIEW
(Mr & Mrs W Wharry), 32 Drumcrow Rd,
BT44 0DX. ☎ (0574) 841225.
B&B s£15 d£25. BB&M s£18 d£30. Rooms
3, ensuite 1. High tea £3.50. Dinner £5.
Last orders 2130 hrs. Open all year.

P ✿ ♣ ⚶ ⛤ 👓 🐕 🏠 ✂ U ✓ ⚓ 👤

PORTREE
(EE Mairs), 419 Coast Rd. ☎ (0574) 841503.
B&B s£18. d£36. Rooms 2. Open all year.

P 🏨 ✿ ♣ ⚶ 👓 🏠 ✂ 🏌

Facilities are liable to change. Check prices when you book. Key to symbols is on the back flap.

ISLANDMAGEE

Bed & Breakfast

HILL VIEW
(Maureen Reid), 30 Middle Rd, BT40 3SL.
☎ (0960) 372581.
B&B s£15 d£26. BB&M s£22 d£40. Rooms
3, ensuite 1. High tea £7. Dinner £8.50.
Last orders 1630 hrs. Open all year.
Off A2, 7m S of Larne

🖵 ❋ ♣ ⚘ ⛄ ▦ ⎗ ⌂

THE FARM
(Mr & Mrs C L Crawford), 69 Portmuck Rd.
BT40 3TP. ☎ (0960) 382252.
B&B s£15 d£30. Rooms 2, ensuite 1. Open
all year.

🆃 🅿 🏠 ❋ ♣ ⚘ ⛄ DAP ✂ ♪ ⌂ ♦

LARNE

Hotels

MAGHERAMORNE HOUSE HOTEL   **
59 Shore Rd, BT40 3HW.
☎ (0574) 279444. Fax 260138.
B&B s£48.50 d£66. Rooms 22, ensuite
22. High tea £10.50. Dinner £13.95.
Last orders 2130 hrs. Open all year.

🆃 🅿 🏠 ❋ ♣ ⚘ ▼ ⛄ 🖩 ▦ ⎗ ⌣ ⛎ ♨ å
🆔

HIGHWAYS HOTEL   *
Donaghy's Lane, Ballyloran BT40 2SU.
☎ (0574) 272272/3.
B&B s£28 d£42. BB&M s£35.50 d£49.50.
Rooms 12, ensuite 12. Last orders 2100
hrs. Open all year.

🅿 ❋ ♣ ▼ ⛄ ▦ ⎗ ⌣ ⌂ ♨ 🆔

Guesthouses

DERRIN HOUSE   (A)
(Mrs E Mills), 2 Prince's Gardens,
BT40 1RQ. ☎ (0574) 273269/273762.
B&B s£17 d£30. Rooms 7, ensuite 4.
Open all year.

🆃 🅿 ⛄ ♞ 🖩 ⎗ ♪ ⌂

MANOR GUEST HOUSE (B)
(Miss A Graham), 23 Olderfleet Rd,
BT40 1AS. ☎ (0574) 273305.
B&B s£15 d£27. Rooms 8, ensuite 8.
Open all year.

🆃 🅿 🏠 ⚘ ⛄ ♞ 🖩 ✂ 🆔

SEAVIEW GUEST HOUSE   (B)
(Miss M Muir), 156 Curran Rd, BT40 1BX.
☎ (0574) 272438/275397.
B&B s£16 d£32. Rooms 8, ensuite 4.
Open all year.

🅿 ⛄ ♞ 🖩 ⎗ ♪ ⌂ 🆔

DAN CAMPBELLS (U)
2 Bridge St, BT40 1LN. ☎ (0574) 277222.
B&B s£21 d£42. Rooms 10, ensuite 10.
High tea £10. Dinner £15. Last orders
2100 hrs. Open all year.

🅿 🏠 ▼ ⛄ 🆔 🖩 ⎗ ⌣ ✂ ♪ ⌂ ♨ 🆔

Bed & Breakfast

BELLEVUE
(Mrs P McKeen), 35 Olderfleet Rd,
BT40 1AS. ☎ (0574) 270233.
B&B s£11.50 d£23. Rooms 3.
Open all year.

🅿 🏠 ❋ ♣ ⚘ ⛄ DAP ♞ 🖩 ♪ ⌂

Facilities are liable to change. Check prices when you book. Key to symbols is on the back flap.

DRUMAHOE HOUSE
(Mrs R Wilson), 110 Drumahoe Rd,
Millbrook, BT40 2SN.
☎ (0574) 273397.
B&B s£12 d£24. Rooms 4. Open Apr-Sept.

🅿 🏠 ✿ ♣ ☀ ⌚ 🖵 ✂

ELMWOOD
(Mr & Mrs Weston), 69 Glenarm Rd,
BT40 1DX. ☎ (0574) 276263.
B&B s£13 d£26. Rooms 2. Open May-Sept.

🅿 ✿ ♣ ☀ ⌚ 🖵 ✂

GRASSY BANKS
(Mr & Mrs McMullan) 5 Cairnbeg Crescent,
Larne BT40 1OH. ☎ (0574) 274394.
B&B s£13 d£26. Rooms 2. Open all year.

✿ ♣ ☀ ⌚ OAP 🖵 ✂ ⌐

HARBOUR INN
(S Dempsey) 25 Olderfleet Rd, BT40 1AS.
☎ (0574) 272386.
B&B s£13 d£26. Rooms 5, ensuite 2. High
tea £4.50, Dinner £7. Last orders 2145 hrs.
Open all year.

🅿 ♣ ☀ ⌚ OAP 🐎 🖵 ✂ ⌐

HILLVIEW
(Mrs M Rainey), 36 Belfast Rd, BT40 2PH.
☎ (0574) 260584.
B&B s£15 d£27. Rooms 4, ensuite 3.
Open Mar-Oct.

🆃 ✿ ♣ ☀ ⌚ 🖵 ✂ ♪

INVERBANN
(Joy Scott), 7 Glenarm Rd, BT40 1BN.
☎ (0574) 272524.
B&B s£15 d£30. Rooms 2, ensuite 1.
Open all year.

🅿 ✿ ♣ ☀ OAP ⌚ 🖵 ✂ ⌐ △

KILLYNEEDAN
(Mrs M McKane), 52 Bay Rd, BT40 1DG.
☎ (0574) 274943.
B&B s£12 d£24.   Rooms 2. Open all year.

🅿 ✿ ☀ 🐎 ⌚ 🖵 ✂

LYNDEN
(Ms S Thompson), 65 Glenarm Rd,
BT40 1DX. ☎ (0574) 272626.
B&B s£12.50 d£ 25. Rooms 1. Open all
year.

🅿 ✿ ♣ ⌚ 🖵 ♪

MILLBROOK HOUSE
(Mrs A Fulton), 62 Ballyhampton Rd,
BT40 2SP. ☎ (0574) 278942. Fax 260288.
B&B s£12.50 d£25. Rooms 3. Open all
year.

🅿 ✿ ♣ ☀ 🐎 ⌚ 🖵 ✂

MONEYDARA
(Mrs A Parker), 149 Curran Rd, BT40 1DD.
☎ (0574) 272912.
B&B s£15 d£26. Rooms 4, ensuite 4.
Open all year.

🅿 ✿ ☀ 🐎 ⌚ 🖵 ✂

LISBURN

Guesthouses

LAUREL HOUSE   (A)
(Mr N J Stephens), 99 Carryduff Rd,
Temple, BT27 6YL.
☎ (0846) 638422. Fax 638422.
B&B s£30 d£40. Rooms 7. High tea £7.
Dinner £9.50. Last orders 2130 hrs.
Open all year.

🅿 ✿ ♣ ❗ ☀ 🖵 🖵 ♪ ⌐ ✎ △ 🔲

B&B = bed and breakfast   s = single   d = double   BB&M = bed, breakfast & evening meal

BROOK LODGE (B)
(Mrs H Moore), 79 Old Ballynahinch Rd,
BT27 6TH. ☎ (0846) 638454.
B&B s£15 d£32. BB&M s£21, d£44.
Rooms 5, ensuite 3. High tea £4.50.
Dinner £6. Open all year.
5 ½ m NW of Ballynahinch

🅿 ❄ ♣ ☼ ♨ 🕮 ⅄ ♪ ☝ ⟋ ⚞

Bed & Breakfast

BRESAGH FARM
(Mrs E Girvin), 55 Bresagh Rd, Boardmills,
BT27 6TU. ☎ (0846) 638316.
B&B s£16 d£32. Rooms 2. Open all year.
Off A24 S of Belfast

🅿 ♣ ☼ 🕮 ⅄

GREENACRES
(Mrs P Irwin), 56 Ballymullan Rd, BT27
5PJ. ☎ (0846) 665328.
B&B s£15 d£30. Rooms 2. Open all year.

🅿 ❄ ♣ ☼ 🕮 ⅄ 🎫

OVERDALE HOUSE
(Mrs N McMullan), 150 Belsize Rd,
BT27 4DR. ☎ (0846) 672275.
B&B s£16 d£32. Rooms 6, ensuite 3.
Open all year.

🅿 ♿ ❄ ♣ ☼ ♨ 🅾 🐎 🕮 ▢ ⅄ ☝

THE PADDOCK
36a Clontara Pk, Belsize Rd, BT27 4LB.
☎ (0846) 601507.
B&B s£15 d£30. Rooms 3.
Open all year.

🅿 ❄ ♣ ♨ 🕮 ▢ ⅄

Mr & Mrs J REID
115a Carryduff Rd, Boardmills, BT27 6YL.
☎ (0846) 638631.
B&B s£15 d£30. Rooms 2, ensuite 1.
Open all year.
3 ½ m NE of Ballynahinch

🅿 ❄ ♣ ☼ ♨ 🕮 ▢ ⅄ ♪ ∪ ⚞

STRATHEARN HOUSE
(Mr & Mrs D McKeown), 19 Antrim Rd,
BT28 3ED. ☎ (0846) 601661.
B&B s£20 d£36. BB&M s£30
d£56. Rooms 3, ensuite 1. Dinner £10
Last orders 2100 hrs. Open all year.

🅿 ❄ ☼ 🕮 ▢ ⅄ ♪ ☝ ∪ ⟋ ♨ ⚞

Hotels

CHIMNEY CORNER HOTEL   ***
630 Antrim Rd, BT36 8RF.
☎ (0232) 844925/844851.
Fax 844352/842058.
B&B s£66 d£80. BB&M s£81 d£110.
Rooms 63, ensuite 63. High tea £12.50.
Dinner £15. Last orders 2130 hrs.
Open all year.

🅿 ♿ ❄ ♣ ♟ ☼ 🕮 ▢ ☎ 🗲 ● ✎ ☝ 🍴 🎫

Bed & Breakfast

IONA
(Mrs P Kelly), 161 Antrim Rd, BT36 7QR.
☎ (0232) 842256.
B&B s£18 d£32. Rooms 4. Open all year.

🅿 ❄ ♣ ☼ ☼ 🅾 🕮 ▢ ☎ ⅄ ☝ ⚞

Facilities are liable to change. Check prices when you book. Key to symbols is on the back flap.

Mrs G McCABE
109 Jordanstown Rd, BT37 0NT.
☎ (0232) 864702.
B&B s£14 d£28. Rooms 2, ensuite 1. Open all year.

🅿 ✿ ♣ ⚹ ⏃ 🎑 ♉ ❑ ⊁ ♪ ⎰ ∪ ⬥ ⚲ 🈷

PERPETUA HOUSE
(Mrs D Robinson), 57 Collinbridge Park, BT36 7SY.
☎ (0232) 833041.
B&B s£18 d£32. Rooms 2. Open all year.

🆃 🅿 ✿ ⚹ ♉ OAP 🎑 ❑ ⊁ ♪ ⎰ ✓ ⬥ ⟟ ⚲

UNIVERSITY OF ULSTER
Shore Rd, Jordanstown, BT37 0QB.
☎ (0232) 365131. Fax 747493.
(Groups only) B&B s£16.02 d£23.82.
BB&M s£22.22 d£36.22. Rooms 660, ensuite 3. Dinner £6.20.
Last orders 1800 hrs. Open Jul-Sept.

🅿 ✿ ♣ ⚹ ⚑ ♉ 🎑 ⌗ ☜ ⚘ ⚴ ⚙

PORTBALLINTRAE

Hotels

BAYVIEW HOTEL **
2 Bayhead Rd, BT57 8RZ.
☎ (026 57) 31453 Fax 32360.
B&B s£35 d£60. BB&M s£55 d£80.
Rooms 16, ensuite 16. High tea £8.50.
Dinner £11.50. Last orders 2130 hrs.
Open all year.

🅿 ✿ ♣ ⚹ ⚑ ♉ OAP ⚞ 🎑 ❑ ☜ ⊁ ⌗ ⚘ ⚴ ⚙
♪ ⎰ ∪ ✓ ⬥ ⟟ ⚲ ⚲

BEACH HOUSE HOTEL **
61 Beach Rd, BT57 8RT.
☎ (026 57) 31214/31380. Fax 31664.
B&B s£45 d£75. BB&M s£54 d£92.
Rooms 32, ensuite 32. High tea £7.
Dinner £16. Last orders 2100 hrs.
Open all year.

🆃 🅿 ⚞ ♣ ⚹ ⚑ ♉ OAP 🎑 ❑ ☜ ⚘ ♪ ⎰ ∪ ⬥
⟟ ⚲ ⚲ 🈷

Guesthouses

WHITE GABLES   (A)
(Mrs R Johnston), 83 Dunluce Rd, BT57 8SJ.
☎ (026 57) 31611.
B&B s£22 d£39. BB&M s£34 d£63.
Rooms 4, ensuite 3. Dinner £12. Last orders 1630 hrs. Open Mar-Oct.

🅿 ✿ ♣ ⚹ ♉ OAP 🎑 ⊁ ♪ ⎰ ⚲

Bed & Breakfast

BAYHEAD HOUSE
(Mr & Mrs Cooke), 8 Bayhead Rd, BT57 8RZ. ☎ (026 57) 31441.
B&B s£26 d£40. Rooms 7, ensuite 7.
Open Mar-Oct.

🅿 ⚹ ♉ 🎑 ❑ ⊁ ♪ ⎰ ∪ ✓ ⬥ ⟟ ⚲ 🈷

CEDAR LODGE
(Mrs M S Wilson), 44 Ballaghmore Rd, BT57 8RL. ☎ (026 57) 31763.
B&B s£17 d£27. Rooms 2. Open all year.

🅿 ✿ ♣ ♉ ⚞ 🎑 ⊁ ♪ ⎰ ∪ ⬥ ⚲

KEEVE-NA
(Mrs H Wilkinson), 62 Ballaghmore Rd, BT57 8RL. ☎ (026 57) 32184.
B&B s£15 d£30. Rooms 3. Open all year.
(ex Christmas).

🅿 ⚹ ♉ 🎑 ⊁ ⚲

B&B = bed and breakfast   s = single   d = double   BB&M = bed, breakfast & evening meal

KENBAAN
(Mrs E Morgan), 55 Bayhead Rd, BT57 8SA.
☎ (026 57) 31534.
B&B s£20 d£32. Rooms 4.
Open all year.
½m from Bushmills

Bed & Breakfast

BANNSIDE FARMHOUSE
(Misses E & A Lowry), 268 Gortgole Rd,
BT44 8AT. ☎ (0266) 821262.
B&B s£11.50 d£ 22.50. Rooms 3.
Open all year.

SPRUCEBANK
(Mrs T Sibbett), 41 Ballymacombs Rd, BT44
8NR. ☎ (0266) 822150/821422.
B&B s£16, d£32. Rooms 4, ensuite 1.
Open all year.

Hotels

CAUSEWAY COAST HOTEL ***
36 Ballyreagh Rd, BT56 8LR.
☎ (0265) 822435. Fax 824495.
B&B s£45 d£60. BB&M s£57 d£84. Rooms
21, ensuite 21. High tea £8. Dinner £12
Last orders 2130 hrs. Open all year.

MAGHERABUOY HOUSE HOTEL ***
41 Magheraboy Rd, BT56 8NX.
☎ (0265) 823507. Fax 824687.
B&B s£50 d£75. Rooms 38, ensuite 38.
High tea £7.50. Dinner £15.
Last orders 2130 hrs. Open all year.

EGLINTON HOTEL **
49 Eglinton St, BT56 8DZ.
☎ (0265) 822371. Fax 823155.
B&B s£45 d£65. BB&M s£55 d£79. Rooms
28, ensuite 28. High tea £8. Dinner £15.
Last orders 2130hrs. Open all year.

Guesthouses

ABERCORN HOUSE (A)
(Mrs L Paul), 57 Coleraine Rd, BT56 8HR.
☎ (0265) 825014/825136.
B&B s£22 d£33. BB&M s£28.50 d£46.
Rooms 10, ensuite 10.

BLACK SWAN HOUSE (A)
(Mr M Dadd), 61 Coleraine Rd, BT56 8HR.
☎ (0265) 823678.
B&B s£18 d£36. Rooms 6, ensuite 6.
Dinner £12. Last orders 1830 hrs.
Open all year.

Facilities are liable to change. Check prices when you book. Key to symbols is on the back flap.

51

BROWN'S COUNTRY HOUSE (A)
(Mrs J Brown), 174 Ballybogey Rd,
Ballywatt, Coleraine, BT52 2LP.
☎ (026 57) 31627.
B&B s£18 d£35. BB&M s£27 d£53. Rooms
8, ensuite 8. Dinner £9. Last orders
1200hrs. Open all year (ex Christmas &
New Year).
Off B62, 5m NE of Ballymoney

CARRICK-DHU GUEST HOUSE (A)
(Mrs H McClay), 6 Ballyreagh Rd,
BT56 8LP. ☎ (0265) 823666.
B&B s£19.50 d£39. BB&M s£31 d£62.
Rooms 7, ensuite 7. High tea £9.50. Dinner
£13. Last orders 1400 hrs. Open all year.

GLENKEEN GUEST HOUSE (A)
(Mrs R Little), 59 Coleraine Rd, BT56 8HR.
☎ (0265) 822279.
B&B s£21 d£36. BB&M s£28.50 d£51.
Rooms 9, ensuite 9. High tea £5.50.
Dinner £7.50. Open all year.

HAYESBANK KANTARA (A)
(Mr & Mrs J Milliken), 5 Ramore Avenue,
BT56 8BB. ☎ (0265) 823823.
B&B s£18 d£36. BB&M s£24 d£48.
Rooms 36, ensuite 5 Dinner £6.
Last orders 1630 hrs. Open all year.

ALEXANDRA (B)
(Mr R Taylor), 11 Lansdowne Crescent,
BT56 8AY. ☎ (0265) 822284.
B&B s£20 d£34. BB&M s£28 d£50. Rooms
8, ensuite 1. Last orders 1800 hrs. Open all
year.

BELVEDERE TOWN HOUSE (B)
(Mrs Dunn), 15 Lansdowne Crescent,
BT56 8AY. ☎ (0265) 822771.
B&B s£15 d£30. BB&M s£30 d£60. Rooms
14, ensuite 7. Open all year.

CASA-A-LA-MAR (B)
(Mrs R Larner), 21 Kerr St, BT56 8DG.
☎ (0265) 822617.
B&B s£12.50 d£25. BB&M s£18
d£36. Rooms 7, ensuite 2. Dinner £5.50.
Last orders 1800 hrs. Open all year.

CASTLE ERIN (B)
Castle Erin Rd, BT56 8DH.
☎ (0265) 822744.
B&B s£15 d£30. BB&M s£20 d£40. Rooms
40, ensuite 11. High tea £6.50. Dinner
£7.50. Open all year.

CLARMONT (B)
(Mr & Mrs Duggan), 10 Lansdowne
Crescent, BT56 8AY.
☎ (0265) 822397. Fax 822397.
B&B s£18 d£40. Rooms 14, ensuite 7.
Open Jan-Nov.

GLENCROFT (B)
(JE & Mrs M I Henderson), 95 Coleraine Rd,
BT56 8HN. ☎ (0265) 822902.
B&B s£17 d£34. BB&M s£28 d£56. Rooms
5, ensuite 2. High tea £6.50. Dinner £8.
Open all year.

B&B = bed and breakfast　s = single　d = double　BB&M = bed, breakfast & evening meal

MA-RING GUEST HOUSE (B)
(Mr & Mrs J Ring), 17 Kerr St, BT56 8OT.
☎ (0265) 822765.
B&B s£20 d£35. BB&M s£25 d£45. Rooms
13, ensuite 8. Open all year.

THE MOUNT ROYAL (B)
(Mrs L Hoy), 2 Eglinton St, BT56 8DX.
☎ (0265) 823342.
B&B s£20 d£34. BB&M s£28 d£50. Rooms
8, ensuite 1. High tea £6.50. Dinner £8.50.
Last orders 2100 hrs. Open all year.

OLD MANSE (B)
(Miss M Owler), 3 Main St, BT56 8BL.
☎ (0265) 824118.
B&B s£20 d£34. BB&M s£28 d£50. Rooms
6. Last orders 1930 hrs. Open all year.

PROSPECT HOUSE (B)
(Mr & Mrs D McKenzie), 20 Lansdowne
Crescent, BT56 8AY. ☎ (0265) 822299.
B&B s£16 d£32. BB&M s£ 22 d£44.
Rooms 14. Dinner £6. Last orders
1730hrs. Open Mar-Nov.

WEST STRAND GUEST HOUSE (B)
(Miss M Robinson), 18 Kerr St, BT56 8DG.
☎ (0265) 822270.
B&B s£15 d£30. BB&M s£20 d£40. Rooms
15. High tea £6. Dinner £8. Last orders
1930 hrs. Open Feb-Nov.

WINDSOR GUEST HOUSE (B)
(Mr & Mrs J Knox), 67 Main St, BT56 8BN.
☎ (0265) 823793.
B&B s£18 d£35. BB&M s£23 d£45. Rooms
26, ensuite 4. Open Jan-Nov.

ABBEYDEAN (U)
(Mrs B Paul), 9 Ramore Avenue, BT56 8BB.
☎ (0265) 822645.
B&B s£12.50 d£ 25. BB&M s£18.50
d£37. Rooms 12. High tea £3. Dinner £6.
Last orders 1600 hrs. Open all year.

BALLYMAGARRY COUNTRY
  HOUSE (U)
(Mrs A Leckey), 46 Leeke Rd, BT56 8NH.
☎ (0265) 823737. Fax 822681.
B&B s£35 d£45. BB&M s£50 d£75.
Rooms 4, ensuite 4. Dinner £15. Last
orders 1930 hrs. Open Feb-Oct.
2m E of Portrush

WEST BAY VIEW (U)
(H S Cunningham), 48 Mark St,
BT56 8BU. ☎ (0265) 823375.
B&B s£19 d£36. BB&M s£22, d£42.
Rooms 38, ensuite 13. Dinner £8. Last
orders 1830 hrs. Open all year.

Bed & Breakfast

AGHALUN
(Mrs A Ebbitt) 2 Caldwell Park BT56 8LZ.
☎ (0265) 823166.
B&B s£15 d£30. Rooms 3. Open Mar-Oct.

Facilities are liable to change. Check prices when you book. Key to symbols is on the back flap.

53

AN ULADH
(Mrs M Mair), 73 Eglinton St, Golf Terrace,
BT56 8DZ. ☎ (0265) 822221.
B&B s£15 d£36. Rooms 11, ensuite 4.
Open all year.

ARDNAREE
(Mrs E Rankin), 105 Dunluce Rd,
BT56 8NB. ☎ (0265) 823407.
B&B s£17.50. d£35. Rooms 5, ensuite 2.
Open all year.
On A2, 1m E of Portrush

A-REST-A-WHILE
(Mr & Mrs R Torrens), 6 Bath Terrace,
BT56 8AN. ☎ (0265) 822827.
B&B s£12 d£24. BB&M s£15 d£30.
Rooms 10. High tea £5. Dinner £6.
Last orders 1600 hrs. Open all year.

ARRONDALE
(B Shields & Miss Duff), 21 Coleraine Rd,
BT56 8EA. ☎ (0265) 824289.
B&B s£13 d£26. Rooms 4. Open all year.

ATLANTIC VIEW
(J&D Britton), 103 Eglinton St, BT56 8DZ.
☎ (0265) 823647.
B&B s£15 d£26. Rooms 8. Open all year.

ATLANTIS
(Mr & Mrs N Torrens), 10 Ramore Avenue,
BT56 8BB. ☎ (0265) 824583.
B&B s£14 d£24. BB&M s£19 d£34.
Rooms 13. Dinner £5. Open all year.

BALLYWILLAN FARM
(Mrs F Nevin), 201 Ballywillan Rd,
BT56 8NT. ☎ (0265) 823291.
B&B s£13 d£26. Rooms 3. Open Apr-Sept.

BETHEL
(Rev & Mrs T Cross), 7 Lansdowne
Crescent, BT56 8AY. ☎ (0265)
822354/823716.
B&B s£12.50 d£25. BB&M s£18
d£36. Rooms 17. High tea £3.50.
Dinner £6.50. Open Jul/Aug.

BEULAH HOUSE
(J&R Anderson), 16 Causeway St,
BT56 8AB. ☎ (0265) 822413.
B&B s£13.50 d£27. BB&M s£20
d£40. Rooms 12. Dinner £6.50.
Open all year.

BONITA VISTA
(Mrs E Allen), 5 Strand Avenue,
Whiterocks, BT56 8ND. ☎ (0265) 823411.
B&B s£14 d£28. BB&M s£20 d£40.
Rooms 4, ensuite 1. Last orders 1900 hrs.
Open May-Aug.
1m E of Portrush

BRAVELLAN
(Mrs M Davison), 130 Coleraine Rd,
BT56 8HN. ☎ (0265) 823245.
B&B s£13.50 d£27. Rooms 3.
Open all year.

Facilities are liable to change. Check prices when you book. Key to symbols is on the back flap.

BROOKHAVEN
(Mrs E Goligher), 99 Coleraine Rd,
BT56 8HN. ☎ (0265) 824164.
B&B s£14 d£28. Rooms 3, ensuite 1.
Open all year.

BROOKSIDE HOUSE
(Mrs P Kennedy), 46 Mark St, BT56 8BU.
☎ (0265) 824498.
B&B s£12.50 d£25. BB&M s£19 d£38.
Rooms 17, ensuite 2. Open Apr-Nov.

CAUSEWAY HOUSE
(M & J Collins), 26 Kerr St, BT56 8DG.
☎ (0265) 824847.
B&B s£13 d£26. Rooms 6. Open all year.

THE DINGLE
(Mrs F O Hume), 8 Bushmills Rd, BT56 8JF.
☎ (0265) 822089.
B&B s£16 d£28. Rooms 3. Open Apr-Sept.

DRUMLEE
(Mr & Mrs R Torrens), 50 Mark St,
BT56 8BU. ☎ (0265) 823133.
B&B s£13 d£26. BB&M s£17 d£34.
Rooms 27. Dinner £5. Open all year.

ELM HOUSE
(Mrs T Murphy), 28 Mark St, BT56 8BT.
☎ (0265) 822360/824114.
B&B s£12.50 d£24. BB&M s£17 d£34.
Rooms 12. High tea £5. Dinner £5.
Last orders 1830 hrs. Open all year.

Mrs H HAMILL
8 Ballyreagh Rd, ☎ (0265) 824030.
B&B s£16 d£28. Rooms 3. Open Jun-Oct.

HARBOUR VIEW
(Mr & Mrs Medcalf), 8 Dhu Varren,
BT56 8EN. ☎ (0265) 824921.
B&B s£12 d£28. BB&M s£18.50 d£41.
Rooms 3, ensuite 2. High tea £6.50.
Dinner £6.50. Last orders 1600 hrs.
Open Feb-Nov.

HOYLAKE HOUSE
(Mrs M Laverty), 10 Victoria St, BT56 8DL.
☎ (0265) 824374.
B&B s£15 d£25. BB&M s£17.50. d£35.
Rooms 3. Open all year.

INVERSHIEL
(Mrs S Allen), 16 Coleraine Rd, BT56 8EA.
☎ (0265) 823861.
B&B s£20 d£33. Rooms 3, ensuite 3.
Open all year.

ISLAY-VIEW
(Mrs E Smith), 36 Leeke Rd, BT56 8NH.
☎ (0265) 823220.
B&B s£17.50 d£35. Rooms 3, ensuite 1.
Open Apr-Sept.
Off B62, 2½m from Portrush

B&B = bed and breakfast   s = single   d = double   BB&M = bed, breakfast & evening meal

LOGUESTOWN FARM
(Mrs M Adams), 59 Magheraboy Rd,
BT56 8NY. ☎ (0265) 822742.
B&B s£14 d£26. Rooms 4, ensuite 1.
Open Jan-Nov.
Off A29, 1m S of Portrush

MADDYBENNY FARM HOUSE
(Mrs R White), 18 Maddybenny Park,
Coleraine Rd, BT52 2PT. ☎ (0265)
823394/823603.
B&B s£25 d£40. Rooms 3, ensuite 3.
Open all year (ex Christmas & New Year).
Off A29, 2m S of Portrush

MALVERN HOUSE
(Mrs J Hassin), 36 Mark St, BT56 8BT.
☎ (0265) 823435.
B&B s£12 d£24. BB&M s£17 d£34.
Rooms 9. Open all year.

MONTANA
(Mr & Mrs M Smyth), 16 Mark St,
BT56 8BT. ☎ (0265) 824884.
B&B s£13 d£26. Rooms 3. Open Apr-Sept.

OAKDENE
(Mr & Mrs C Francey), 6 Lansdowne
Crescent, BT56 8AY. ☎ (0265) 824629.
B&B s£14 d£26. BB&M s£20
d£38. Rooms 16. Open Jan-Nov.

PADORA HOUSE
(Misses Humphries & Todd), 50 Salisbury
Terrace, BT56 8HR. ☎ (0265) 822891.
B&B s£16 d£28. BB&M s£20 d£36.
Rooms 10. Open all year.

PORT-NA-GLAS
(Mrs J Hamill), 111 Eglinton St, BT56 8DZ.
☎ (0265) 824352.
B&B s£15 d£23. Rooms 14, ensuite 1.
Open Mar-Sept.

PORT O CALL
(Mr & Mrs M Moffett), 28 Dhu Varren,
BT56 8EN. ☎ (0265) 822570.
B&B s£12.50 d£25. Rooms 5. Open Apr-
Sept.

RAMONA
(Mr & Mrs J McKibbin), 8 Ramore Avenue,
BT56 8BB. ☎ (0265) 824734.
B&B s£15 d£25. BB&M s£21 d£36.
Rooms 11. Dinner £6. Open all year.

Mrs A RANKIN
184 Ballybogey Rd, Bushmills, BT57 8UH.
☎ (026 57) 32295.
B&B s£13 d£26. Rooms 2. Open all year.

RATHLIN HOUSE
(Mr D & Mrs H Davidson), 2 Ramore
Avenue, BT56 8BB. ☎ (0265) 824834.
B&B s£15 d£30 . BB&M s£20 d£40.
Rooms 17. High tea £6. Dinner £6.
Last orders 1930 hrs. Open all year.

Facilities are liable to change. Check prices when you book. Key to symbols is on the back flap.

Mr & Mrs M ROBINSON
88 Coleraine Rd, BT56 8HA. ☎ (0265)
822733.
B&B s£15 d£30. Rooms 2. Open all year.

🄿 🐎 🄾🄰🄿 🎚 ❏ ⅍ ♩ 👆 ♨ 🜨

ROCHESTER
(Mr & Mrs A Barr), 6 Mount Royal,
Eglinton St, BT56 8DZ. ☎ (0265) 822778.
B&B s£14.50 d£29. BB&M s£20 d£40.
Rooms 8, ensuite 1. Dinner £5.50.
Last orders 1700 hrs. Open Jan-Oct.

🔆 🐎 🄾🄰🄿 🎚 ⅍ 🜨

ROSS-ERNE
(Mrs L Ramage), 18 Coleraine Rd,
BT56 8EA. ☎ (0265) 825171.
B&B s£17.50 d£35. Rooms 2, ensuite 1.
Open Jan-Nov.

🄿 ✿ ♣ 🐎 🎚 🜨

SANDHAVEN
(Kathleen Patterson), 77 Eglinton St, BT56
8DZ. ☎ (0256) 822731.
B&B s£12 d£24. Rooms 4. Open Jun-Aug.

🔆 🎚 ⅍ 🜨

SEAMARA
(Mr I Taggart), 26 Mark St, BT56 8BT.
☎ (0265) 822541.
B&B s£13 d£26. Rooms 12, ensuite 1.
Open all year.

🔆 🐎 🎚 ⅍ ♩ 👆 ♨ 🜨

SUMMER-ISLAND HOUSE
(Mrs A Armstrong), 14 Coleraine Rd,
BT56 8EA. ☎ (0265) 824640.
B&B s£20 d£36. Rooms 3, ensuite 3.
Open Jan-Nov.

🄿 ✿ 🐎 🄾🄰🄿 ♨ ♩ 👆 ♨ 🜨

Bed & Breakfast

Mrs C BAILIE
46b Tamlough Rd. ☎ (084 94) 79719.
B&B s£18 d£36. Rooms 2, ensuite 1.
Open all year.

🄿 ✿ ♣ 🔆 🎚 ❏ ⅍ ♩ 👆

Guesthouses

RATHLIN GUEST HOUSE   (B)
(Mr & Mrs D McCurdy), The Quay,
BT54 6RT. ☎ (026 57) 63917.
B&B s£12 d£24. BB&M s£20 d£40.
Rooms 4. Dinner £8. Last orders 1900 hrs.
Open Mar-Sept.

✿ ♣ 🔆 🐎 🎚 🄴🄱

Hotels

TEMPLETON HOTEL   **
882 Antrim Rd, BT39 0AH. ☎ (0849)
432984. Fax 433406.
B&B s£95 d£110. BB&M s£110 d£140.
Rooms 20, ensuite 20. High tea £10.
Dinner £17. Last orders 2145 hrs.
Open all year.

🄿 🕮 ✿ ♣ 🔆 🍽 🐎 🄳 🎚 ❏ ☏ ♩ 👆 ♨ 🜩
🍴 🄴🄱

B&B = bed and breakfast   s = single   d = double   BB&M = bed, breakfast & evening meal

Bed & Breakfast

TOBERAGNEE DAIRY FARM
(Mr & Mrs W Hyde), 54 Lylehill Rd,
BT39 0ES. ☎ (084 94) 32389.
B&B s£13.50 d£27. Rooms 3.
Open all year.

🅿 ❄ ♣ ⚶ 🐴 OAP ⏸ ⅍ ⌑

TOOMEBRIDGE

Hotels

O'NEILL ARMS HOTEL   *
20 Main St, BT41 3TQ.
☎ (0648) 50202/50885. Fax 50970.
B&B s£20 d£40. BB&M s£27 d£54.
Rooms 11, ensuite 5. High tea £8.
Dinner £13. Last orders 2200 hrs.
Open all year.

🅿 ❄ ♣ ⚶ ⏲ 🐴 🖵 ☏ ⅍ ♪ ⌑ ✦ ⌂ ♟ ⑀

WHITEHEAD

Bed & Breakfast

CRESTBANK
(Kathleen Rigby), 13 Marine Parade,
BT38 9QP. ☎ (0960) 372338.
B&B s£15 d£30. BB&M s£20 d£40.
Rooms 4. Open all year.

🅿 ⌂ ♣ ⚶ 🐴 OAP ⏸ ⅍ ♪ ⌑ ∪ △ ⏚ ⑀

Facilities are liable to change. Check prices when you book. Key to symbols is on the back flap.

County Armagh

Hotels

CHARLEMONT ARMS HOTEL   *
63 Lower English St, BT61 7LB.
☎ (0861) 522028/522719.
B&B s£22 d£40. Rooms 12, ensuite 9. High
tea £8. Dinner £12.50. Last orders 2030
hrs. Open all year.

⊡ ₽ ♠ ❀ ❢ ঠ ◧ ▥ ▢ ᄔ ⅛ ♪ ↑ ∪ ⁄ ❢
⊞

Bed & Breakfast

CLONHUGH HOUSE
(Mrs P McKenna), 1 College Hill,
BT61 9DN. ☎ (0861) 522693.
B&B s£14 d£25. Rooms 5, ensuite 1.
Open all year.

₽ ♠ ❀ ঠ ▥ ⅛ ♪ ↑ ◎

DESART
(Mrs S McRoberts), 99 Cathedral Rd,
BT61 8AE. ☎ (0861) 522387.
B&B s£15 d£30. Rooms 5. Open all year.

₽ ❀ ♠ ঠ ⋔ ▥ ⅛ ♪ ↑ ∪ ⁄ ▵ ⁊

PADUA HOUSE
(Kathleen O'Hagan), 63 Cathedral Rd,
BT61 7QX. ☎ (0861) 522039/523584. Fax
527426.
B&B s£12 d£24. Rooms 3. Open all year.

₽ ♠ ❀ ♠ ❢ ঠ ▥ ▢ ⅛

ST MICHAEL'S
(Mrs J McFarland), 1 Mullinure Lane,
BT61 7RT. ☎ (0861) 527958.
B&B s£15 d£30. Rooms 2, ensuite 2. High
tea £8.50. Dinner £10. Last orders
1000 hrs. Open all year.

₽ ❀ ♠ ❢ ঠ ▥ ⅛ ♪ ↑ ∪

VICTORIA
(Mrs M Hanson), 33 Tullysaran Rd,
Cloughfin, BT61 8HB. ☎ (0861) 525925.
B&B s£14 d£26. BB&M s£22 d£42. Rooms
3. Dinner £8. Last orders 1800 hrs. Open
Mar-Oct.
3m NW of Armagh

₽ ❀ ♠ ❢ ঠ ▥ ⅛ ♪ ↑ ∪ ▵ ⁊

Hotels

SILVERWOOD HOTEL   *
Kiln Rd, Silverwood, Lurgan, BT66 6NF.
☎ (0762) 327722. Fax 325290.
B&B s£46 d£65. BB&M s£58 d£90. Rooms
28 , ensuite 28. High tea £7.50. Dinner
£14. Last orders 2115 hrs. Open all year.

₽ ❀ ♠ ❢ ঠ ▥ ▢ ᄔ ♪ ↑ ▵ ⁊ ⁊ ⊞

Bed & Breakfast

GLENSIDE HOUSE
(Mrs N Quinn), 22a Tullynavall Rd,
Cullyhanna, BT35 0PZ. ☎ (0693) 861075.
B&B s£11 d£22. BB&M s£16 d£32. Rooms
2. High tea £5. Dinner £5. Open all year.

₽ ♠ ❀ ♠ ❢ ঠ ▥ ▢ ⅛ ♪ ↑ ∪ ⁄ ▵ ⁊

LIKANE FARMHOUSE
(Mr & Mrs T Forde), 10 Corliss Rd,
BT35 9AY. ☎ (0693) 868348.
B&B s£10 d£20. Rooms 2. Open all year.

₽ ❀ ♠ ❢ ঠ ▥ ⅛ ♪ ↑ ∪ ▵ ⁊

Facilities are liable to change. Check prices when you book. Key to symbols is on the back flap.

LIMA
(Mrs E Ryan), 16 Drumalt Rd, Silverbridge,
BT35 9LQ. ☎ (0693) 861944.
B&B s£12 d£24. BB&M s£20 d£36. Rooms
3, ensuite 1. High tea £8. Dinner £10. Last
orders 2100 hrs. Open all year.

KILLYLEA

Bed & Breakfast

HEIMAT
(Mrs D McLoughlin), 6 Polnagh Rd,
BT60 4NW. ☎ (0861) 568661.
B&B s£11.50 d£23. Rooms 4.
Open all year.

LURGAN
(See also Craigavon)

Hotels

ASHBURN HOTEL   *
81 William St, BT66 6JB. ☎ (0762) 325711.
B&B s£28 d£46. BB&M s£35 d£60. Rooms
12, ensuite 12. Dinner £15. Last orders
2115 hrs. Open all year.

PORTADOWN
(See also Craigavon)

Hotels

CARNGROVE HOTEL   **
2 Charlestown Rd, BT63 5PW. ☎ (0762)
339222. Fax 332899
B&B s£ 42.95 d£61.90. Rooms 35, ensuite
35. High tea £10. Dinner £18. Open all
year.

SEAGOE HOTEL **
Upper Church Lane, BT63 5JE. ☎ (0762)
333076. Fax 350210.
B&B s£46.50 d£66. BB&M s£71.50 d£116.
Rooms 37, ensuite 37. High tea £15.
Dinner £25. Last orders 2145 hrs. Open all
year.

Guesthouses

DRUMCREE HOUSE   (B)
(Mrs A O'Neill), 38 Ashgrove Rd,
BT62 1PA. ☎ (0762) 338655.
B&B s£15 d£28. BB&M s£22.50 d£43.
Rooms 5, ensuite 2. High tea £7.50.
Dinner £7.50. Last orders 2000 hrs.
Open all year.

B&B = bed and breakfast   s = single   d = double   BB&M = bed, breakfast & evening meal

Bed & Breakfast

BANNVIEW SQUASH CLUB
60 Portmore St, BT62 3NF. ☎ (0762)
336666.
B&B s£24 d£40. Rooms 10, ensuite 10.
High tea £6. Dinner £7.50. Last orders
2100 hrs. Open all year.

🅿 ❀ ⚘ ❗ ❦ ☺ [OAP] ▥ ☐ ✆ ⚥ 🎁 ♣ ♪ ▶ ✒ ⬦
⚏ ♞ ⚑ ⊞

BAWNBOY HOUSE
(Miss M Reilly), 30 Corbrackey Rd,
BT62 1PG. ☎ (0762) 332674.
B&B s£12 d£24. BB&M s£16 d£30. Rooms
3. High tea £5.50, Dinner £7.50. Last
orders 2000 hrs. Open all year.
3m NW of Portadown

Ⓣ 🅿 ❀ ♣ ❦ [OAP] ▥ ⚥

CEDARBROOK FARM
(Mrs M Irwin), 84 Brackagh Rd, BT62 3RP.
☎ (0762) 840347.
B&B s£12 d£24. Rooms 3. Open all year.

🅿 ❀ ♣ ⚘ ❦ ▥ ⚥ ♞

GREENACRES
(Mrs F Hampton), 57 Red Lion Rd,
BT62 4HR. ☎ (0762) 352610.
B&B s£13 d£26. Rooms 3. Open all year.
On B77, 3m W of Portadown

🅿 ❀ ♣ ❦ [OAP] ▥ ⚥ ♪ ▶ ∪

Mrs E NEVILLE
125 Summerisland Rd, Annaghmore,
BT62 1SJ. ☎ (0762) 851437.
B&B s£12 d£24. BB&M s£17 d£34.
Rooms 2. Open all year.

🅿 ♣ ▥

REDBRICK HOUSE
(Mrs M Stephenson), Corbrackey Lane,
BT62 1PQ. ☎ (0762) 335268.
B&B s£12 d£24. BB&M s£15 d£30.
Rooms 4, ensuite 1. Open all year.

🅿 ❀ ♣ ⚘ ❦ [OAP] ▥ ⚥ ♪ ▶ ∪ ✒ ⬦ ⚏

SLANTRY HOUSE
(Mr & Mrs P McKeever), 113 Charlestown
Rd, BT63 5PR. ☎ (0762) 333391.
B&B s£20 d£36. BB&M s£28 d£44. Rooms
3, ensuite 1. High tea £8. Dinner £8. Last
orders 1900 hrs. Open Apr-Sept.

🅿 ❀ ♣ ⚘ ❦ [OAP] ▥ ⚥ ♪ ▶ ∪ ⬦ ⚏ ♞

Guesthouses

BALLINAHINCH HOUSE   (B)
(Mrs E Kee), 47 Ballygroobany Rd,
BT61 9NA. ☎ (0762) 870081.
B&B s£14 d£27. Rooms 4. Open May-Sept.
Off A3, SW of Portadown (B131 Richhill)

🅿 🏠 ♣ ⚘ ❦ ▥ ⚥ ♪ ▶ ∪ ✒ ⬦ ⚏

Bed & Breakfast

Mrs J BINGHAM
69 Sleepy Valley, BT61 9LH.
☎ (0762) 871387.
B&B s£15 d£30. Rooms 2, ensuite 1.
Open all year.

🅿 ❀ ♣ ❦ ▥ ⚥

Facilities are liable to change. Check prices when you book. Key to symbols is on the back flap.

TANDRAGEE

Bed & Breakfast

ARNSHEEN
(Anna Norris), 11 Mullavilly Heights,
BT62 2NH. ☎ (0762) 841770.
B&B s£15 d£28. BB&M s£19 d£38. Rooms
3, ensuite 1. High tea £4. Dinner £5.
Open all year.

🆃 🅿 ❄ ♣ ⛷ 🐾 🐴 🏠 ❏ ⚰ ⚲

WARINGSTOWN

Bed & Breakfast

THE CURATAGE
(Mrs E Turkington), 6 Banbridge Rd,
BT66 7QA. ☎ (0762) 882285.
B&B s£17.50 d£30. BB&M s£23 d£46.
Rooms 4, ensuite 4. High tea £5.50. Dinner
£7.50. Last orders 2030 hrs. Open all year.

🅿 ❄ ♣ ⛷ 🐾 🏠 ⚰ ♪ 🏌 ∪ 💷

IVANHOE
(Mrs F Dewart), 10 Valley Lane,
BT66 7SR.
☎ (0762) 881287.
B&B s£12 d£24. Rooms 3. Open all year.

🅿 ♣ ⛷ 🏠

B&B = bed and breakfast   s = single   d = double   BB&M = bed, breakfast & evening meal

County Down

Guesthouses

GLASSDRUMMAN LODGE   (A)
85 Mill Rd, BT34 4RH. ☎ (039 67) 68451.
Fax 67041.
B&B s£65 d£85. BB&M s£85 d£105.
Rooms 10, ensuite 10. Dinner £20. Last
orders 2000 hrs. Open all year.

🕇 🅿 ✿ ♣ 🔆 🐎 🏢 ⌨ ☎ ✂ ⚲ ♪ ⌐ ∪ ⬥ 🔁

Bed & Breakfast

DAIRY FARM
(Mrs C Gordon), 52a Majors Hill,
BT34 4QR. ☎ (039 67) 68433.
B&B s£14 d£28. Rooms 2. Open all year.

🅿 ✿ ♣ 🔆 🐎 OAP 🏢 ✂

FOUR WINDS
(Mrs D Stevenson), 237 Kilkeel Rd,
BT34 4TW. ☎ (039 67) 68345.
B&B s£13.50 d£27. Rooms 3, ensuite 2.
Open all year.

🅿 ✿ ♣ 🔆 🐎 🐴 🏢 ⌐ ⌐ ∪ ⬥ 🌀

Mrs I JARDINE
16 Moneydarragh Rd, BT34 4TY.
☎ (039 67) 68153.
B&B s£13.50 d£27. BB&M s£20.50 d£41.
Rooms 2, ensuite 1. High tea £7, Dinner
£7. Open Apr-Sept.

🕇 🅿 ✿ ♣ 🔆 🐎 🏢 ✂ ⌐ ∪

THE SYCAMORES
(Mrs A McKee), 52 Majors Hill, BT34 4QR.
☎ (039 67) 68279.
B&B s£15 d£30. BB&M s£23 d£46. Rooms
2, ensuite 2. Dinner £8. Open all year.

🕇 🅿 ✿ ♣ 🔆 🐎 OAP 🏢 ⌐ ✂ ♪ ⌐ ∪ ⬥

Bed & Breakfast

STRAND
(Mrs M Donnan), 231 Ardglass Rd,
BT30 7UL. ☎ (0396) 841446.
B&B s£12 d£23. Rooms 2. High tea £5.
Dinner £6. Open all year.
On B1, 1¹/₂m NW of Ardglass

🅿 ✿ ♣ 🔆 🐎 OAP ✂ ♪ ⌐ ∪ ⬥ ⬥

Bed & Breakfast

BAYVIEW
(Mrs E Patton), 187 Harbour Rd BT22 1BP.
☎ (024 77) 58908.
B&B s£12.50, d£25. Rooms 3. High tea
£4.50. Dinner £7.50. Last orders 1800 hrs.
Open all year.

🅿 ✿ ♣ 🔆 🐎 OAP 🏢 ✂

Hotels

MILLBROOK LODGE HOTEL   *
5 Drumaness Rd, BT24 8LS.
☎ (0238) 562828. Fax 565402.
B&B s£27.50 d£47. BB&M s£37.50 d£57.
Rooms 16, ensuite 16. High tea £6. Dinner
£10. Last orders 2115 hrs. Open all year.

🅿 🛏 ✿ ♣ 🔆 🍴 🐎 OAP 🏢 ⌐ ☎ ♪ ⌐ ∪ ✓ 🍸 🔁

Facilities are liable to change. Check prices when you book. Key to symbols is on the back flap.

WHITE HORSE HOTEL　*
17 High St, BT24 8AB. ☎ (0238) 562225.
B&B s£28 d£48. BB&M s£38 d£64. Rooms
12, ensuite 6. High tea £8.50. Dinner
£12.50. Last orders 2100 hrs. Open all
year.

Bed & Breakfast

BUSHYMEAD COUNTRY HOUSE
(Mrs S Murphy), 86 Drumaness Rd,
BT24 8LT. ☎ (0238) 561171.
B&B s£15 d£30. BB&M s£18.50 d£37.
Rooms 5.　Dinner £3.50.
Last orders 2200 hrs. Open all year.

CORNERHOUSE
(Mrs M Rogan), 182 Dunmore Rd,
BT24 8QQ. ☎ (0238) 562670.
B&B s£12.50 d£25. Rooms 2.
Open Jun-Oct.
Off A24, 3m S of Ballynahinch

CUMBER HOUSE
(Mrs E Clements), 58 Crabtree Rd,
BT24 8RJ. ☎ (0238) 562286.
B&B s£12 d£24. Rooms 2. Open all year.

DAIRY LAKE HOUSE
(Mrs V Hawthorne), 172 Old Belfast Rd,
BT24 8YJ. ☎ (0238) 561543.
B&B s£13 d£26. BB&M s£20 d£40.
Rooms 3, ensuite 1. Dinner £10.
Last orders 2100 hrs. Open all year.

EDENAVADDY HOUSE
(Mrs M Reid), 6 Edenavaddy Rd, BT24 8JJ.
☎ (0238) 562962.
B&B s£12.50 d£25. BB&M s£20 d£40.
Rooms 3. High tea £7.50. Dinner £7.50
Open all year.

GLENVIEW
(Mrs E Skelly), 40 Ballymaglave Rd, Spa,
BT24 8QB. ☎ (0238) 562684.
B&B s£12.50 d£24. Rooms 2. Open Feb-
Nov.

MOUNT ELEANOR
(Mr & Mrs N McCord), 28b Main St,
BT24 8DN. ☎ (0238) 562468.
B&B s£15 d£30. Rooms 2, ensuite 1.
Open all year.

NUMBER THIRTY
(Mrs M E Reid), 30 Mountview Rd,
BT24 8JR. ☎ (0238) 562956.
B&B s£15 d£30. Rooms 3, ensuite 1.
High tea £6.50. Last orders 1200 hrs.
Open all year.

PEAR TREE FARM
(Mrs J Metcalfe), 10 Peartree Rd,
BT24 7JY. ☎ (0238) 510437.
B&B s£13 d£26. BB&M s£23 d£46.
Rooms 2, ensuite 2. Dinner £10. Last
orders 1200 hrs. Open all year.

B&B = bed and breakfast　　s = single　　d = double　　BB&M = bed, breakfast & evening meal

BALLYWALTER

County DOWN

BALLYWALTER

Bed & Breakfast

GREENLEA
(Mrs E McIvor), 48 Dunover Rd, BT22 2LE.
☎ (024 77) 58218.
B&B s£13 d£25. BB&M s£20 d£38. Rooms
5. High tea £6.50. Dinner £8. Open all
year.
Off A2, ½ m N of Ballywalter

ROCKDENE
(Mrs F Dickson), 4 Springvale Rd,
BT22 2PE. ☎ (024 77) 58205.
B&B s£12.50. d£25. Rooms 2. Open
Mar-Sept.

WINDMILL HOLLOW
(Mr K B Sloan), 166 Whitechurch Rd,
BT19 1RR. ☎ (024 77) 58755.
Fax 58755.
B&B s£20 d£40. BB&M s£32 d£64.
Rooms 2. Dinner £12. Last orders 1500 hrs.
Open all year.
On A2, N of Ballywalter

BANBRIDGE

Hotels

BELMONT HOTEL *
Rathfriland Rd, BT32 3LH. ☎ (082 06)
62517. Fax 62517.
B&B s£30 d£40. Rooms 12, ensuite 12.
High tea £8.75. Dinner £10. Last orders
2130 hrs. Open all year.

Bed & Breakfast

BELLA VISTA
(Mr B McDonnell), 107 Scarva Rd,
BT32 3QD. ☎ (082 06) 27066.
B&B s£17, d£30. Rooms 5, ensuite 3.
Open all year.
On B10, 1m W of Banbridge

GREENACRES
(Mr & Mrs R Mayne), 15 Brague Rd,
Corbet, BT32 5JZ. ☎ (082 06) 23328.
B&B s£15 d£30. BB&M s£21 d£42.
Rooms 3, ensuite 2. High tea £4. Dinner
£6. Last orders 2100 hrs. Open all year.

HEATHMAR
(Mrs J Fleming), 37 Corbet Rd, BT32 3SH.
☎ (082 06) 22348.
B&B s£12 d£24. Rooms 2, ensuite 1.
Open all year.
Off B25, 4m N of Banbridge

LISDRUM
(Mrs E Campbell), 189 Newry Rd,
BT32 3NB. ☎ (082 06) 22663.
B&B s£15 d£28. Rooms 1, ensuite 1. Open
all year.

MEADOWVIEW
(Michael & Margaret McAvoy)
26a Monteith Rd, Annaclone, BT32 5LS.
☎ (082 06) 71141.
B&B s£13 d£24. Rooms 2. High tea £5.
Dinner £5. Last orders 2000 hrs. Open all
year.

Facilities are liable to change. Check prices when you book. Key to symbols is on the back flap.

67

MOOR LODGE
(Mr & Mrs J McClory), 20 Ballynafern Rd,
Annaclone, BT32 5AE. ☎ (082 06) 71516.
B&B s£13 d£25. BB&M s£21 d£40.
Rooms 4. High tea £7. Dinner £8. Last
orders 1800 hrs. Open all year.
½m off B10

🆃 🅿 ❄ ♣ ⚹ ☆ OAP ▥ ⊬ ♪ ↑ ∪ ⬥ ⊞

MOURNEVIEW
(Mrs N Kerr), 32 Drumnascamph Rd,
Laurencetown, BT63 6DU. ☎ (082 06)
26270/24251.
B&B s£12 d£24. Rooms 7, ensuite 4.
Open all year.
2½m NW of Banbridge

🆃 🅿 ❄ ♣ ⚹ ☆ ▥ ⊬ ♪ ↑ ∪ ✓

SPRINGHILL
(Mrs D Shanks), 132 Ballygowan Rd,
BT32 3QX. ☎ (082 06) 23882.
B&B s£12.50 d£25. Rooms 2. Open all
year.
1m from Banbridge

🅿 🏠 ❄ ♣ ⚹ ☆ OAP ▥ ⊬ ♪ ↑ ∪

Hotels

O'HARA'S ROYAL HOTEL   **
26 Quay St, BT20 5ED. ☎ (0247) 271866.
Fax 467810.
B&B s£61.50 d£74.50. Rooms 34, ensuite
34. High tea £12.50. Dinner £17.50.
Last orders 2115 hrs. Open all year.

🆃 ⚹ ❗ ☆ 🆖 ▥ ⊡ ↻ ♪ ↑ ⬥ ⚛ ❦ ⊞

SANDS HOTEL   *
10 Seacliff Rd, BT20 5EY.
☎ (0247) 270696. Fax 271678.
B&B s£51 d£70. Rooms 12, ensuite 12.
High tea £8.50. Dinner £12.95.
Last orders 2115 hrs. Open all year.

🆃 🅿 ⚹ ❗ ☆ OAP ▥ ⊡ ↻ ⊬ ♪ ↑ ⬥ ❦ ⊞

TEDWORTH HOTEL   *
Lorelei, Princetown Rd, BT20 3TF.
☎ (0247) 463928. Fax 463954.
B&B s£35 d£55. BB&M s£47.95 d£67.95.
Rooms 26, ensuite 24. High tea £7. Dinner
£13. Last orders 2130 hrs. Open all year.

🅿 🏠 ♣ ⚹ ❗ ☆ ▥ ⊡ ↻ ⊬ ♪ ↑ ⬥ ⚛ ❦ ⊞

WINSTON HOTEL   *
19 Queen's Parade, BT20 3BJ.
☎ (0247) 454575. Fax 454575.
B&B s£40 d£55. Rooms 27, ensuite 2.
High tea £7. Dinner £9.50. Last orders
2130 hrs. Open all year.

🆃 🅿 ⚹ ❗ ☆ OAP ⇥ ▥ ⊡ ↻ ⊬ ♪ ↑ ∪ ✓ ⬥
⚛ ❦ ⊞

SHELLEVEN HOUSE   (A)
(Mrs F Davis), 61 Princetown Rd,
BT20 3TA. ☎ (0247) 271777. Fax 271777.
B&B s£20 d£40. BB&M s£32.50 d£65.
Rooms 12, ensuite 8. High tea £8.50.
Dinner £12.50. Last orders 1900 hrs.
Open all year.

🆃 🅿 ❄ ⚹ ☆ OAP ▥ ⊡ ⊬ ♪ ↑ ∪ ✓ ⬥ ⚛ ❦
⊞

B&B = bed and breakfast   s = single   d = double   BB&M = bed, breakfast & evening meal

BATTERSEA GUEST HOUSE (B)
(Mrs J Hanna), 47 Queen's Parade,
BT20 3BH. ☎ (0247) 461643.
B&B s£15 d£26. BB&M s£21
d£32. Rooms 3. Dinner £6.
Open all year.

BEACHCROFT (B)
(Mrs M Keery), 5 Princetown Terrace,
BT20 3BE. ☎ (0247) 473516.
B&B s£13 d£26. BB&M s£17.50 d£35.
Rooms 4. Dinner £4.50. Open all year.

ENNISLARE GUEST HOUSE (B)
(Mr & Mrs B Walsh), 9 Princetown Rd,
BT20 3TA. ☎ (0247) 270858.
B&B s£14 d£26. Rooms 8. Dinner £6.
Open all year.

LYN-LEY (B)
(Mr & Mrs B McCamley), 53 Queen's
Parade, BT20 3BH. ☎ (0247) 469505.
B&B s£15 d£26. BB&M s£21 d£38.
Rooms 3, Dinner £6. Last orders 1900 hrs.
Open all year.

MARDEE GUEST HOUSE (B)
(Mr W Loughrey), 58 Queen's Parade,
BT20 3BH. ☎ (0247) 457733.
B&B s£13 d£26. Rooms 4, ensuite 1.
Open all year.

ROSEWOOD HOUSE (B)
(Mrs M McKeen), 41 Princetown Rd,
BT20 3TA. ☎ (0247) 450029.
B&B s£15 d£25. BB&M s£22 d£39.
Rooms 5. High tea £5. Dinner £7.
Last orders 2000 hrs. Open all year.

SEACLIFF GUEST HOUSE (B)
(Mrs P Foster), 74 Seacliff Rd, BT20 5EZ.
☎ (0247) 453104.
B&B s£12 d£24. BB&M s£22 d£44.
Rooms 5. Dinner £10. Open all year.

TARA (B)
(Mr W Spence), 51 Princetown Rd,
BT20 3TA. ☎ (0247) 468924/(0850) 422067.
B&B s£16 d£30. Rooms 10, ensuite 4.
High tea £12.50. Dinner £12.50.
Open all year.

BERESFORD HOUSE (U)
(Mrs J Anderson), 45 Queen's Parade,
BT20 3BH. ☎ (0247) 472143. Fax 435167.
B&B s£14.50 d£28. BB&M s£22 d£40.
Rooms 16, ensuite 5. High tea £7.50.
Dinner £8. Last orders 1830 hrs.
Open all year.

Bed & Breakfast

ABBEYVIEW HEIGHTS
(Mrs E McClenaghan), 38 Bryansburn Rd,
BT20 3SE. ☎ (0247) 472119.
B&B s£18 d£36. Rooms 5, ensuite 2.
Open all year.

Facilities are liable to change. Check prices when you book. Key to symbols is on the back flap.

A .L. S. O. D. ZION-KERN
18 Prospect Rd, BT20 5DA.
☎ (0247) 461309.
B&B s£12 d£24. Rooms 4. Open all year.

ALTON
(Mrs M Lyle), 1 Bryansburn Rd, BT20 3RY.
☎ (0247) 457924.
B&B s£15 d£26. Rooms 3. Open all year.

ANCHORAGE
(Mrs E Erskine), 36 Seacliff Rd, BT20 5EY.
☎ (0247) 461326.
B&B s£13 d£26. BB&M s£19 d£38. Rooms
5. High tea £6. Dinner £6. Open all year.

ARMELL
(Mrs A Armstrong), 30 Donaghadee Rd,
BT20 5RU. ☎ (0247) 461903.
B&B s£11 d£22. BB&M s£15 d£25. Rooms
4. High tea £4. Dinner £5. Open Jun-Aug
& Easter.

ASLAN
(Mr & Mrs T Duncan), 24 Southwell Rd,
BT20 3AQ. ☎ (0247) 451156.
B&B s£12 d£24. BB&M s£18 d£36.
Rooms 7, ensuite 1. Open all year.

BRABAZON
(Mrs A Speers), 126 Seacliff Rd, BT20 5EZ.
☎ (0247) 452329.
B&B s£13 d£25. BB&M s£18 d£36.
Rooms 3. Open all year.

BRACKNEY HOUSE
(Mrs A Thompson), 2 Green Rd, Conlig,
BT23 3PZ. ☎ (0247) 461423.
B&B s£17 d£30. Rooms 3, ensuite 2.
Open all year.
Off A21, 1 m S of Bangor

CAMELOT
(Mrs M Hewitt), 83 Abbey Park,
BT20 4BZ. ☎ (0247) 451985.
B&B s£12 d£24. BB&M s£18 d£36.
Rooms 3. Open all year.

CAROLESTA
(Mrs B G Spence), 17 Southwell Rd,
BT20 3AQ. ☎ (0247) 460640.
B&B s£12 d£24. BB&M s£18.50 d£37.
Rooms 4. Dinner £7. Open all year.

CLIFFSIDE
(Mrs C Deacon), 140 Seacliff Rd,
BT20 5EZ. ☎ (0247) 454726/464545.
B&B s£12 d£24. BB&M s£18 d£30.
Rooms 4. Dinner £6. Last orders 2000 hrs.
Open all year.

EMMAUS
(Mrs S Campbell), 53 Holborn Avenue,
BT20 5ET. ☎ (0247) 456887.
B&B s£11 d£21. BB&M s£17 d£33.
Rooms 5. High tea £6. Open all year.

GLENALLEN HOUSE
(Mr & Mrs J Patterson), 16 Seacliff Rd,
BT20 5EY. ☎ (0247) 473964.
B&B s£12 d£24. Rooms 4, ensuite 1.
Open all year.

Facilities are liable to change. Check prices when you book. Key to symbols is on the back flap.

GLENDALE HOUSE
(Mrs A Blachford), 77 Southwell Rd,
BT20 3AE. ☎ (0247) 468613.
B&B s£12 d£24. BB&M s£18 d£36.
Rooms 3. High tea £4, Dinner £6.
Last orders 1900 hrs. Open all year.

HEBRON HOUSE
(Margaret McClure), 59 Queen's Parade,
BT20 3BH. ☎ (0247) 463126.
B&B s£11 d£22. Rooms 3. Open all year.

HIGHFIELD COUNTRY HOUSE
(Mrs E Finlay), 531 Belfast Rd, BT19 1UN.
☎ (0247) 853693.
B&B s£18 d£34. Rooms 3. Open all year.

KILDARA
(Mrs T Hughes), 51 Prospect Rd,
BT20 5DA. ☎ (0247) 461245.
B&B s£12 d£24. Rooms 3, ensuite 1.
Open Apr-Sept.

LEASIDE
(Mrs C Royle), 22 Southwell Rd,
BT20 3AQ. ☎ (0247) 472360.
B&B s£12 d£24. BB&M s£18 d£36.
Rooms 4. Dinner £6. Open all year.

LISMORE
(Mrs L Lowry), 74 Southwell Rd, BT20 3AE.
☎ (0247) 473862.
B&B s£11.50 d£22. Rooms 4. High tea £5.
Dinner £6. Open all year.

LISNACREE
(Mr & Mrs M Conway), 53 Princetown Rd,
BT20 3TA. ☎ (0247) 462571.
B&B s£14 d£26. BB&M s£20.50 d£39.
Rooms 6. High tea £6.50. Dinner £8.50.
Open all year.

PIER VIEW HOUSE
(Mrs R Watts), 28 Seacliff Rd, BT20 5EY.
☎ (0247) 463381.
B&B s£13 d£26. Rooms 5, ensuite 2.
Open all year.

RHO-MAR-TO LODGE
(Mrs M Davison), 79 Ballycrochan Rd,
BT19 6NF. ☎ (0247) 461921.
B&B s£15 d£30. BB&M s£27 d£54 :
Rooms 5, ensuite 2. High tea £8. Dinner
£12. Last orders 2200 hrs. Open all year.

SEACREST
(Mrs I Marsden), 98 Seacliff Rd, BT20 5EZ.
☎ (0247) 461935.
B&B s£15 d£26. BB&M s£24 d£44.
Rooms 4. Dinner £9. Open all year.

SNUG HARBOUR
(Mrs P McKenna), 144 Seacliff Rd,
BT20 5EZ. ☎ (0247) 454238.
B&B s£11 d£22. BB&M £18 d£36.
Rooms 3. Open all year.

B&B = bed and breakfast   s = single   d = double   BB&M = bed, breakfast & evening meal

ST IVES
(Mrs I Artt), 58 Seacliff Rd, BT20 5EZ.
☎ (0247) 469444.
B&B s£13 d£25. BB&M s£19 d£37. Rooms
5, ensuite 1. High tea £5. Dinner £6. Last
orders 1830 hrs. Open all year.

WHITE O'MORN
(Mr & Mrs H Dunlop), 30 Seacliff Rd,
BT20 5EY. ☎ (0247) 468400.
B&B s£13 d£26. Rooms 5. Open all year.

CASTLEWELLAN

Guesthouses

CHESTNUT INN   (B)
(Mr & Mrs G King), 28 Lower Square,
BT31 9DW. ☎ (039 67) 78247/78344.
B&B s£18 d£36. BB&M s£26.50 d£33.
Rooms 7, ensuite 7. High tea £6.50. Dinner
£9.50. Last orders 2045 hrs. Open all year.

Bed & Breakfast

ARDNARI HOUSE
(Miss F King), 67 Newcastle Rd, BT31 9DS.
☎ (039 67) 78058/78239. Fax 71524.
B&B s£13.50 d£27. Rooms 2.
Open Mar-Oct.

BEAFORTE
(Mrs A King), 17 Upper Square,
BT31 9DD. ☎ (039 67) 71478.
B&B s£12 d£24. BB&M s£19 d£38.
Rooms 3. Open all year.

TREETOPS
(Mrs J King), 39 Circular Rd, BT31 9ED.
☎ (039 67) 78132.
B&B s£13 d£26. Rooms 4, ensuite 1.
Open all year.

CLOUGH

Bed & Breakfast

Mrs B HAMILTON
21 Dundrum Rd, BT30 8SH.
☎ (039 687) 521.
B&B s£13.50 d£27. BB&M s£20
d£40. Rooms 2. Dinner £6.50.
Open Apr-Oct.
7m SW of Downpatrick

COMBER

Bed & Breakfast

FLAX MILL HOUSE
(Mrs I McEntee), 117 Glen Rd, BT23 5QT.
☎ (0247) 873253.
B&B s£17 d£32. Rooms 2. Open all year.

MOSSBANK
(Mrs N E Erskine), 54b Ballycreely Rd,
BT23 5PX. ☎ (0232) 448245.
B&B s£14 d£26. Rooms 2. Open all year.

Facilities are liable to change. Check prices when you book. Key to symbols is on the back flap.

OLD SCHOOL HOUSE
(Mr & Mrs T Brown), 100 Ballydrain Rd.
BT23 6EA. ☎ (0238) 541182.
B&B s£25 d£40. BB&M s£37.95 d£65.90.
Rooms 4, ensuite 2. Dinner £15. Last
orders 2230 hrs. Open all year.

Ⓣ Ⓟ 🏮 ❊ ♣ ☀ ⚡ ⛺ 🏞 ⚑ ✁ ♪ ⌐ ∪ ⚓ ⚔ 🏵
⚱

TRENCH FARM
(Mrs M Hamilton), 35 Ringcreevy Rd,
BT23 5JR. ☎ (0247) 872558. B&B s£15
d£30. BB&M s£25 d£50. Rooms 3. High
tea £8. Dinner £10. Open all year.
Off A21, 3 m E of Comber

Ⓟ ❊ ♣ ☀ 🏞 ⚑ ✁ 🏵

CRAWFORDSBURN

Hotels

OLD INN   ***
15 Main St, BT19 1JH. ☎ (0247) 853255.
Fax 852775.
B&B s£70 d£90. Rooms 32, ensuite 32.
High tea £7.50. Dinner £17. Last orders
2130 hrs. Open all year.

Ⓟ 🏮 ❊ ♣ ♥ ☀ 🏞 ⚑ ⌐ ↾ ∪ ⚓ ⚔ 🏵 ⚱

Guesthouses

GLEN HOUSE   (U)
(Mrs N Harte), 212 Crawfordsburn Rd,
BT19 1HY. ☎ (0247) 852610.
Fax 852229.
B&B s£25 d£45. BB&M s£40 d£75. Rooms
5, ensuite 5. High tea £12. Dinner £15.
Last orders 2000 hrs. Open all year.

Ⓟ ❊ ♣ ☀ ☀ 🏞 ⚑ ✁ ♪ ↾ ∪ ✓ ⚓ 🏵 ⚱

CROSSGAR

Bed & Breakfast

HILLHOUSE
(Mrs M Davison), 53 Killyleagh Rd,
BT30 9EE. ☎ (0396) 830792.
B&B s£16 d£30. BB&M s£22 d£42. Rooms
4, ensuite 2. High tea £6. Dinner £9.
Last orders 1900 hrs. Open all year.

Ⓣ Ⓟ 🏮 ❊ ♣ ☀ ☀ 🏞 ⚑ ✁ ♪ ↾ ∪ ✓ ⚓ ⚔

MONDARA HOUSE
(Mrs H A Steele), 4 Creevy Rd, BT30 9HX.
☎ (0396) 830444.
B&B s£15 d£30. BB&M s£20 d£40.
Rooms 2. High tea £5. Dinner £5.
Last orders 2200 hrs. Open all year.

Ⓟ 🏮 ❊ ♣ ☀ 🏞 ⚑ ✁ ♪ ↾ ∪ ✓ ⚓ ⚔

DONAGHADEE

Hotels

COPELANDS HOTEL   **
60 Warren Rd, BT21 0PD. ☎ (0247)
888189. Fax 888344.
B&B s£35 d£45. Rooms 16, ensuite 16.
High tea £9. Dinner £13. Last orders 2130
hrs. Open all year.

Ⓟ ❊ ♣ ☀ ♥ ☀ 🏞 ⚑ ⌐ ✁ ♪ ↾ ∪ ⚓ ⚔ 🏵 ⚱

Bed & Breakfast

BRIDGE HOUSE
(Mrs F Logan), 93 Windmill Rd, BT21
0NQ. ☎ (0247) 883348.
B&B s£14 d£26. Rooms 2. Open all year.
2 m W of Donaghadee

Ⓟ ❊ ♣ ☀ ☀ 🏞 ⚑ ● ♪ ↾ ∪ ⚓

B&B = bed and breakfast   s = single   d = double   BB&M = bed, breakfast & evening meal

THE DEANS
(Mrs S Wilson), 52 Northfield Rd, BT21
0BD. ☎ (0247) 882204.
B&B s£15 d£28. BB&M s£22 d£42. Rooms
3. High tea £6. Dinner £7.50. Last orders
1930 hrs. Open all year.

🅿 ❄ 🕭 ᴰᴬᴾ ▦ ☐ ☏ ⚲ ↑

WATERSIDE
(Mrs A Dalzell), 11 New Rd, BT21 0AH.
☎ (0247) 888305.
B&B s£14 d£28. Rooms 2. Open May-Sept.

🏠 ❄ ♣ ☇ 🕭 ᴰᴬᴾ ▦ ☐ ⚲ ♪ ↑

WATERSIDE SHANAGHAN
(Mrs M Beattie), 154 Warren Rd,
BT21 0PN. ☎ (0247) 888167.
B&B s£16.50 d£30. BB&M s£23, d£45.
Rooms 3. High tea £6.50. Dinner £10.
Open all year.

Ⓣ 🅿 ❄ ♣ ☇ 🕭 ᴰᴬᴾ 🛌 ▦ ☏ ⚲ ♪ ↑ U ✓ ⌂ ⚡

WOODSIDE
(Mrs J Caddoo), 7 Newtownards Rd,
BT21 0PN. ☎ (0247) 883653.
B&B s£14 d£28. Rooms 2. Open all year.

🅿 ❄ ♣ ▦ ⚲

DOWNPATRICK

Hotels

ABBEY LODGE HOTEL   **
Belfast Rd, BT30 9AU. ☎ (0396) 614511.
Fax 616415.
B&B s£35 d£45. BB&M s£46 d£67. Rooms
21, ensuite 21. High tea £6. Dinner £10.
Last orders 2130 hrs. Open all year.

❄ ♣ ☇ ❗ 🕭 ▦ ☐ ☏ ⚲ ♪ ↑ U ✓ ⌂ ⚡ ♟ ⚔ 🏃
🆓

Bed & Breakfast

Mrs E COBURN, 47 Roughal Park, BT30
6HB. ☎ (0396) 612656.
B&B s£13 d£26. BB&M s£20 d£40. Rooms
2, ensuite 2. Dinner £7. Last orders
1200 hrs. Open all year.

🅿 ❄ ♣ ☇ 🕭 ▦ ☐ ⚲ ♪ ↑ U ✓ ⌂ ⚡ 🏃

HAVINE FARM
(Mrs M Macauley), 51 Ballydonnell Rd,
BT30 8EP. ☎ (039 685) 242.
B&B s£14.50 d£28. Rooms 6. High tea
£6.50. Dinner £9.50. Last orders 1530 hrs.
Open all year ex Christmas.
Off A25, 4 ¾ m S of Downpatrick

🅿 🏠 ♣ ☇ 🕭 ᴰᴬᴾ ♪ ↑ U 🏃

HILLCREST
(Mrs F Fitzsimons), 157 Strangford Rd,
BT30 7JZ. ☎ (0396) 612583.
B&B s£12 d£24. Rooms 3, ensuite 1.
Open all year.

🅿 ❄ ♣ ☇ 🕭 ᴰᴬᴾ ▦ ⚲ ♪ ↑ ✓ ⌂ 🏃

LISNAMOYLE
(Mrs M Doran), 1 Folly Lane, BT30 6NF.
☎ (0396) 615335.
B&B s£12 d£24. Rooms 1. Open Jan-Dec.

🅿 ❄ ♣ ☇ ➤ ▦ ☐ ♪ ↑ U ✓ ⌂ ⚡ 🏃

RATHTULLA
(Mr & Mrs McMullan), 29 Rathkeltair Rd,
BT30 6SA. ☎ (0396) 612068.
B&B s£13 d£26. Rooms 3, ensuite 1.
Open Mar-Sept.

🅿 ❄ ♣ ☇ ☇ 🕭 ᴰᴬᴾ ▦ ☐ ⚲ ⚫ ♪ ↑ U ✓ ⌂ ⚡
🏃

B&B = bed and breakfast   s = single   d = double   BB&M = bed, breakfast & evening meal

TYRELLA HOUSE
(Mr & Mrs Corbett), Clanmaghery Rd,
Tyrella, BT30 8SU. ☎ (0396) 85422.
B&B s£35 d£60. BB&M s£53 d£96.
Rooms 3, ensuite 2. Dinner £18.
Last orders 1600 hrs. Open all year.

🔲 🅿 ✿ ♣ ☀ ➢ ᠁ ✂ ↗ � 🌂

DROMORE

Bed & Breakfast

THE MAGGIMINN
(Mr & Mrs W Mark), 11 Bishopswell Rd,
BT25 1ST. ☎ (0846) 693520.
B&B s£18.50 d£32. BB&M s£28 d£50.
Rooms 4, ensuite 1. High tea £6. Dinner
£10. Open all year.

🔲 🅿 ✿ ♣ ☀➢ ᠁ ✂ ↗ ☝

SYLVAN HILL HOUSE
(Mr & Mrs J Coburn), 76 Kilntown Rd,
BT25 1HS.
☎ (0846) 692321.
B&B s£18 d£32. BB&M s£29 d£54.
Rooms 3. High tea £7. Dinner £11.
Open all year.

🅿 🏠 ✿ ♣ ☀ ⭐ ᠁ ✂ ↗ ☝ U ✓ 🌢

WIN-STAFF
(Mrs E Erwin), 45 Banbridge Rd,
BT25 1NE. ☎ (0846) 692252.
B&B s£17 d£34. BB&M s£25 d£50.
Rooms 6, ensuite 3. Open all year.

🅿 ✿ ♣ ➢ ᠁ ☐ �

DUNDRUM

Bed & Breakfast

BAY INN
169 Main St, BT33 0LY. ☎ (039 675) 209.
B&B s£10 d£20. Rooms 4. Open all year.

🅿 ♣ ☀ ❢ ➢ 0AP ᠁ ↗ ☝ U ✓ 🌢⛵🌂

MOURNEVIEW HOUSE
(Mrs S McKeating), 16 Main St, BT33 0LU.
☎ (039 675) 457.
B&B s£12 d£24. Rooms 4. Open all year.

🅿 🏠 ✿ ♣ ☀ ➢ 🐎 ᠁ ✂ 🌢 ☺ 🌂

GILFORD

Bed & Breakfast

MOUNT PLEASANT
(Mrs M Buller), 38 Banbridge Rd,
BT63 6DJ. ☎ (0762) 831522.
B&B s£12 d£24. Rooms 5. Open all year.

🏠 ✿ ♣ ➢ ᠁ ✂ ↗ ☝ ✓ 🌢 🌂

GREYABBEY

Bed & Breakfast

ABBEY FARM
(Mrs M Hall), 17 Ballywalter Rd, BT22 2RF.
☎ (024 77) 88207.
B&B s£14 d£28. BB&M s£22 d£44. Rooms
2. High tea £9. Dinner £9.50. Last orders
1900 hrs. Open all year.
On B5

🔲 🅿 ✿ ♣ ➢ ᠁ ☐ ✂ ↗ ☝ U 🌢

B&B = bed and breakfast   s = single   d = double   BB&M = bed, breakfast & evening meal

BRIMAR
(Mrs M Dixon) 4 Cardy Rd, BT22 2LS.
☎ (02477) 88681.
B&B s£17 d£34. Rooms 5, ensuite 5.
Dinner £10. Last orders 1200 hrs.
Open all year.

P ✿ ♣ ⅍ ⅗ DAP ⅏ ▢ ✁ ♪ ⌐ ∪ ∕ △⅄ ☺

GORDONALL FARM
(Mrs A Martin), 93 Newtownards Rd,
BT22 2QJ. ☎ (024 77) 88325.
B&B s£14 d£27. Rooms 2. Open all year.
On A20, 1m from Greyabbey

P ✿ ♣ ⅍ ⅗ ⅏ ✁ ♪ ⌐ △

MERVUE
(Mrs A Heron), 28 Portaferry Rd, BT22
2RX. ☎ (024 77) 88619.
B&B s£15 d£30. Rooms 3, ensuite 3.
Open all year.

P ⅋ ✿ ♣ ⅍ DAP ⅃ ⅏ ✁ ♪ ⌐ ∪ ∕ △⅄

Guesthouses

SANDEEL LODGE (U)
(Mrs A Briers), Orlock, BT19 6LP.
☎ (0247) 883139.
B&B s£45 d£70. BB&M s£57.50 d£110.
Rooms 3, ensuite 2. Dinner £12.50.
Open all year.

☎ P ✿ ♣ ⅍ ⅏ ▢ ✁ ⅌ ✆ ⅏ ♪ ⌐ ∪ ∕ △
⅄ ⊞

ISLET HILL
(Mr D Mayne), 21 Bangor Rd, BT19 6JF.
☎ (0247) 464435.
B&B s£17 d£34. Rooms1, ensuite 1.
Open all year.

☎ P ⅋ ✿ ♣ ⅍ ⅗ ⅏ ♪ ⌐ ∪ ∕ △⅄

TANNER COTTAGE
(Mrs S Walker), 5 Main St, BT19 6JR.
☎ (0247) 464534.
B&B s£22.50 d£35. Rooms 2, ensuite 2.
Open all year.

P ⅍ ⅏ ▢ ✁

Bed & Breakfast

CARRIG-GORM
(Mrs E Eves), 27 Bridge Rd, BT19 1TS.
☎ (0247) 853680.
B&B s£20 d£36. Rooms 2, ensuite 1.
Open all year.

☎ P ✿ ♣ ⅍ ⅗ ⅏ ▢ ✁ ⌐ △⅄

Hotels

WHITE GABLES HOTEL   ***
14 Dromore Rd, BT26 6HU. ☎ (0846)
682755. Fax 689532.
B&B s£68 d£86. Rooms 31, ensuite 31.
Dinner £19. Last orders 2115 hrs.
Open all year.

☎ P ✿ ♣ ♨ ⅗ ⅏ ▢ ⅃ ⅌ ♪ ⌐ ∕ △⅄⅂ ⊞

Facilities are liable to change. Check prices when you book. Key to symbols is on the back flap.

Bed & Breakfast

CASHEL-EANEN
(Mrs M Shannon), 26 Comber Rd,
BT26 6LN. ☎ (0846) 682380.
B&B s£20 d£35. BB&M s£30 d£50. Rooms
2, ensuite 1. High tea £6. Dinner £10.
Open all year.

FORTWILLIAM
(Mrs M Dunlop), 210 Ballynahinch Rd,
BT26 8BH. ☎ (0846) 682255/683401.
Fax 689608.
B&B s£25 d£35. BB&M s£35 d£55. Rooms
4, ensuite 3. High tea £7.50. Dinner £10.
Last orders 2030 hrs. Open all year.

GRANIDA
(Mrs A McKeag), 65 Dromore Rd,
BT26 6HQ. ☎ (0846) 682210.
B&B s£16 d£32. Rooms 2. Open all year.

MRS JANET SILCOCK.
16 Lisburn St, BT26 6AB. ☎ (0846)
683334.
B&B s£15 d£30. Rooms 2. Open all year.

HILLTOWN

Bed & Breakfast

GRITAR HEIGHTS
(Mrs C Devlin), 49 Sandbank Rd, Leitrim,
BT34 5XS. ☎ (082 06) 38002.
B&B s£12.50 d£25. BB&M 20.50 d£41.
Rooms 3, ensuite 1. High tea £5. Dinner
£8. Last orders 2000 hrs. Open all year.

HOLYWOOD

Guesthouses

ARDSHANE COUNTRY HOUSE (A)
5 Bangor Rd, Holywood, BT18 0NU.
☎ (023 17) 422044. Fax 427506.
B&B s£50 d£70. Rooms 8, ensuite 7. Last
orders 2000 hrs. Open all year.

RAYANNE HOUSE (A)
(Mr & Mrs R McClelland), 60 Demesne
Rd, BT18 9EX. ☎ (0232) 425859/423364.
Fax (0232) 425859.
B&B s£45 d£70. BB&M s£65 d£110.
Rooms 6, ensuite 6. Dinner £20. Last
orders 2100 hrs. Open all year.

Bed & Breakfast

CHURCHILL HOUSE
(Mrs C Blackwell), 1 Churchill, BT18 9DS.
☎ (0232) 424658/423749.
B&B s£18 d£34. Rooms 6, ensuite 4. Open
all year.

NUMBER TWO
(Mrs J Walker), 2 Victoria Rd, Holywood,
BT18 6BA. ☎ (0232) 422662.
B&B s£25 d£35. Rooms 3, ensuite 3.
Open all year.

Facilities are liable to change. Check prices when you book. Key to symbols is on the back flap.

KILKEEL

Hotels

KILMOREY ARMS HOTEL **
41 Greencastle St, BT34 4BH. ☎ (069 37)
62220/62801. Fax 65399.
B&B s£27 d£42. BB&M s£35 d£58. Rooms
27, ensuite 26. High tea £7.50. Dinner
£11. Last orders 2100 hrs. Open all year.

Guesthouses

WYNCREST (A)
(Mrs I Adair), 30 Main Rd, BT34 4NU.
☎ (069 37) 63012. Fax 63012.
B&B s£18.50 d£37. BB&M s£31 d£62.
Rooms 6, ensuite 4. Dinner £12.50.
Open Apr-Sept.
On A2, 3m NE of Kilkeel

MORNE ABBEY (B)
(Mrs A Shannon), 16 Greencastle Rd,
BT34 4DE. ☎ (069 37) 62426.
B&B s£13.50 d£33. BB&M s£22 d£48.
Rooms 5, ensuite 3. Dinner £8.50.
Open Apr-Sept.
Off B27, ½m from Kilkeel

Bed & Breakfast

ASHCROFT
(Miss E Orr), 12 Ballykeel Rd, Ballymartin,
BT34 4PL. ☎ (069 37) 62736.
B&B s£15 d£30. Rooms 4, ensuite 1.
Open Apr-Sept.
Off A2, 3m NE of Kilkeel

BARNESCROFT
(Mrs H Barnes), 37 Dunaval Rd, Ballyardle,
BT34 4JT. ☎ (069 37) 64519.
B&B s£16.50 d£33. Rooms 3, ensuite 1.
High tea £5.50. Dinner £8. Open all year.

CARGINAGH LODGE
(Mrs S Stronge), 195 Carginagh Rd,
BT34 4QA. ☎ (069 37) 62085.
B&B s£12 d£24. BB&M s£20 d£40.
Rooms 3. Dinner £8. Open all year.
Off A2, 3¼m from Kilkeel

EASTWOOD
(Mrs J Bonnargent), 8 Cranfield Rd.
☎ (069 37) 65162.
B&B s£12.50 d£25. BB&M s£19.50 d£39.
Rooms 3. Dinner £7.50. Last orders 2000
hrs. Open Apr-Sept.

HEATH HALL
(Mrs M McGlue), 160 Moyadd Rd, BT34
4HJ. ☎ (069 37) 62612.
B&B s£13 d£26. BB&M s£20 d£40. Rooms
3. Dinner £7. Last orders 1200 hrs. Open
Jan-Oct.
On B27, ½m N of Kilkeel

HILLVIEW
(Mrs M Trainor), 18 Bog Rd, Attical,
BT34 4HT. ☎ (069 37) 64269.
B&B s£12.50 d£25. BB&M s£17.50 d£40.
Rooms 3, ensuite 1. High tea £4.50.
Dinner £7.50. Last orders 2200 hrs.
Open all year.
Off B27, 4m NW of Kilkeel

B&B = bed and breakfast   s = single   d = double   BB&M = bed, breakfast & evening meal

HOMESYDE
(Mrs E Haugh), 7 Shandon Drive,
BT34 4DF. ☎ (069 37) 62676.
B&B s£12 d£24. Rooms 2. Open all year.

🅿 ✿ ♣ ☀ ⏰ [OAP] 🛏 ☐ ✂

IONA
(Mrs M Fitzpatrick), 161 Newcastle Rd,
BT34 4NN. ☎ (069 37) 62586.
B&B s£22 d£35. BB&M s£27 d£45.
Rooms 4. Open all year.

🆃 🅿 🏠 ✿ ♣ ☀ ⏰ [OAP] 🛏 ☐ ✆ ✈ ⚓ ⛵ ∪ ✓ ♠ ⚡

Mrs S MULLIGAN
66 Annalong Rd, Ballymartin BT34 4PG.
☎ (039 67) 68326.
B&B s£12 d£24. Rooms 2. Open Apr-Oct.

✿ ☀ ⏰ 🛏 ✈ ⚓ ∪

ROSETTA
(Mrs B McManus), 33 Newry Rd.
☎ (069 37) 63501/62258.
B&B s£12.50 d£25. Rooms 3. Open all year.

🅿 ✿ ♣ ☀ ⏰ 🛏 ✂ ✈ ⚓ ∪ ✓ ♠ ⚡

SHARON
(Mrs M Bingham), 6 Ballykeel Rd,
Ballymartin BT34 4PL. ☎ (069 37) 62521.
B&B s£15 d£28. Rooms 3. Open all year.

🆃 🅿 ✿ ♣ ☀ ⏰ 🛏 ✂ Ⓖ

Bed & Breakfast

BARNAGEEHA
(Mr & Mrs D Crawford), 90 Ardmillan Rd,
BT23 6QN. ☎ (0238) 541011.
B&B s£20 d£40. BB&M s£30 d£60.
Rooms 3, ensuite 3. Dinner £15. Last orders
2030 hrs. Open all year.

🅿 ✿ ♣ ☀ ⏰ 🛏 ☐ ✆ ✂ ⚲ ✈ ⚓ ∪ ✓ ♠ ⚡ ♠ 🆓

TIDES REACH
(Mr G Booth & Mrs H Booth),
107 Whiterock Rd, BT23 6PU.
☎ (0238) 541347.
B&B s£20 d£35. Rooms 3, ensuite 3.
Open all year.

🆃 🅿 ✿ ♣ ☀ ⏰ [OAP] 🛏 ☐ ✂ ✈ ⚓ ∪ ♠ ♠ 🆓

Bed & Breakfast

LOUGH VIEW
(Mrs E McCullough), 31 Rowreagh Rd,
BT22 1AS. ☎ (024 77) 38324.
Fax 38708.
B&B s£15 d£30. Rooms 3, ensuite 1.
Open all year.

🅿 ✿ ♣ ☀ [OAP] ⏰ ✂

SCHOOL HOUSE
(Mrs G Palmer), 12 Manse Rd BT22 1DR.
☎ (024 77) 38563.
B&B s£12.50 d£25. BB&M s£22 d£44.
Rooms 2, ensuite 1. High tea £9.50. Dinner
£9.50. Open all year.

🅿 ✿ ♣ ☀ [OAP] ⏰ ✂

Facilities are liable to change. Check prices when you book. Key to symbols is on the back flap.

MILLISLE

Bed & Breakfast

CROSSDONEY
(Mrs M Galloway), 216 Abbey Rd,
BT22 2DH. ☎ (0247) 861526.
B&B s£13.50 d£27. BB&M s£21.50 d£43.
Rooms 2. Open all year.

MOIRA

Guesthouses

BALLYCANAL MANOR   (B)
(Mrs P Brown), 2 Glenavy Rd, BT67 0LT.
☎ (0846) 611923.
B&B s£23 d£37. BB&M s£30 d£50. Rooms
5, ensuite 3. High tea £5. Dinner £7. Last
orders 2230 hrs. Open all year.

NEWCASTLE

Hotels

BURRENDALE HOTEL
 & COUNTRY CLUB   ***
51 Castlewellan Rd, BT33 0JY.
☎ (039 67) 22599. Fax 22328.
B&B s£55 d£80. BB&M s£ 65 d£104.
Rooms 51 ensuite 51. High tea £7.50.
Dinner £16. Last orders 2130 hrs.
Open all year.

SLIEVE DONARD HOTEL   ***
Downs Rd, BT33 0AH. ☎ (039 67) 23681.
Fax 24830.
B&B s£65 d£98. BB&M s£82.50 d£133.
Rooms 120, ensuite 120. High tea £8.50.
Dinner £17.50. Last orders 2130 hrs.
Open all year.

ENNISKEEN HOUSE HOTEL   **
98 Bryansford Rd, BT33 0LF.
☎ (039 67) 22392. Fax 24084.
B&B s£42 d£70. BB&M s£53 d£92. Rooms
12, ensuite 12. High tea £7.50. Dinner
£12.50. Last orders 2030 hrs. Open Mar-
Nov.

BROOK COTTAGE HOTEL   *
58 Bryansford Rd, BT33 0LD.
☎ (039 67) 22204/23508. Fax 22204.
B&B s£38 d£60. BB&M s£50 d£84 .
Rooms 8, ensuite 5. High tea £7.50.
Dinner £10.50. Last orders 2100 hrs.
Open all year.

DONARD HOTEL   *
27 Main St, BT33 0AD.
☎ (039 67) 22203/22501. Fax 22203.
B&B s£28 d£45. BB&M s£35 d£60. Rooms
13, ensuite 13. High tea £6.50. Dinner £9.
Last orders 2115 hrs. Open all year.

B&B = bed and breakfast   s = single   d = double   BB&M = bed, breakfast & evening meal

Guesthouses

ARUNDEL GUEST HOUSE (B)
(Mrs D Priestley), 23 Bryansford Rd,
BT33 0AX. ☎ (039 67) 22232.
B&B s£14 d£28. BB&M s£20.50 d£41.
Rooms 6. Dinner £6.50. Last orders 1730
hrs. Open all year.

HARBOUR HOUSE (B)
(Mr & Mrs Connolly), 4 South Promenade,
Kilkeel Rd, BT33 0EX.
☎ (039 67) 23445/23535.
B&B s£25 d£40. BB&M s£30 d£60. Rooms
4 , ensuite 4. High tea £8. Dinner £10.
Last orders 2130 hrs. Open all year.

SAVOY GUEST HOUSE (B)
(Mr & Mrs Keogh), 20 Downs Rd,
BT33 0AG. ☎ (039 67) 22513.
B&B s£22 d£30. BB&M s£30.50 d£47.
Rooms 9. Dinner £7.50. Open May-Oct.

THE BRIERS (U)
(Mrs M Bowater), 39 Middle Tollymore Rd,
BT33 0JJ. ☎ (039 67) 24347.
B&B s£20 d£32. BB&M s£30 d£52. Rooms
7, ensuite 7. High tea £6. Dinner £10. Last
orders 2000 hrs. Open all year.
Off B180, ¼ m from forest park

THE COTTAGE (U)
(M Railton), 81 Burrenreagh Rd,
Bryansford, BT33 0PU. ☎ (039 67) 24698.
Fax 24698.
B&B s£30.50, d£45. BB&M s£45.50 d£75.
Rooms 4, ensuite 4. Dinner £15. Last
orders 1200 hrs. Open Feb-Nov.

Bed & Breakfast

ARMORS COVE HOUSE
(Mr & Mrs W Rooney), 26 Ballagh Rd,
BT33 0LA. ☎ (039 67) 23814.
B&B s£13 d£26. Rooms 4. High tea £8.50.
Dinner £10.50. Last orders 2030 hrs.
Open Mar-Nov.

ASHMOUNT
(Mr & Mrs A Biggerstaff), 19 Bryansford Rd,
BT33 0HJ. ☎ (039 67) 25074.
B&B s£13.50 d£27. BB&M s£23.50 d£47.
Rooms 3. High tea £10. Dinner £10.
Last orders 1800 hrs. Open all year.

BEACH HOUSE
(Mrs M Macauley), 22 Downs Rd,
BT33 0AG. ☎ (039 67) 22345.
B&B s£18 d£30. BB&M s£28 d£50. Rooms
3. High tea £8. Dinner £10. Last orders
1830 hrs. Open Jan-Nov.

CARLTON HOUSE
(Mrs V Gray), 15 South Promenade,
BT33 0EX. ☎ (039 67) 22123.
B&B s£13 d£26. Rooms 2. Open all year.

Facilities are liable to change. Check prices when you book. Key to symbols is on the back flap.

CASTLEBRIDGE HOUSE
(Mrs KC Lynch), 2 Central Promenade,
BT33 0AB. ☎ (039 67) 23209.
B&B s£14 d£28. Rooms 5. Open all year.

CHERRY VILLA
(Mrs G Keown), 12 Bryansford Gardens,
BT33 0EQ. ☎ (039 67) 24128.
B&B s£13.50 d£27. Rooms 3. Open all
year.

EVERGREENS
(Ann Herron) 122 Bryansford Rd, BT33
0PP. ☎ (039 67) 24212/23252.
B&B s£18.50 d£35. Rooms 8, ensuite 3.
Open all year.

FÁILTE
(J&K Moclair), 28 Shimna Rd, BT33 0EE.
☎ (039 67) 23559.
B&B s£12.50 d£25. Rooms 2, ensuite 1.
Open all year.

FERN VIEW
(Mrs E O'Hare), 101 Tullybrannigan Rd,
BT33 0PW. ☎ (039 67) 23949.
B&B s£14 d£27. Rooms 4, ensuite 1.
Open Apr-Nov.

FIR LODGE
(Mrs A Herron), 124 Bryansford Rd,
BT33 0PP. ☎ (039 67) 24212/23252.
B&B s£20 d£40. Rooms 1, ensuite 1.
Open all year.

FOUNTAINVILLE HOUSE
(Mr & Mrs N Neill), 103 Central
Promenade, BT33 0HH. ☎ (039 67)
24312/22317.
B&B s£14 d£27. BB&M s£17.50 d£34.
Rooms 7, ensuite 1. Open Apr-Oct.

GLENSIDE FARMHOUSE
(Mrs M Murray), 136 Tullybrannigan Rd,
BT33 0PW. ☎ (039 67) 22628.
B&B s£8 d£16. Rooms 3. Open all year.

GOLFLINKS HOUSE
(Mrs E McPolin), 109 Dundrum Rd,
BT33 0LN. ☎ (039 67) 22054.
B&B s£13 d£25. BB&M s£20 d£40. Rooms
6, ensuite 6. High tea £5. Dinner £7. Open
all year.

HOMELEIGH
(Mrs M McBride), 7 Slievemoyne Park,
BT33 0JD. ☎ (039 67) 22305.
B&B s£13 d£24. Rooms 3. Open all year.

INNISFREE HOUSE
(Mrs M Dornan), 7 Dundrum Rd,
BT33 0BG. ☎ (039 67) 23303.
B&B s£15 d£25. Rooms 3. Open all year.

Mr & Mrs D KING.
2 Tullybrannigan Rd, ☎ (039 67) 24474.
B&B s£12.50 d£25. Rooms 2.
Open Jun-Sept.

B&B = bed and breakfast   s = single   d = double   BB&M = bed, breakfast & evening meal

Mrs M LAVERY
12 Linkside Park, Dundrum Rd, BT33 0LR.
☎ (039 67) 23638.
B&B s£15 d£28. Rooms 2. Open all year.

🅿 ❀ ♣ ⚳ ☙ ☝ ♠

MONEYCARA
(Mrs N Ritchie), 11 Sunningdale Park,
Tullybrannigan Rd, BT33 0GL. ☎ (039 67)
22586.
B&B s£13 d£24. Rooms 2. Open Apr-Sept.

🅿 ❀ ⚳ ☙ OAP ▥ ⅍ ♠

MOUNTAINSIDE LODGE
(Mrs K Keown), 154 Tullybrannigan Rd,
BT33 0PW. ☎ (039 67) 22672/22844.
B&B s£18 d£30. Rooms 3, ensuite 1.
Open May-Aug.

🅿 ❀ ♣ ⚳ ☙ ▥ ☐ ⅍ ☝ ∪ ◬ ♠ ⊞

OLD TOWN FARM
(Mrs W Annett), 25 Corrigs Rd, BT33 0JZ.
☎ (039 67) 22740.
B&B s£18 d£36. Rooms 3, ensuite 1.
Open Apr-Sept.

🅿 ❀ ♣ ⚳ ☙ ▥ ⅍ ♠

QUAY LODGE
(Mrs P Deery), 31 South Promenade BT33
0EX. ☎ (039 67) 23054.
B&B s£15 d£30. Rooms 3. Open Apr-Aug.

🅿 ❀ ♣ ⚳ ☙ ▥ ☐ ⅍ ☝ ∪ ♠

YMCA/YWCA
Glenada House, 29 South Promenade,
BT33 0EY. ☎ (039 67) 22402. Fax 26229.
B&B s£17.50 d£28. BB&M s£26 d£35.
Rooms 25, ensuite 9. High tea £6.50.
Dinner £7.50. Open all year.

🅿 ♫ ❀ ⚳ ☙ OAP ▥ ☐ ℄ ⅍ ♠ ♪ ☝ ∪ ◬ ⚡
♥ ♠ ⊞

Hotels

MOURNE COUNTRY HOTEL   **
52 Belfast Rd, BT34 1TR. ☎ (0693) 67922.
Fax 62659.
B&B s£42 d£55. BB&M s£52 d£65. Rooms
42, ensuite 42. High tea £12. Dinner £10.
Last orders 2030 hrs. Open all year.

🅿 ❀ ♣ ♥ ⚳ ☙ OAP ▥ ☐ ℄ ⅍ ♥ ⊕ ♠ ⊞

Guesthouses

ARD-MHUIRE GUEST HOUSE   (B)
(Mr & Mrs J Cunningham), 27
Carrickasticken Rd, Forkhill, BT35 9RJ.
☎ (0693) 888316.
B&B s£12.50 d£25. BB&M s£18 d£36.
Rooms 4. High tea £6. Dinner £7.50.
Open Mar-Oct.

🅿 ❀ ♣ ⚳ ☙ OAP ▥ ⅍ ☝ ∪ ∕ ◬ ⚡

ASHTON HOUSE   (B)
(Mrs B Heaney), 37 Omeath Rd, Fathom
Line,
BT35 8QN. ☎ (0693) 62120.
B&B s£15 d£28. BB&M s£23 d£44. Rooms
6, ensuite 6. Dinner £8. Open all year.

🆃 🅿 ♫ ❀ ♣ ⚳ ☙ ▥ ☐ ⅍ ♪ ☝ ∪ ∕ ◬ ⚡
♠

HILLSIDE   (U)
(Mrs J McNally), 1 Rock Rd, BT34 1PL.
☎ (0693) 65484/61430.
B&B s£15 d£28. BB&M s£22 d£42. Rooms
5 ensuite 3. Dinner £7. Open all year.

🆃 🅿 ❀ ♣ ⚳ ☙ OAP ▥ ⅍ ♠

B&B = bed and breakfast   s = single   d = double   BB&M = bed, breakfast & evening meal

Bed & Breakfast

CASTLE VIEW
(Mrs C Gracey), 89a High Walk, Chapel St,
BT34 2DN. ☎ (0693) 68786/69130.
B&B s£15 d£30. BB&M s£20 d£40.
Rooms 3, ensuite 1. Dinner £6. Last orders
1900 hrs. Open all year.

DRUMCONRATH
(Mrs A Magennis), 28 Ballymacdermot Rd,
BT35 8NA. ☎ (0693) 63508.
B&B s£14 d£28. BB&M s£18
d£36. Rooms 2. High tea £4. Dinner £4.
Last orders 1900 hrs. Open all year.

MR and MRS GORMAN
6 Highfields Avenue ☎ (0693) 65883.
B&B s£15 d£28. BB&M s£20, d£38.
Rooms 3, ensuite 1. Open all year.

GREEN GABLES
(Mrs B Tiernan), 2 Tiffcrum Rd, BT35 9RU.
☎ (0693) 888589.
B&B s£12 d£24. BB&M s£18 d£36. High
tea £6. Last orders 2100 hrs. Open Apr-
Sept.

LAKEVIEW
(Mr & Mrs O'Neill), 34 Church Rd Forkhill.
☎ (0693) 888382.
B&B s£12 d£28. Rooms 2, ensuite 1. Open
all year.

LAVENGRO
(Mrs A O'Rourke), 5 Liska Rd, Cloughoge,
BT35 8NH. ☎ (0693) 63773.
B&B s£12.50 d£25. Rooms 3. Open all
year.

Hotels

STRANGFORD ARMS HOTEL ***
92 Church St, BT23 4AL. ☎ (0247)
814141. Fax 818846.
B&B s£63.75 d£87.50. BB&M s£73.75
d£107.50. Rooms 40, ensuite 40. High tea
£6. Dinner £10. Last orders 2130 hrs.
Open all year.

Guesthouses

GREENACRES (A)
(Mrs D Long), 5 Manse Rd, BT23 4TP.
☎ (0247) 816193.
B&B s£18 d£30. BB&M s£28 d£50. Rooms
4, ensuite 4. High tea £7.50. Dinner £10.
Last orders 1830 hrs. Open all year.
Off A20, ¼ m from N'ards

Bed & Breakfast

ARD CUAN
(Mrs V Kerr), 3 Manse Rd, BT23 4TP.
☎ (0247) 811302.
B&B s£15 d£30. Rooms 1. Open all year.

Facilities are liable to change. Check prices when you book. Key to symbols is on the back flap.

87

ARD NUA
(Mrs D E Cochrane), 217 Scrabo Rd,
BT23 4SJ. ☎ (0247) 812377.
B&B s£13.50 d£27. BB&M s£22 d£44.
Rooms 2. Dinner £8.50. Open all year.

🅿 ❀ ♣ ⚘ ☎ 🏛 ✂ ♪ 🏳 ∪ ◬ ⚡ ⚕

BALLYCASTLE HOUSE
(Mrs M Deering), 20 Mountstewart Rd,
BT22 2AL. ☎ (024 77) 88357.
B&B s£16 d£32. Rooms 3, ensuite 3.
Open all year.
5m SE of Newtownards

🆃 🅿 ♨ ❀ ♣ ⚘ ☎ OAP 🏛 ✂ ♪ 🏳 ∪ ╱ ◬ ⚡

BEECHHILL FARM
(Mrs J McKee), 10 Loughries Rd, BT23
3RN. ☎ (0247) 818404. Fax 812820.
B&B s£14 d£28. BB&M s£24 d£48. Rooms
2. High tea £8.50. Dinner £10. Last orders
1830 hrs. Open all year ex Christmas.
Off A20, 4m from Newtownards

🅿 ❀ ♣ ⚘ ☎ 🏛 ✂ ♪ 🏳 ∪ ╱ ◬ ⚡

BURNSIDE
(Mrs J Bartholomew), 26 Ballyblack Rd,
BT22 2AP. ☎ (0247) 812920.
B&B s£12 d£24. Rooms 3. Open all year.
3m E of Newtownards

🅿 ❀ ♣ ☎ 🏛 ✂ ♪ 🏳

CUAN CHALET
(Mrs W Cochrane), 41 Milecross Rd,
BT23 4SR. ☎ (0247) 812302.
B&B s£12.50 d£25. BB&M s£21.50 d£43.
Rooms 2. Dinner £9. Open all year.
Off A20, ¼m W of town centre

🅿 ❀ ♣ ⚘ ☎ OAP 🏛 ✂ ♪ 🏳 ∪ ◬ ⚡ ⚕

DRUMCREE HOUSE
(Mrs E Forde), 18A Ballyblack Rd East,
BT22 2AB. ☎ (0247) 862198.
B&B s£13.50 d£27. Rooms 3. Open all
year.

🅿 ❀ ♣ ☎ OAP 🏛 ✂ ♪ 🏳 ∪

EDENVALE HOUSE
(Mrs D Whyte), 130 Portaferry Rd,
BT22 2AH. ☎ (0247) 814881.
B&B s£15 d£35. BB&M s£30 d£50. Rooms
3, ensuite 2. Dinner £15. Open all year.

🅿 ♨ ❀ ♣ ⚘ ☎ 🏛 ⬚ ✂ ♪ 🏳 ∪ ╱ ◬ ⚕

ERNSDALE
(Mrs D McCullagh), 120 Mountstewart Rd,
Carrowdore, BT22 2ES. ☎ (0247) 861208.
B&B s£12.50 d£25. Rooms 2.
Open Apr-Oct.
5½m SE of Newtownards

🅿 ❀ ♣ ☎ 🏛 ✂ ♪ 🏳 ∪ ╱ ◬ ⚡ ◉

MAYNARD
(Mr & Mrs R Morrison), 19 Old Belfast Rd,
BT23 4SG. ☎ (0247) 812069.
B&B s£15 d£30. Rooms 3. Open all year.
Off A20

🅿 ❀ ♣ ⚘ ☎ 🏛 ✂ 🏳 ∪ ╱ ◬ ⚡ ⚕

Mrs A McKIBBIN
17 Ballyrogan Rd, BT23 4ST. ☎ (0247)
811693.
B&B s£15 d£30. Rooms 2. Open all year.

🅿 ❀ ♣ ☎ 🏛 ⬚ ✂ 🏳 ◬ ◉ ⚕

B&B = bed and breakfast   s = single   d = double   BB&M = bed, breakfast & evening meal

PORTAFERRY

Hotels

PORTAFERRY HOTEL   ***
10 The Strand, BT22 1PE. ☎ (024 77)
28231. Fax 28999.
B&B s£45 d£80. BB&M s£62.50 d£57.50.
Rooms 14, ensuite 14. High tea £12.
Dinner £17.50. Last orders 2100 hrs.
Open all year.

Bed & Breakfast

Mr & Mrs T ADAIR
22 The Square, BT22 1LW. ☎ (024 77)
28412.
B&B s£12 d£24. Rooms 3. Open all year.

BERNADETTE WHITTAKER
15 High St, BT22 1QT. ☎ (024 77) 28580.
B&B s£12 d£24. BB&M s£20 d£40. Rooms
3. Dinner £8. Last orders 1900 hrs. Open
all year.

LOUGH COWEY LODGE
(Mrs F Taggart), 9 Lough Cowey Rd,
BT22 1PJ. ☎ (024 77) 28263.
B&B s£12.50 d£25. Rooms 2. High tea
£7.50. Dinner £10. Last orders 2000 hrs.
Open all year.

TULLYNACREW FARM
(Mrs A Wilson), 16 Ballyblack Rd,
BT22 1PY. ☎ (024 77) 28377.
B&B s£13 d£26. Rooms 2. Open Apr-Oct.

RATHFRILAND

Guesthouses

RATHGLEN VILLA   (A)
(Mrs M Maginn), 7 Hilltown Rd,
BT34 5NA. ☎ (082 06) 38090.
B&B s£16 d£28. BB&M s£24 d£44.
Rooms 4, ensuite 1. Open all year.

Bed & Breakfast

RUELLEN
(Mrs M H Bickerstaff), 56 Dromore St,
BT34 5LU. ☎ (082 06) 30761.
B&B s£12 d£24. BB&M s£18 d£36. Rooms
2. Dinner £6. Last orders 1800 hrs. Open
all year.

ROSTREVOR

Bed & Breakfast

CARRIGANEAN HOUSE
(Mrs A McElroy), 137 Killowen Rd,
BT34 3AQ. ☎ (069 37) 39536.
B&B s£13 d£26. Rooms 3, ensuite 1.
Open all year.

FORESTBROOK HOUSE
(Mrs E Henshaw), 11 Forestbrook Rd,
BT34 3BT. ☎ (069 37) 38105.
B&B s£13 d£26. BB&M s£20 d£40. Rooms
6. High tea £5. Dinner £7. Open all year.

Facilities are liable to change. Check prices when you book. Key to symbols is on the back flap.

HILLCREST FARMHOUSE
(Mrs M Murphy), 12 Kilfeaghan Rd,
Killowen, BT34 3AW. ☎ (069 37) 38114.
B&B s£15 d£25. BB&M s£20 d£30. Rooms
3, ensuite 1. High tea £6. Dinner £7. Open
Apr-Oct.

🅣 🅿 ❁ ♣ ⚜ ⛵ 🆊 🎨 🍴 ⚓ ♪ ⌐ ◢ 🐾

STILL WATERS
(Mrs E McCabe), 14 Killowen Rd,
BT34 3AF. ☎ (069 37) 38743.
B&B s£12 d£24. Rooms 3. Open Apr-Oct.

🅿 ❁ ♣ ⚜ ⛵ 🎨 🍴 ♪ ⌐ ∪ ◢ △ ⚡ 🐾

SAINTFIELD

Bed & Breakfast

THE HILL
(Mrs M Rice), Peartree Rd, BT24 7JY.
☎ (0238) 511330.
B&B s£12.50 d£25. BB&M s£18 d£36.
Rooms 4. High tea £5. Dinner £6. Last
orders 1200 hrs. Open Apr-Oct.

🅿 ❁ ♣ ⚜ ⛵ 🎨 ♪ ⌐ ∪ ◢ △ ⚡

WARRENPOINT

Guesthouses

FERNHILL HOUSE (B)
(Mr & Mrs P McCullough), 90 Clonallon
Rd, BT34 3HQ. ☎ (069 37) 72677.
B&B s£14 d£28. BB&M s£21d£42. Rooms
4, ensuite 1. High tea £4.50. Dinner £7.
Open all year.

🅿 ❁ ♣ ⚜ ⛵ 🆊 🎨 ⬜ 🍴 ♪ ⌐ ∪ △ ⚡

Bed & Breakfast

FIRÓNE
(Mr & Mrs T McQuillan), 74 Upper
Dromore Rd, BT34 3PN. ☎ (069 37)
74293.
B&B s£13.50 d£27. Rooms 3. High tea £8.
Dinner £8. Last orders 2100 hrs. Open all
year.

🅿 ❁ ♣ ⚜ ⛵ 🎨 🍴 ♪ ⌐ ∪ ◢ △ ⚡

GLEN ROSA
(Mrs C Carr), 4 Gt George's St South,
BT34 3NF. ☎ (069 37) 72589.
B&B s£13 d£25. Open all year.

⚜ ⛵ 🍴

THE VICTORIA
(Mr & Mrs P Dowdall), The Square,
BT34 3LZ. ☎ (069 37)53687/53448.
B&B s£15 d£25. Dinner £10. Rooms 4.
Open all year.

🅣 🏮 ⚜ 🍷 ⛵ 🎨 🍴 ♦ ⌐ ∪ ◢ △ ⚡ 🍴 🈸

B&B = bed and breakfast   s = single   d = double   BB&M = bed, breakfast & evening meal

County Fermanagh

BALLINAMALLARD

Guesthouses

JAMESTOWN HOUSE   (U)
(Mr & Mrs A Stuart), Magheracross,
BT94 2JP. ☎ (036 581) 209.
B&B s£25 d£50. BB&M s£40 d£80. Rooms
3, ensuite 3. Dinner £15. Open all year (ex
Christmas).
1m NE of Ballinamallard

🅿 🏠 ✿ ♣ 🔆 🐴 🛏 🍴 🔍 🔍 🎵 🏌 ∪ 🏊 ⚓ 🛥

Bed & Breakfast

JEANVILLE
(Mrs J McFarland), Goblusk, BT92 2LW.
☎ (036 581) 424.
B&B s£15 d£30. Rooms 2, ensuite 2.
Open all year.

🅿 ✿ ♣ 🔆 🐴 🛏 🔲 🍴 🎵 🏌 ∪ ⚓ 🛥

BELCOO

Guesthouses

CORRALEA FOREST LODGE (A)
(Mr & Mrs P Catterall), Corralea,
BT93 5DZ. ☎ (036 586) 325.
B&B s£21 d£36. BB&M s£32 d£58. Rooms
4, ensuite 4. Dinner £11. Open Mar-Oct.
2½m NW of Belcoo

🆃 🅿 ✿ ♣ 🔆 🐴 🛏 🔲 🎵 ⚓ 🏊

Bed & Breakfast

BELCOO HOUSE
(Mrs K Sweeney), 31 Main St, BT93 5FB.
☎ (036 586) 304.
B&B s£10 d£20. Rooms 2. Open all year.

🏠 ♣ 🔆 🐴 🅟 🐴 🛏 🔲 🍴 🏌 ⚓ 🏊

BELLEEK

Guesthouses

MOOHANS FIDDLESTONE   (U)
(Messrs J & M McCann), 15 Main St,
BT93 5XX. ☎ (036 56) 58008.
B&B s£15 d£30. BB&M s£27 d£54. Rooms
5, ensuite 5. Dinner £12. Open all year.

🆃 ✿ 🔆 🍴 🐴 🛏 🍴 🎵 🏌 ∪ 🏊 ⚓ 🏊 🅴

Bed & Breakfast

THE CARLTON
2 Main St, BT93 9XX. ☎ (036 56)
58282/285.
B&B s£15 d£30. BB&M s£20 d£35. Rooms
5, ensuite 3. High tea £5. Dinner £10.
Last orders 2200 hrs. Open all year.

🅿 ✿ ♣ 🔆 🍴 🐴 🅿 🛏 🎵 🏌 ∪ 🏊 ⚓ 🏊 🅴

ERNEVILLE
(Mrs M Brennan), Garrison Rd, Corry,
BT93 3FU. ☎ (036 56) 58025.
B&B s£12 d£24. Rooms 3. Open May-Oct.

🅿 ✿ ♣ 🔆 🐴 🅿 🛏 🍴 🎵 🏌 ∪ 🏊 ⚓ 🏊 🅴

Mrs C MULLIN
190 Garrison Rd, Corry, BT93 3FU.
☎ (036 56) 58588.
B&B s£11.50 d£23. Rooms 3. Open May-
Sept.

🅿 ✿ ♣ 🔆 🐴 🛏 🍴 🎵 🏌 ∪ 🌐 🏊

RIVERSIDE HOUSE
(Ms G McGuinness), 601 Lough Shore Rd,
Drumbadreevagh, BT93 3FT.
☎ (036 56) 58649.
B&B s£15 d£30. BB&M s£25 d£50. Rooms
2, ensuite 1. High tea £8. Dinner £10.
Last orders 1900 hrs. Open Mar-Sept.

♣ 🔆 🐴 🛏 🎵 ⚓ 🏊

Facilities are liable to change. Check prices when you book. Key to symbols is on the back flap.

BROOKEBOROUGH

Bed & Breakfast

NORFOLK HOUSE
(Evelyn Norton), Killykeeran, BT94 4AQ.
☎ (036 553) 681.
B&B s£13 d£26. BB&M s£20 d£40. Rooms
4. High tea £5. Dinner £7. Last orders 1700
hrs. Open all year.

COLEBROOKE PARK.
(Viscount & Viscountess Brookeborough).
☎ (036553) 402. Fax 686.
BB&M s£80 d£160. Rooms 10, ensuite 4.
Open all year.

DERRYGONNELLY

Guesthouses

NAVAR GUEST HOUSE (A)
(Mr & Mrs P Love), Derryvarey, BT93
6HW. ☎ (036 564) 384.
B&B s£14.50 d£29. BB&M s£21.50 d£43.
Rooms 5, ensuite 2. High tea £6. Dinner
£8. Open all year.

Bed & Breakfast

DRUMARY FARM HOUSE
(Mr & Mrs J Elliott), Glenasheever Rd,
Drumary North, BT93 6GA.
☎ (036 564) 420.
B&B s£20 d£30. BB&M s£27 d£44. Rooms
3, ensuite 3. High tea £3.50. Dinner £7.
Open all year.
Off A46, 9m NW of Enniskillen

MEADOW VIEW
(Mr & Mrs J Wray), Sandhill, BT93 6ER.
☎ (036 564) 233.
B&B s£12.50 d£25. BB&M s£17.50 d£36.
Rooms 2. High tea £6. Dinner £7. Last
orders 1700 hrs. Open Mar/Apr & Jul/Aug.

ENNISKILLEN

Hotels

KILLYHEVLIN HOTEL ***
Dublin Rd, BT74 4AU. ☎ (0365) 323481.
Fax 324726.
B&B s£55 d£90. Rooms 22, ensuite 22.
High tea £10. Dinner £14.50. Last orders
2115 hrs. Open all year.

MANOR HOUSE COUNTRY HOTEL ***
Killadeas, BT94 1NY. ☎ (036 56) 21561.
Fax 21545.
B&B s£50 d£75. Rooms 50, ensuite 50.
High tea £7.50. Dinner £15. Last orders
2130 hrs. Open all year.
5½ m N of Enniskillen

FORT LODGE HOTEL **
72 Forthill St, BT74 6AJ. ☎ (0365) 323275.
Fax 323275.
B&B s£30 d£60. BB&M s£40 d£80. Rooms
36, ensuite 36. High tea £8. Dinner
£11.50.
Last orders 2130 hrs. Open all year.

B&B = bed and breakfast   s = single   d = double   BB&M = bed, breakfast & evening meal

RAILWAY HOTEL *
34 Forthill St, BT74 6AJ. ☎ (0365) 322084.
Fax 327480.
B&B s£30 d£58. Rooms 19, ensuite 18.
Open all year.

🆃 🅿 🏧 ❗ 💺 🔟 ⬛ 🔗 ⛵ ✝ ∪ ⚓ 🎣 ⛴ 🔲

Guesthouses

ASHWOOD GUEST HOUSE (A)
(Mrs B Harris), Sligo Rd, BT74 7JY.
☎ (0365) 323019.
B&B s£15 d£28. BB&M s£24 d£46. Rooms
7, ensuite 3. Dinner £9. Last orders 1630
hrs. Open all year.

🆃 🅿 ✿ ♣ ⚒ 💺 🔟 ⅍ ⛵ ✝ ∪ ⟋ ⚓ 🎣 🔲

BAYVIEW GUEST HOUSE (A)
(Mrs E Hassard), Tully, Church Hill,
BT93 6HP. ☎ (036 564) 250.
B&B s£16 d£30. BB&M s£23 d£44. Rooms
4, ensuite 2. High tea £5. Dinner £7. Last
orders 1800 hrs. Open Jan-Nov.
On A46, 11m NE of Enniskillen

🅿 ✿ ♣ ⚒ 💺 🔟 ⛵ ✝ ∪ ⚓

BRINDLEY GUEST HOUSE (A)
(Mr & Mrs D Flood), Tully, Killadeas,
BT94 1RE. ☎ (036 56) 28065.
B&B s£19 d£34. BB&M s£29 d£54. Rooms
8, ensuite 6. High tea £7. Dinner £10.
Open all year.
Off B82, 7m NE of Enniskillen

🅿 ✿ ♣ ⚒ 💺 🆖 🔟 ⛵ ✝ ∪ ⚓ ☺ 🎣

LACKABOY FARM HOUSE (A)
(Mrs D Noble), Tempo Rd, BT74 6EB.
☎ (0365) 322488.
B&B s£15 d£26. BB&M s£23 d£42. Rooms
10, ensuite 4. High tea £6. Dinner £8.
Last orders 1700 hrs. Open all year.
½ m NE of Enniskillen

🅿 ✿ ♣ 💺 🔟 ⅍ 🔲

LAKEVIEW FARM HOUSE (A)
(Mrs J Hassard), Drumcrow, Blaney,
BT93 7EY. ☎ (036 564) 263.
B&B s£15 d£28 BB&M s£23 d£44. Rooms
4, ensuite 1. High tea £7. Dinner £8.
Last orders 1400 hrs. Open Jan-Nov.
10m NW of Enniskillen

🅿 🏧 ✿ ♣ ⚒ 💺 🔟 ⅍ 🔲

MOUNTVIEW (A)
(Mrs W McChesney), 61 Irvinestown Rd,
Drumclay, BT74 6DN. ☎ (0365) 323147.
B&B s£19.50 d£32. BB&M s£30 d£54.
Rooms 3, ensuite 2. Dinner £11. Last
orders 1700 hrs. Open all year.
1m N of Enniskillen

🆃 🅿 ✿ ♣ ⚒ 💺 🆖 🔟 ⬛ ⅍ ☺ ⛵ ✝

TULLYHONA HOUSE (A)
(Mr & Mrs G Armstrong), 59 Marble Arch
Rd, Florencecourt, BT92 1DE.
☎ (0365) 348452.
B&B s£19 d£34. BB&M s£26 d£48. Rooms
7, ensuite 4. High tea £5.50. Dinner £7.50
Last orders 1900 hrs. Open all year.
7 ½ m SW of Enniskillen

🅿 🏧 ✿ ♣ ⚒ 💺 🔟 ⬛ ⅍ ⛵ ✝ ∪ ⟋ ⚓ 🎣 ⛴ ☂
🔲

Facilities are liable to change. Check prices when you book. Key to symbols is on the back flap.

93

Fair Days & Hey Days

There's always something happening at the Buttermarket

Craft Workshops - *come & see the crafts people at work*
Rebecca's Place Coffee Shop - *relax & enjoy the taste of home cooking*
Boston Quay Craft Shop - *some of the best of Fermanagh's craft & design*
Exhibitions of local craft work
Art & Craft Fairs - *stall in courtyard*
Street Entertainment - *buskers etc.*
STAR Room - *come & see the latest in advanced telecommunications*

★ *Watch local press for details - Mon-Sat, 9.30 am-5.30 pm*

**The Buttermarket, Enniskillen Craft & Design Centre
Down Street, Enniskillen. Tel: (0365) 324499**

FORT LODGE HOTEL
72 FORTHILL STREET, ENNISKILLEN CO. FERMANAGH
Telephone: (0365) 323275

John and Mary Sheerin welcome you to the Fort Lodge Hotel situated in historic Enniskillen, the heart of Ulster Lakeland and the ideal centre for a touring or fishing holiday, a leisure week or just an overnight stay.

● **MODERN AND COMFORTABLE** ●

All 35 bedrooms with private bathroom or shower, Sky TV, radio, video, direct-dial telephone, tea/coffee maker.

● *Function room for 250 people*
● *Car parking facilities*

★ **Weekend entertainment** ★

Dancing Saturday & Sunday night
Our Bailey Restaurant open to non-residents breakfasts, morning coffee, lunch, dinner, bar snacks all day.

Bar and lounge where you can enjoy an evening drink

DERRYAD HOLIDAY COTTAGES
FERMANAGH LAKELAND
ON SHORES OF UPPER LOUGH ERNE
Derryad Quay, Lisnaskea

* Probably Lough Erne's most exclusive self-catering location!
* Tranquil secluded setting. Picturesque lake/mountain views.
* Each cottage has its own boat and private lakeside garden.
* Bright spacious rooms. Luxury furnishings. Comfortable beds.
* Cosy atmosphere. Central heating & homely open fire.
* Fully equipped kitchens. Washing-machine, fridge, cooker, oven.
* Payphone, colour TV, radio, iron, linen included.
* Superb relaxing, sightseeing, boating
* Free use of 14ft cabin boat & oars. Optional engine.
* Excellent local lake & river fishing. Garden jetty.
* Explore secluded bays & deserted, wooded islands.
* Pets welcome. Over-55's special offer discounts.
* Autumn, winter, spring: much reduced rates.
* Open all year offpeak bargain weekends & midweek breaks.
* Shops/restaurants: 10 mins drive. Air/Seaports apx 2 hrs.

Innisfree sleeps 5. Idlewild: 1-10 (Cheaper: 1-5)
Two cottages only
Please book early to avoid disappointment.
Reservations & Free Brochure:
James Dawson, 1 Bernard Avenue,
Ealing, London W13 9TG
Tel: London (081) 567 4487

BLANEY GUEST HOUSE (B)
(Mr & Mrs T Robinson), Blaney Post Office,
BT93 7ER. ☎ (036 564) 206.
B&B s£12.50 d£25. Rooms 4. High tea £5.
Dinner £6. Open all year.

🆃 🅿 ❋ ♣ 🕊 🦢 ⏾ 🃏 ▯ ✂ 🎵 🏌 ⚲ ⛵ ⚓ 🍴

DRUMCOO HOUSE (B)
(Mrs H Farrell), 32 Cherryville, Cornagrade
Rd, BT74 4FY. ☎ (0365) 326672.
B&B s£17 d£30. Rooms 3, ensuite 3.
Open all year.

🆃 🅿 ❋ ♣ 🦢 🃏 ▯ ✂ 🎵 🌀 🏌 ⚓ 🏢

PINEGROVE GUEST HOUSE (B)
(Mrs A Dixon), 3 Old Enniskillen Rd,
Tamlaght, BT7 4HJ. ☎ (0365)
87057/87279.
B&B s£12 d£24. Rooms 3, ensuite 1. Open
Mar-Sept.

❋ ♣ 🕊 🦢

RIVERSIDE FARM (B)
(Mrs M Fawcett), Gortadrehid, Culkey Post
Office, BT92 2FN. ☎ (0365) 322725.
B&B s£16 d£28. BB&M s£23 d£42. Rooms
6, ensuite 2. High tea £5. Dinner £8.
Last orders 2030 hrs. Open all year.
1¹/₂ m NW of Enniskillen

🅿 ❋ ♣ 🕊 🦢 ⏾ 🃏 ✂ 🎵 🏌 ⚲ ⚓ ⛵ 🏢

ROSSOLE HOUSE (B)
(Mr & Mrs J Sheridan), 85 Sligo Rd,
BT74 7JZ. ☎ (0365) 323462.
B&B s£16 d£27. BB&M s£23 d£45. Rooms
5, ensuite 2. Dinner £10. Last orders 1200
hrs. Open all year.

🆃 🅿 🎹 ❋ ♣ 🕊 🦢 🃏 ▯ ✂ 🎵 🏌 ⚲ ⛵ 🍴 🏢

ABBEYVILLE
(Mrs M McMahon), 1 Willoughby Court,
Portota, BT47 7EX. ☎ (0365) 327033.
B&B s£13.50 d£27. Rooms 3, ensuite 1.
Open all year.

🅿 ♣ 🦢 ⏾ 🃏 ▯ ✂ 🎵 🏌 ⚲ ⚓

ABOCURRAGH FARMHOUSE
Abocurragh, Letterbreen, BT74 9AG.
☎ (0365) 348484.
B&B s£13 d£26. Rooms 2. Open Mar-Dec.

🆃 🅿 ❋ ♣ 🕊 🦢 🃏 🎵 🏌 ⚲ ⛵ ⚓ ⚘

ALEEN HOUSE
Cosbytown, BT93 7ER. ☎ (036 564) 472.
B&B s£15 d£30. BB&M s£25 d£50.
Rooms 3, ensuite 2. High tea £5. Last orders
2000 hrs. Open all year.

🆃 🅿 🎹 ❋ ♣ 🦢 ⏾ 🃏 ▯ 🎵 🏌 ⚲ ⛵ ⚓ ⛵

THE BEECHES
(Mr & Mrs B Ternan), Killadeas
BT94 1NZ. ☎ (036 56) 21557.
B&B s£15, d£26. Rooms 2, ensuite 1.
Open all year.

🅿 ❋ ♣ 🕊 🦢 ⏾ 🃏 ✂ 🎵 🏌 ⚲ ⚓

BELMORE COURT MOTEL
(Mr McCartney), Tempo Rd, BT74 6HR.
☎ (0365) 326633. Fax 326362.
Room only d£38. Rooms 27, ensuite 27.
Open Jan-Nov.

🆃 🅿 ❋ 🐾 ⏾ 🃏 🍷 🎵 🏌 ⚲ ⚓ 🌀 🏢

Facilities are liable to change. Check prices when you book. Key to symbols is on the back flap.

BROADMEADOWS
(Mrs L McKibbin), Cleenish Island Rd,
Bellanaleck, BT92 2AL. ☎ (0365) 348395.
B&B s£15 d£30. BB&M s£25 d£50. Rooms
3, ensuite 1. High tea £8. Dinner £10.
Last orders 1400 hrs. Open all year.
1 ½ m E of Bellanaleck

CARRAIG AONRAI
(Mrs P Mulhern), 19 Sligo Rd, BT74 7JY.
☎ (0365) 324889.
B&B s£10 d£20. Rooms 4. Open Jan-Nov.

CHERRYVILLE
(Mrs F Moore), Bellanaleck, BT92 2BA.
☎ (0365) 348226.
B&B s£12.50 d£25. Rooms 2, ensuite 1.
Open all year.

CORRCLARE HOUSE
(Mr & Mrs McBrien), Derrylin P.O.
Enniskillen . ☎ (0365) 48339.
B&B s£12 d£24. BB&M s£18 d£36. Rooms
3. Dinner £6.50. Last orders 2130 hrs.
Open all year.

THE CREST
(Mrs A Reid), Rossaa, BT92 1BR.
☎ (0365)348317/(0365) 322727.
B&B s£12 d£26. Rooms 3, ensuite 2.
Open Apr-Sept.

DROMARD HOUSE
(Mrs S Weir), Tamlaght, BT74 4HR.
☎ (0365) 87250.
B&B s£16 d£28. Rooms 5, ensuite 4.
Open all year.

DUNROVIN
(Mrs C Harron), Skea, Arney, BT92 2DL.
☎ (0365) 348354. Fax 348446.
B&B s£12 d£24. BB&M s£19 d£38. Rooms
5, ensuite 3. High tea £6. Dinner £7.50.
Last orders 1800 hrs. Open Feb-Dec.
5m SW of Enniskillen

EBENEZER HOUSE
(Mrs J Moore), Ashwoods Rd, Drumawill,
BT74 5HJ. ☎ (0365) 323398.
B&B s£14.50 d£27. Rooms 3. Open Mar-
Sept.

FOUR OAKS
(Mrs E Armstrong), 2 Four Oaks,
Ballycassidy, BT94. ☎ (0365) 328158.
B&B s£12, d£28. Rooms 3, ensuite 1.
Open all year.

HILLCREST
(Mrs J Clements), Bellanaleck, BT92 2BA.
☎ (0365) 348392.
B&B s£12.50 d£25. BB&M s£19 d£38.
Rooms 3. Open all year.

B&B = bed and breakfast   s = single   d = double   BB&M = bed, breakfast & evening meal

LOUGH ERNE HOUSE
(Mrs H Bruce), St Catherines, Blaney,
BT93 7AY. ☎ (036 564) 216.
B&B s£12 d£24. BB&M s£16 d£32. Rooms
3. High tea £6. Dinner £7. Last orders 2100
hrs. Open all year.
Off A46, 9m NW of Enniskillen

P ❖ ♣ ⚘ ☙ OAP ▥ ✂ ♪ ⌐ ✓ ⚊ ⚒

MAGHERA HOUSE
(M G Burns), Magherageeragh. BT74. ☎
(0365) 341662.
B&B s£12.50 d£24. Rooms 4, ensuite 1.

P ⌂ ❖ ♣ ⚘ ☙ OAP ▥ ♪ ⌐ U ⚊ ⚒

ROSSFAD HOUSE
(Mrs L Williams), Killadeas, BT74 2LS.
☎ (036 581) 505.
B&B s£17 d£30. Rooms 2, ensuite 2.
Open Mar-Nov.

T P ⌂ ❖ ♣ ⚘ ☙ OAP ▥ ✂ ♪ ⌐ U ✓ ⚊ ⚒

GARRISON

Guesthouses

HEATHERGROVE GUEST HOUSE   (B)
(Mrs J Duffy), Meenacloybane, BT93 4AT.
☎ (036 56) 58362.
B&B s£15 d£30. BB&M s£30 d£60. Rooms
3, ensuite 3. Dinner £15. Last orders 1600
hrs. Open all year.

T P ❖ ♣ ⚘ ☙ OAP ▥ ⌷ ✂ ♪ ⌐ U ✓ ⚊ ⚒
⚹

Bed & Breakfast

LAKE VIEW HOUSE
(Mr & Mrs P Flanagan), Carran West,
BT93 4EL. ☎ (036 56) 58444.
B&B s£10 d£20. Rooms 3. Open Mar-Nov.

T P ⌂ ❖ ♣ ⚘ ☙ OAP ⚐ ▥ ✂ ♪ ⌐ U

LOUGH MELVIN HOLIDAY CENTRE.
Garrison, BT93 3BX. ☎ (036 56) 58142.
Fax 58719.
B&B s£14 d£26. BB&M s£20 d£38. Rooms
11, ensuite 1. High tea £4.50. Dinner £8.
Last orders 2000 hrs. Open Feb-Dec.

P ♣ ⚘ ☙ ▥ ✂ ♠ ♪ ⌐ U ⚊ ⚒ ⚹ ⊞

MELVINDALE
(Mrs M McGuinness), Melvin Rd,
BT93 4EW. ☎ (03656) 58724.
B&B s£12 d£24. Rooms 3. Open Jan-Oct.

P ❖ ♣ ⚘ ▥ ♪ ⌐ U ✓ ⚊ ⚒

ROSSKIT
(Mrs I Moody), Garrison), BT93 4ET.
☎ (036 56) 58231.
B&B s£25 d£50. BB&M s£40 d£80. Rooms
5, ensuite 3. Dinner £15. Open all year.

T P ❖ ♣ ⚘ ⚐ ▥ ✂ ♪ ⌐ ⚊

IRVINESTOWN

Hotels

MAHON'S HOTEL   *
Mill St, BT74 9XX. ☎ (036 56) 21656.
Fax 28344.
B&B s£29.50 d£56. BB&M s£42 d£84.
Rooms 18, ensuite 18. Dinner £12.50. Last
orders 2100 hrs. Open all year.

T P ♣ ♟ ☙ OAP ⚐ ▥ ⌷ ☎ ✂ ♠ ♪ ⌐ U ⚊
⚒ ⚑ ⊞

Facilities are liable to change. Check prices when you book. Key to symbols is on the back flap.

Bed & Breakfast

FLETCHERS FARM
(Mrs M Knox), Drumadravey, BT94 1LQ. ☎
(036 56) 21351.
B&B s£12 d£ 24. Rooms 4, ensuite 3.
Open all year.

P ❋ ♠ ☡ OAP ▥ ✂ ♫ ☈ ∪ ✓ ⛰ ⚲

GREENACRE
(Mrs J Sloan), 161 Kesh Rd, BT94 1BN.
☎ (036 56) 28287.
B&B s£11 d£22. Rooms 2. Open all year.

♠ ☀ ☡ OAP ▥ ✂

LEN-AIRE
(Mrs E Allen), Kesh Rd, BT94 1FY.
☎ (036 56) 21627.
B&B s£15 d£28. Rooms 4, ensuite 1.
Open Mar-Sept.

P ❋ ♠ ☀ ☡ OAP ⚘ ▥ ✂ ⛰

LETTERMONEY HOUSE
(Mrs J Kinnear), 51 Mossfield Rd, BT94.
☎ (036 581) 347.
B&B s£12 d£24. Rooms 3. Open all year.

P ❋ ♠ ☀ ☡ OAP ⚘ ▥ ☐ ✂ ♫ ☈ ∪ ✓ ⛰ ⚲

ROSEVILLE
(Mrs K Hudson), Dromore Rd, BT94 1ES. ☎
(036 56) 21055.
B&B s£11 d£22. Rooms 2, ensuite 1.
Open Apr-Oct.

P ❋ ♠ ☡ ▥ ✂

WOODHILL FARM
(Mrs M Irwin), Derrynanny, BT94 1QA.
☎ (036 56) 21795.
B&B s£14 d£24. BB&M s£22 d£40. Rooms
4. High tea £8. Dinner £7.50. Last orders
2200 hrs. Open all year.

T P ❋ ♠ ☀ ☡ OAP ▥ ✂ ☈ ∪ ✓ ⛰ ⚲

Hotels

LOUGH ERNE HOTEL   **
Main St, BT93 1TF. ☎ (036 56) 31275.
Fax 31921.
B&B s£30 d£60. Rooms 12, ensuite 12.
High tea £11.75. Dinner £12.50. Last
orders 2100 hrs. Open all year.

P ❋ ♠ ☀ ☂ ☡ ⚘ ▥ ☐ ☍ ♫ ☈ ∪ ⛰ ⚲ ☂
⊞

Guesthouses

MANVILLE HOUSE   (A)
(Mrs M Graham), Aughnablaney, Letter,
BT93 2BB. ☎ (036 56) 31668.
B&B s£14 d£26. Rooms 4. Open all year.
9m W of Kesh

P ❋ ♠ ☀ ☡ ▥ ✂ ♫ ☈ ∪ ⛰ ⚲ ⚱

ARDESS CRAFT CENTRE   (B)
(Mrs D Pendry), Ardess House, BT93 1NX.
☎ (036 56) 31267.
B&B s£22.50 d£39. BB&M s£35 d£64.
Rooms 4, ensuite 4. Dinner £12. Last
orders 1400 hrs. Open Jan-Oct.

T P ⚑ ❋ ♠ ☀ ☡ ▥ ✂ ♫ ☈ ∪ ✓ ⛰ ⚲

GREENWOOD LODGE   (B)
(Mrs E McCord), Erne Drive, Ederney,
BT93 0EF. ☎ (036 56) 31366.
B&B s£16 d£30. BB&M s£24 d£45.
Rooms 7, ensuite 4. Dinner £7.50.
Last orders1900 hrs. Open all year.

T P ❋ ♠ ☀ ☡ ☡ OAP ▥ ✂ ☈

B&B = bed and breakfast   s = single   d = double   BB&M = bed, breakfast & evening meal

MULLYNAVAL LODGE   (U)
(Miss N Grant), Boa Island, BT93 8AN.
☎ (036 56) 31995.
B&B s£16 d£29. BB&M s£25 d£47.
Rooms 5, ensuite 5. Dinner £9. Last orders
1930 hrs. Open all year.

🅿 🏮 ✿ ♣ ⚒ ⏃ 🅓 📠 📖 ⬜ ⅋ 🐚 🔦 ♩ ⌐ ∪
✓ 🔺 ⚱

Bed & Breakfast

CLAREVIEW
(Mr & Mrs M Moore), 85a Crevenish Rd,
BT93 1RQ. ☎ (036 56) 31455.
B&B s£14 d£26. Rooms 3. Open all year.
On scenic route

🅿 ✿ ♣ ⚒ ⏃ 📖 ⅋ ♩ ⌐ ∪ 🔺 ⚱ ⊙ ✿

EDERNEY LODGE
(Mrs S Flack), Ederney, BT93 0EF.
☎ (036 56) 31261.
B&B s£12 d£24. Rooms 2. Open all year.

🅿 ✿ ♣ ⏃ 📠 📖 ⬜ ⅋ ♩

ERNEVALE
(Mr & Mrs M Lee), 26 Main St, BT93 1TF.
☎ (036 56) 31707.
B&B s£12 d£24. Rooms 3. Open all year.

🅿 ✿ ♣ ⏃ 📖 ⅋ ♩ ⌐ ∪ ✓ 🔺 ⚱

HALFWAY INN
(Jas Gamble), Letterbreen, BT74 9FH.
☎ (0365) 341367.
B&B s£12, d£24. BB&M s£18.50 d£37.
Rooms 2, ensuite 1. High tea £10. Dinner
£6.50. Last orders 2200 hrs. Open Mar-
Dec.

🅿 ♣ ⚒ ❗ ⏃ 🅓 🐎 📖 ⬜ 🕯 ⅋ 🔦 ♩ ⌐ ∪ ✓
🔺 ⚱ ⊞

HOLLYFIELD HOUSE
(Mr & Mrs V Loane), Gortnagullion,
BT93 1BT. ☎ (036 56) 32072.
B&B s£12 d£24. Rooms 2. Open all year.

🅿 ✿ ♣ 📖 ⅋ ⚱

MUCKROSS LODGE
(Mrs C Anderson), Muckross Quay,
BT93 1TZ. ☎ (036 56) 31887/31719.
B&B s£13 d£26. Rooms 2, ensuite 2.
Open all year.

🅿 ✿ ♣ ⏃ 🅓 🐎 📖 ⬜ ⅋ ♩ ⌐ ∪ ✓ 🔺 ⚱

NATANNA
(Mrs A Anderson), 38 Main St.
☎ (036 56) 31985.
B&B s£15 d£26. Rooms 2, ensuite 1.
Open all year.

🅿 🏮 ✿ ♣ ⏃ 📖 ⬜ ⅋ ♩ ⌐ ∪ ✓ 🔺 ⚱

ROSCOLBAN HOUSE
(Mrs N Stronge), Enniskillen Rd, BT93
1TF. ☎ (036 56) 31096.
B&B s£12.50 d£25. Rooms 3. Open Mar-
Oct.

🆃 🅿 ✿ ♣ ⚒ ⏃ 📖 ⅋ ♩ ⌐ ∪ ✓ 🔺 ⚱

ROSSCAH LODGE.
(Mrs A Geddes) 11 Crevenish Rd,
☎ (036 56) 31001.
B&B s£13 d£26. Rooms 2. Open Mar-Sept.

🅿 ✿ ⚒ 📖 ⬜ ⅋ ♩ ⌐ ∪ 🔺 ⚱

ROSSCREENAGH HOUSE
(Mr A Lowry), 482 Boa Island Rd, Letter
Post Office, BT93 2AQ. ☎ (036 56) 31373.
B&B s£11 d£22. BB&M s£19 d£38. Rooms
3. Open all year.

🆃 ✿ ♣ ⏃ 📖 ⬜ ♩ ⌐ ∪ ✓ 🔺

Facilities are liable to change. Check prices when you book. Key to symbols is on the back flap.

TUDOR FARM
(Mr S McCreery), 619 Boa Island Rd,
Portinode, BT93 8AQ. ☎ (036 56) 31943.
B&B s£18 d£36. Rooms 6, ensuite 2.
Open all year.

🅣 🅟 ✿ ♣ ⚡ 🐾 🛏 ⊁ ♪ ⌐ ∪ ✓ ⚓ ⚘

VAN-ELM
(Messrs J & E Vance), Pettigo Rd,
BT93 8DD. ☎ (036 56) 31719/31887.
B&B s£13.50 d£27. Rooms 3, ensuite 3.
Open all year.

🅟 ✿ ♣ ⚡ 🐾 🅞🅐🅟 🐴 🛏 ⊡ ♪ ⌐ ∪ ⚓ ⚘

WILLOWDALE
(Mrs S McCubbin), Drumbarna, BT93
1RR. ☎ (036 56) 31596.
B&B s£13.50 d£27. Rooms 2.
Open all year.

🅟 ✿ ♣ ⚡ 🐾 🅞🅐🅟 🛏 ⊡ ⊁ ♪ ⌐ ∪ ✓ ⚓ ⚘

FAIRY TREE HOUSE
(Mrs Keys) Glenarn, Lack. ☎ (036 56)
31015/32185.
B&B s£11 d£22. BB&M s£18 d£36. Rooms
3. Dinner £7. Last orders 1730 hrs. Open
all year.

🅟 ✿ ♣ ⚡ 🐾 🅞🅐🅟 🛏 ⊡ ⊁ ♪ ⌐ ∪ ✓ ⚓ ⚘

Guesthouses

AGHNACARRA HOUSE (A)
(Mrs N Ensor), Carrybridge, BT94 5NF.
☎ (0365) 87077.
B&B s£13 d£26. BB&M s£21 d£42. Rooms
6, ensuite 2. Dinner £8. Open all year.
On B514, S of Lisbellaw

🅣 🅟 ✿ ♣ ⚡ 🐾 🛏 ⊁ ♠ ♪ ⌐

TATNAMALLAGHT HOUSE (U).
(Mrs I Dunlop), 39 Farnamullan Rd.,
Tatnamallaght, BT94 5DY. ☎ (0365)
87174.
B&B s£12 d£22. BB&M s£19 d£37. Rooms
5, ensuite 3.High tea £6.50, Dinner £7.50.
Open all year.

🅣 🅟 ✿ ♣ ⚡ 🐾 🅞🅐🅟 🛏 ⊡ ♪ ⌐

BRAMLEY COTTAGE
(Mr & Mrs R Little), Gola Cross, BT94 5ND.
☎ (0365) 87388.
B&B s£13.50 d£27. Rooms 2. Open all
year.

🅟 ✿ ♣ ⚡ 🐾 🛏 ⊁ ⌐

CLITANA
(Mrs H Beacom), Leambreslin, BT94 5EX.
☎ (0365) 87310.
B&B s£11.50 d£23. BB&M s£20 d£40.
Rooms 4, ensuite 2. Dinner £8.50.
Last orders 1900 hrs. Open all year.

🅟 ✿ 🛏 ⊁ ♪ ⌐ ∪ ✓ ⚓ ⚘

FORTMOUNT
(Mrs E Johnston), Mullybritt Rd, BT94 5ER.
☎ (0365) 87026.
B&B s£11.50 d£23. BB&M s£18.50 d£37.
Rooms 3. Dinner £7. Last orders 1200 hrs.
Open all year.

🅟 ✿ ⚡ 🐾 🅞🅐🅟 🛏 ⊁ ♪ ⌐ ∪ ⚓ ⚘

INNISH VIEW
(Mrs A Brown), Gola, BT94 5ND.
☎ (0365) 87893.
B&B s£12.50 d£25. BB&M s£19.50
d£38.50. Rooms 2. High tea £4.50. Dinner
£7.50. Open all year.

✿ ♣ ⚡ 🐾 🅞🅐🅟 🛏 ⊡ ☏ ⊁ ♪ ⌐ ∪ ✓ ⚓ ⚘

Facilities are liable to change. Check prices when you book. Key to symbols is on the back flap.

MULLAGHKIPPIN FARM
(Mrs H Johnston), Derryharney, BT94 5JH.
☎ (0365) 87419.
B&B s£13 d£26. BB&M s£20 d£40. Rooms
2, ensuite 2. High tea £5. Dinner £8. Last
orders 2100 hrs. Open May-Sept.
On B514, S of Lisbellaw

[icons]

ROSE LODGE
(Mr & Mrs A Hutchinson), Mullybritt,
BT94 5ER. ☎ (0365) 87302.
B&B s£12 d£24. Rooms 3. Open Apr-Sept.

[icons]

WIL-MER LODGE
(Mrs M Mulligan), Carrybridge Rd,
Farnamullen, BT94 5EA. ☎ (0365) 87045.
B&B s£12 d£24. BB&M s£20 d£40. Rooms
3, ensuite 2. High tea £5. Dinner £8. Open
all year.
Off A4, S of Lisbellaw

[icons]

LISNARICK

Hotels

DRUMSHANE HOTEL **
Lisnarick, BT94 1PS. ☎ (036 56) 21146.
Fax 21311.
B&B s£30 d£60. Rooms 10, ensuite 7.
Last orders 2200 hrs. Open all year.

[icons]

Guesthouses

ROSSGWEER HOUSE (A)
(Mrs M Hemphill), 274 Killadeas Rd,
BT94 1PE. ☎ (036 56) 21924.
B&B s£15 d£30. BB&M s£23 d£46. Rooms
7, ensuite 6. High tea £5.50. Dinner £8.
Last orders 1300 hrs. Open Jan-Dec.

[icons]

Bed & Breakfast

ARCHDALE LODGE
(Mr & Mrs N Noble), Drumall, Lisnarick,
BT94 1PG. ☎ (036 56) 28022.
B&B s£14 d£27. Rooms 3, ensuite 3.
Open all year.

[icons]

THE COTTAGE
(Mrs E Armstrong), Carnboy, ☎ (036 56)
21856.
B&B s£11 d£22. Rooms 1. Open all year.

[icons]

DRUMEDEN COUNTRY HOUSE
(Mrs L Noble), Coolisk. ☎ (036 56) 21836.
B&B s£13 d£26. Rooms 2, ensuite 2.
Open Apr-Oct.

[icons]

RUSHINDOO HOUSE
(Mrs L Anderson), 378 Killadeas Rd,
Lisnarick, BT94 1PS. ☎ (036 56) 21220.
B&B s£15 d£26. BB&M s£24 d£48. Rooms
3, ensuite 3. Open all year.

[icons]

B&B = bed and breakfast   s = single   d = double   BB&M = bed, breakfast & evening meal

LISNASKEA

Hotels

ORTINE HOTEL *
Main St, BT92 0GD. ☎ (03657) 21206.
Fax 21206.
B&B s£32.50 d£48. Rooms 18, ensuite 18.
High tea £8.95. Dinner £10.50. Last orders
2100 hrs. Open all year.

🅣 🅿 ✿ ❢ 🐾 ⚓ ᴼᴬᴾ 🐎 ▥ ❑ ☾ ⚡ ✎ ◆ ♩ ⌐ ∪ ✓
⚓ ⚱ 🎩 🚶 ⊞

Guesthouses

COLORADO HOUSE   (A)
(Mr & Mrs J Scott), 102 Lisnagole Rd,
BT92 0QF. ☎ (036 57) 21486.
B&B s£12 d£24. Rooms 8, ensuite 1.
Open all year.
On A34, 1m SE of Lisnaskea

🅿 ✿ ♣ 🐾 ⚓ ▥ ✎ ♩ ⌐ ∪ ✓ ⚓ ⚱ ۞ ٨

MALLARD HOUSE   (A)
(Mrs J McVitty), Drumany, BT92 0EU.
☎ (036 57) 21491.
B&B s£13 d£25. BB&M s£20 d£37.
Rooms 4. Dinner £5. Last orders 1500 hrs.
Open Apr-Oct.

🅿 🏠 ♣ 🐾 ⚓ ᴼᴬᴾ ▥ ❑ ✎ ♩ ⌐ ∪ ✓ ⚓ ⚱

Bed & Breakfast

LEA-VILLE
(Geo & Gladys Kettyle), Cushwash, BT92
0DW. ☎ (036 57) 22800.
B&B s£12.50 d£25. Rooms 4. High tea £5.
Dinner £5. Open all year.

🅿 ♣ ⚓ ▥ ✎ ♩ ⌐ ∪ ✓ ⚓ ⚱ ٨

TEACH A CEILI
(Mr & Mrs J Reihill), Inniscorkish,
BT92 0SA. ☎ (036 57) 21360.
B&B s£14 d£26. BB&M s£24 d£46. Rooms
2. High tea £6. Dinner £10. Last orders
1800 hrs. Open Jan-Nov.
On Inniscorkish Island

🅣 ✿ ◆ 🐾 ⚓ ᴼᴬᴾ ▥ ✎ ♩ ✓ ⚓ ⚱

NEWTOWNBUTLER

Bed & Breakfast

PORTS HOUSE
(Mr K Mewes), Ports, BT92 8DT.
☎ (036 57) 38528.
B&B s£13 d£26. Rooms 3, ensuite 1.
Dinner £11. Open Apr-Sept.

🅿 🏠 ✿ ◆ 🐾 🐚 ♩ ⌐ ⚓ ٨

ROSLEA

Bed & Breakfast

ANNAGULGAN
(Mrs M Callaghan), Roslea, BT92 7FN.
☎ (036 575) 498.
B&B s£11 d£22. BB&M s£18 d£36.
Rooms 2. High tea £7. Dinner £7.
Last orders 1900 hrs. Open Apr-Oct.

🅿 ✿ ◆ 🐾 ⚓ ᴼᴬᴾ ▥ ❑ ✎ ♩ ⌐ ∪ ✓ ⚓ ⚱

Facilities are liable to change. Check prices when you book. Key to symbols is on the back flap.

TEMPO

Bed & Breakfast

THE FORGE
(Mrs C White) 43 Main St. ☎ (036 554) 359.
Fax 359.
B&B s£12.50 d£25. BB&M s£21 d£42.
Rooms 2, ensuite 2. High tea £8.50. Dinner
£8.50. Last orders 1800 hrs. Open all year.

🅿 ♠ ⛄ [OAP] ⚏ ❑ ✄ ♪ ⌐ ∪ ⏴⏵

TEMPO MANOR
(John Langham), ☎ (036 554) 247. Fax 202.
B&B s£60 d£104. BB&M s£81 d£146.
Rooms 4, ensuite 2. Dinner £21. Last
orders 1200 hrs. Open Mar-Dec.

🆃 🅿 🏠 ❋ ♠ 🎿 ⛄ ⛺ ⚏ ✄ ♪ ⌐ ∪ ✓ ⏴⏵
✝

County Londonderry

AGHADOWEY

Hotel

BROWN TROUT GOLF & COUNTRY
  INN **
(Mr & Mrs B O'Hara), 209 Agivey Rd,
BT51 4AY. ☎ (0265) 868209. Fax 868878.
B&B s£40 d£65. BB&M s£50 d£75. Rooms
15, ensuite 15. High tea £8. Dinner £12.
Last orders 2130 hrs. Open all year.

🕆 🅿 🏦 ❊ ♣ 🌺 🍴 🐂 🐎 🔟 ▢ 🕻 ⚷ 🎵 🏳 ✓
⚓ 🎣 🏇 🛈 🈹

Bed & Breakfast

INCHADOGHILL HOUSE
(Mrs M McIlroy), 196 Agivey Rd,
BT51 4AD. ☎ (0265) 868250/868232.
B&B s£12 d£24. Rooms 3. Open all year.
9m S of Coleraine

🏦 ❊ ♣ 🐂 🛈

CASTLEDAWSON

Guesthouse

MOYOLA LODGE (B)
(Mr & Mrs L Swinerton), 9 Brough Rd,
BT45 8ER. ☎ (0648) 68224/68573.
B&B s£20 d£36. BB&M s£33 d£62.
Rooms 3. Dinner £13. Last orders 2130 hrs.
Open all year.

🅿 🏦 ❊ ♣ 🍴 🐂 🛈 🎵 🏳 ∪ ⚓ 🎣 🍴

Bed & Breakfast

Mr & Mrs R BUCHANAN
99 Old Town Rd, BT45 8BZ.
☎ (0648) 68741.
B&B s£10 d£20. Rooms 3. Open all year.

🅿 ❊ ♣ 🌺 🐂 🆑 🛈 ⚷ 🎵 🏳 ⚓

DAWSON ARMS

(Mrs B Garvin), 31 Main St, BT45 8AA.
☎ (0648) 68269.
B&B s£12.50 d£19. Rooms 3.
Open all year.

🕆 🅿 🏦 ❊ 🍴 🆑 🛈 ⚷ 🎵 🏳 ∪

CASTLEROCK

Hotels

GOLF HOTEL *
17 Main St, BT51 4RA. ☎ (0265) 848204.
Fax 848295.
B&B s£35 d£55. BB&M s£45 d£75.
Rooms 16, ensuite 16. High tea £6.50.
Dinner £12.50. Last orders 2100 hrs.
Open all year.

🕆 🅿 ❊ ♣ 🌺 🍴 🐂 🆑 🛈 ▢ 🕻 ⚷ 🎵 🏳 ∪ ✓
⚓ 🎣 🏇 🈹

Guesthouses

MARINE INN (A)
(Mr Des McAfee), 9 Main St, BT51 4RA.
☎ (0265) 848456.
B&B s£20 d£36. BB&M s£26 d£48. Rooms
9, ensuite 9. High tea £6.50. Dinner £8.50.
Last orders 2130 hrs. Open all year.

🕆 🅿 🌺 🍴 🐂 🆑 🐕 🛈 ▢ ⚷ ♦ 🎵 🏳 ∪ 🍴

Bed & Breakfast

BANNVIEW
(Mrs M Henry), 14 Exorna Lane, BT51 4UA.
☎ (0265) 848033.
B&B s£14 d£28. Rooms 3. Open Mar-Oct.

🅿 ❊ ♣ 🌺 🐂 🐕 🛈 ⚷ 🎵 ∪ ⚓ 🍴

Facilities are liable to change. Check prices when you book. Key to symbols is on the back flap.

CARNEETY HOUSE
(Mrs C Henry), 120 Mussenden Rd,
BT51 4TX. ☎ (0265) 848640.
B&B s£15 d£30. Rooms 3, ensuite 1.
Open all year.
On A2, 5m from Coleraine

🅿 ❄ ♣ ⅍ ⋟ 📠 ▥ ☐ ✁ ♪ ↾ ∪ ✿

CRAIGHEAD HOUSE
(Mrs J McConkey), 8 Circular Rd,
BT51 4XA. ☎ (0265) 848273/848701.
B&B s£20 d£30. Rooms 3, ensuite 2.
Open all year.

🅿 🏠 ❄ ♣ ⅍ 📠 🐎 ▥ ☐ ↾ ∪ ✿

KENMUIR HOUSE
(Mrs E Norwell), 10 Sea Rd, BT51 4TL.
☎ (0265) 848345.
B&B s£15.50 d£31. Rooms 2.
Open all year.

🅿 ♣ ⅍ ⋟ ▥ ☐ ✁ ♪ ↾ ∪ ✿

MARITIMA HOUSE
(Mrs J Caulfield), 43 Main St, BT51 4RA.
☎ (0265) 848388.
B&B s£17 d£34. Rooms 3, ensuite 3.
Open all year.

🅿 ❄ ♣ ⅍ ⋟ 📠 🐕 ▥ ✁ ✿

Guesthouses

BEAUFORT HOUSE (B)
(Avril Gibson), 11 Church St, BT47 4AA.
☎ (0504) 338248.
B&B s£12 d£24. Rooms 4. High tea £5.
Dinner £6. Last orders 1900 hrs.
Open all year.
Centre of village

🅿 🏠 ❄ ♣ ⅍ ❢ ⋟ 📠 ▥ ✁ ♦ ♪ ↾ ∪ ⟋ ⬠
⁊

Bed & Breakfast

MUNREARY LODGE
(Mr & Mrs G Hayes), 241 Foreglen Rd,
BT47 4EE. ☎ (0504) 338803.
B&B s£13 d£25. BB&M s£18 d£33.
Rooms 3. Dinner £5. Last orders 2000 hrs.
Open all year.
On A6, 5m W of Dungiven

🆃 🅿 ❄ ♣ ⅍ ⋟ 📠 ▥ ☐ ✁ ↾ ∪ ⦿

COLERAINE

Hotels

BOHILL HOTEL
& COUNTRY CLUB **
69 Cloyfin Rd, BT52 2NY.
☎ (0265) 44406/7. Fax 52424.
B&B s£38 d£66. BB&M s£50 d£90. Rooms
36, ensuite 36. High tea £8. Dinner £14.
Last orders 2115 hrs. Open all year.

🆃 🅿 ❄ ♣ ❢ ⋟ ▥ ☐ ☎ ✆ ♦ ⚲ ↾ ⚓ ⦿

B&B = bed and breakfast   s = single   d = double   BB&M = bed, breakfast & evening meal

BUSHTOWN HOUSE
COUNTRY HOTEL   **
283 Drumcrone Rd.
☎ (0265) 58367. Fax 320909.
B&B s£45 d£65. BB&M s£60 d£95.
Rooms 21, ensuite 21. High tea £9. Dinner
£15. Last orders 2130 hrs. Open all year.

▣ ▣ ❈ ♣ ⚡ ❢ ☞ ↑ ▦ ☐ ⌕ ✿ ◈ ↑ ❢ ⦿
☒

LODGE HOTEL · **
Lodge Rd, BT52 1NF.
☎ (0265) 44848. Fax 54555.
B&B s£39 d£60. Rooms 20, ensuite 20.
High tea £8. Dinner £11.50. Last orders
2100 hrs. Open all year.

▣ ❈ ♣ ❢ ☞ ↑ ▦ ☐ ⌕ ↑ ∪ ⟋ ◬ ᴢ ❢ ᴤ ☒

Guesthouses

BLACKHEATH HOUSE   (A)
(Mr & Mrs J Erwin), 112 Killeague Rd,
Blackhill, BT51 4HH.
☎ (0265) 868433. Fax 868433.
B&B s£35 d£60. Rooms 5, ensuite 5.
Dinner £18. Last orders 2130 hrs.
Open all year.
7m S of Coleraine

▣ ▣ ⌂ ❈ ♣ ⚡ ❢ ▦ ☐ ⌕ ◆ ↗ ↑ ∪ ⟋ ☒

GREENHILL HOUSE   (A)
(Mrs J Hegarty), 24 Greenhill Rd,
Aghadowey, BT51 4EU.
☎ (0265) 868241.
B&B s£25 d£40. Rooms 6, ensuite 6.
Dinner £12.50. Last orders 1200 hrs.
Open Mar-Oct.
3m NE of Garvagh

▣ ▣ ⌂ ❈ ♣ ☞ ㏇ ▦ ☐ ⤢ ↗ ↑ ∪ ☒

Bed & Breakfast

BALLYLAGAN HOUSE
(Mrs J Lyons), 31 Ballylagan Rd, BT52 2PQ.
☎ (0265) 822487.
B&B s£16 d£32. Rooms 5, ensuite 2.
Open all year (ex Christmas & New Year).
Off B17, 2½ m from Coleraine

▣ ♣ ⚡ ☞ ㏇ ▦ ⤢ ↗ ↑ ∪ ⟋ ◬ ᴢ

BEARDIVILLE NURSERY
(Mr & Mrs A Badger), 9 Ballyhome Rd,
BT52 2LU. ☎ (026 57) 31816.
B&B s£17 d£34. Rooms 3, ensuite 2.
Open all year.
Off B62, off B17, 3m NE of Coleraine

▣ ▣ ❈ ♣ ☞ ㏇ ▦ ⤢ ⦿

BELLE VUE
(Mrs E Morrison), 43 Greenhill Rd,
Coleraine   BT51 4EU. ☎ (0265) 868797.
B&B s£15 d£30. B&B s£23 d£46. Rooms 5.
Dinner £8. Open all year.

▣ ⌂ ❈ ♣ ⚡ ☞ ㏇ ▦ ⤢ ↗ ↑ ∪ ◬ ᴢ ᴤ

CAIRNDHU
(Mr & Mrs R Eyre), 4 Cairn Court,
Ballycairn Rd, BT51 3BW.
☎ (0265) 42854.
B&B s£15 d£26. BB&M s£22 d£40.
Rooms 2. Open all year.

▣ ▣ ❈ ☞ ▦ ⤢ ⦿ ᴤ

CAMUS HOUSE
(Mrs J King), 27 Curragh Rd, BT51 3RY.
☎ (0265) 42982.
B&B s£20 d£34. BB&M s£22 d£40.
Rooms 3. Open all year.
Off A54, 3m S of Coleraine

▣ ▣ ⌂ ❈ ♣ ⚡ ▦ ☐ ⤢ ↗ ↑ ∪ ⟋ ◬ ᴢ

Facilities are liable to change. Check prices when you book. Key to symbols is on the back flap.

COOLBEG
(Mrs D Chandler), 2e Grange Rd,
BT52 1NG. ☎ (0265) 44961.
B&B s£20 d£34. Rooms 5, ensuite 3.
Open all year.

🆃 🅿 ❄ ▥ ⌷ ⏾⚡

DUNDERG COTTAGE
(Mrs R Armour), 251 Dunhill Rd, BT51
3QJ. ☎ (0265) 43183.
B&B s£12 d£24. Rooms 3. Open all year.

🅿 ❄ ♣ ⛷ ▥ ⚡

ERNEVILLE
(Mrs H Boyd), 59 Nursery Avenue,
BT52 1LP. ☎ (0265) 55972.
B&B s£15 d£29. Rooms 4. Open all year.

🅿 ❄ OAP ▥ ⚡ ♩ ⚓⚡

HEATHFIELD HOUSE
(Mrs H Torrens), 3.1 Drumcroon Rd,
Killykergan, Garvagh, BT51 4EB.
☎ (02665) 58245.
B&B s£16 d£32. BB&M s£25 d£50.
Rooms 3, ensuite 2. Dinner £9.
Open all year.
On A29, 7m S of Coleraine

🆃 🅿 ❄ ♣ ☆ ⛷ 🐎 ▥ ⌷ ⚡ ♩ ⏂ ∪ ⚓ ⚡
🆙

HILLVIEW FARM
(Mrs L Neely), 40 Gateside Rd, BT52 2PB.
☎ (0265) 43992.
B&B s£15 d£30. Rooms 3, ensuite 1.
Open all year.

🅿 ❄ ♣ ☆ ▥ ⚡ ∪ ⚓⚡

KILLEAGUE HOUSE
(Mrs M Moore), 156 Drumcroon Rd,
Blackhill, BT51 4HJ. ☎ (0265) 868229.
B&B s£17 d£30. BB&M s£27 d£50.
Rooms 3, ensuite 2. Dinner £10.
Last orders 1600 hrs. Open all year.
On A29, 7m S of Coleraine

🆃 🅿 🏠 ❄ ♣ ⛷ OAP ▥ ⚡ ∪

MANOR COTTAGE
(Mrs N Roulston), 44 Cranagh Rd,
BT51 3NN. ☎ (0265) 44001.
B&B s£15 d£30. Rooms 3, ensuite 1.
Open Apr-Sept.

🅿 ❄ ♣ ☆ ⛷ 🐎 ▥ ⚡ ♩ ⏂ ∪ ⚓⚡

MARTINDALE
(Mrs M Wilson), 70 Newbridge Rd,
BT52 2LB. ☎ (0265) 55175.
B&B s£14 d£19.50. Rooms 3, ensuite 1.
Open all year.

🅿 ❄ ♣ ⛷ OAP ▥ ⌷ ⚡ ♩ ⏂ ∪ ⚡

Mrs S NEELY
52a Gateside Rd, BT52 2PB. ☎ (0265)
57185. B&B s£15 d£30. Rooms 3, ensuite
1. Open Apr-Sept.

🅿 ❄ ♣ ⛷ OAP ▥ ⚡ ⏾⚡

ROCKMOUNT
(Mrs J Kerr), 241 Windyhill Rd, Ballinrees,
BT51 4JN. ☎ (0265) 42914.
B&B s£12 d£24. BB&M s£17 d£34.
Rooms 2. Open Apr-Oct.
4m SW of Coleraine

🅿 ❄ ♣ ☆ ⛷ ▥ ⚡ ⚡

TRAMALIS
(Mrs J Doak) 5 Ballindreen Rd, BT52 2JU.
☎ (0265) 55204. B&B s£12 d£24.
BB&M s£18 d£36. Rooms 2. Dinner £6.
Open all year.

🅿 ❄ ♣ ☆ ⛷ OAP ▥ ⌷ ⚡ ♩ ⏂ ∪ ⚓⚡

Facilities are liable to change. Check prices when you book. Key to symbols is on the back flap.

TULLAN'S FARM
(Mrs D McClelland), 46 Newmills Rd,
BT52 2JB. ☎ (0265) 42309.
B&B s£15 d£30. Rooms 3, ensuite 1.
Open all year.

🖵 🅿 ✿ ♣ ⛺ DAP ▥ ⊁ ⤴ ⌐ ∪ ✓ ⬙ ⤢ ⚲

UNIVERSITY OF ULSTER
Cromore Rd, BT52 1SA.
☎ (0265) 44141 (ext 4567). Fax 40903.
B&B s£16.02 d£23.82. BB&M s£22.22
d£36.22. Rooms 300, ensuite 12.
Dinner £6.20. Last orders 1800 hrs.
Open July-Sept.

🅿 ✿ ♣ ⚡ ❗ ⛺ ▥ ● ◐ ◀ ◉

Bed & Breakfast

BRADAGH
(Maura McMacken)
132 Main St, BT47 4LG. ☎ (050 47) 41346.
B&B s£11 d£22. Rooms 3. Open all year.

🖵 🅿 ✿ ♣ ⛺ 🐴 ▥ ⊡ ⚲

WHITEHILL HOUSE
(Mrs N Fulton), 74 Altmover Rd,
Derrylane, BT47 4QD. ☎ (050 47) 41211.
B&B s£12 d£24. Rooms 3. Open all year.

🅿 ✿ ♣ ⛺ DAP ▥ ⊁ ⤴ ⌐ ∪ ✓

Bed & Breakfast

MOYOLA VIEW
(Patricia Flanagan), 35 Tobermore Rd,
BT45 7HJ. ☎ (0648) 28495.
B&B s£12 d£24. Rooms 2. Open Jan-Dec.

🅿 ✿ ♣ ⚡ ⛺ ▥ ⊡ ⊁ ⤴ ⌐ ⚲

PINE VIEW HOUSE
(Mrs B Convery), 57 Derrynoid Rd,
BT45 7DW. ☎ (0648) 28337.
B&B s£12 d£24. Rooms 2.
Open May-Oct.

🅿 ✿ ♣ ⚡ ⛺ ▥ ⊁ ⚲

Hotels

GLEN HOUSE HOTEL **
9 Main St, BT47 3AA. ☎ (0504) 810527.
B&B s£36.50 d£50. BB&M s£48.50 d£64.
Rooms 16, ensuite 16. High tea £6.50.
Dinner £12. Last orders 2145 hrs.
Open all year.

🖵 🅿 ♿ ♣ ❗ ⛺ DAP ▥ ⊡ ⚬ ⊁ ⤴ ⌐ ∪ ✓ ⊤
💷

Bed & Breakfast

CARMONEY HOUSE
(Mrs F Dinsmore), 34 Carmoney Rd,
BT47 3JJ. ☎ (0504) 810276.
B&B s£13.50 d£25. Rooms 2.
Open all year.

🅿 ✿ ♣ ⚡ ⛺ ▥ ⊁

B&B = bed and breakfast   s = single   d = double   BB&M = bed, breakfast & evening meal

GREENAN FARM
(Mrs E Montgomery), 25 Carmoney Rd,
BT47 3JJ. ☎ (0504) 810422.
B&B s£12.50 d£25. BB&M s£18 d£36.
Rooms 3, ensuite 1. High tea £6.
Open all year.

TAMNEYMORE HOUSE
(Mrs P Gordon), 77 Limavady Rd,
Tamneymor, BT51 5ED. ☎ (026 65) 58333.
B&B s£11 d£22. Rooms 2. Open Jun-Sept.

LONGFIELD FARM
(Mrs E Hunter), 132 Clooney Rd,
BT47 3DX. ☎ (0504) 810210.
B&B s£14 d£26. Rooms 3. High tea £5.
Dinner £6.50. Open Apr-Oct.
1m W of Eglinton

WILD GEESE CENTRE
Movenis Airfield, 116 Carrowreagh Rd,
BT51 5LQ.
☎ (026 65) 58609. Fax (026 65) 57050.
B&B s£5. Rooms 34. High tea £2.50.
Dinner £2.50. Last orders 2100 hrs.
Open all year.

Mrs M McCARTER
6 Manor Park, BT47 3DL.
☎ (0504) 810598.
B&B s£12 d£24. Rooms 2. Open all year.

KILREA

Bed & Breakfast

BEECHMOUNT
(Mrs A Palmer), 197 Drumagarner Rd,
BT51 5TP. ☎ (026 65) 40293.
B&B s£12.50 d£25. BB&M s£20 d£40.
Rooms 3. High tea £5.50. Dinner £7.50.
Last orders 1930 hrs. Open all year.

ONCHAN
(Mrs K McCauley), 3 Ballygudden Rd,
BT47 3AD. ☎ (0504) 810377.
B&B s£14 d£25. Rooms 3, ensuite 1.
Open all year.
8m NE of Londonderry

LIMAVADY

Hotels

GORTEEN HOUSE HOTEL   *
187 Roe Mill Rd, BT49 9EX.
☎ (050 47) 22333. Fax 22333.
B&B s£26 d£40. BB&M s£36 d£60. Rooms
32, ensuite 32. High tea £6. Dinner £10.
Last orders 2200 hrs. Open all year.

GARVAGH

Bed & Breakfast

FAIRVIEW
(Mr & Mrs J Stewart) 53 Grove Rd,
BT51 5NY. ☎ (026 65) 58240.
B&B s£12 d£24. Rooms 2. Open all year.

Facilities are liable to change. Check prices when you book. Key to symbols is on the back flap.

Bed & Breakfast

ALEXANDER ARMS
(Mr R Jefferies & Mr D Morgan), 34 Main
St, BT49 0EP.
☎ (050 47) 63443/62660.
B&B s£18.50 d£37. BB&M s£25 d£43.50.
Rooms 6, ensuite 2. Dinner £8. Last orders
2200 hrs. Open all year.

🅿 🏠 ❗ 🛆 🕮 ⬛ 🍷

BALLYCARTON FARM HOUSE
(Mrs E Craig), 239 Seacoast Rd, Bellarena,
BT49 0HZ. ☎ (050 47) 50216.
B&B s£13 d£26. BB&M s£19 d£38.
Rooms 5. High tea £5. Dinner £6.
Last orders 1600 hrs. Open all year.
Off A2, 5m N of Limavady

🅿 🏠 ✿ ♣ � 🛆 🆑 🕮 ♪ ↑

BALLYHENRY HOUSE
(Mrs R Kane), 172 Seacoast Rd, BT49 9EF.
☎ (050 47) 22657.
B&B s£15 d£30. BB&M s£23.50 d£45.
Rooms 3, ensuite 1. High tea £5. Dinner
£8.50. Last orders 1700 hrs. Open all year.
On B69, 3m N of Limavady

🆃 🅿 🏠 ✿ ♣ � 🛆 🕮 ⚡ ✎ ♪ ↑ ∪ 🛆ⓩ

BALLYMULHOLLAND HOUSE
(Mrs D Morrison), 474 Seacoast Rd,
BT49 0LF. ☎ (050 47) 50227.
B&B s£12 d£24. BB&M s£18 d£36.
Rooms 2. Dinner £6. Last orders 1200 hrs.
Open all year.

🅿 ✿ ♣ � 🛆 🆑 🐕 🕮 ✎ ♪ ↑ ∪

BENONE HOUSE
(Mr T Deighan), 5 Benone Ave, Magilligan,
BT49 0LQ. ☎ (050 47) 50284.
B&B s£20 d£40. Rooms 3, ensuite 3. Open
Mar-Oct.

🆃 ✿ ♣ � 🛆 🆑 🕮 ⚡ ✎ ♪ ↑ ∪ ✓ 🛆

DRENAGH
(Mr & Mrs P Welsh), 17 Dowland Rd,
BT49 0HP. ☎ (050 47) 22649.
B&B s£40 d£100. BB&M s£65 d£150.
Rooms 6, ensuite 4. Dinner £25.
Last orders 1200 hrs. Open Feb-Nov.

🆃 🅿 🏠 ✿ ♣ � 🛆 🕮 ✎ ● ⚲ ♪ ↑ ∪ ✓ 🍷 🆓

Mr & Mrs E HARPUR
100 Highlands Rd, BT49 9LY.
☎ (050 47) 64701.
B&B s£13 d£26. Rooms 2. Open all year.

🅿 🏠 ✿ ♣ 🛆 🕮

Mrs D McDAID
1 Rush Hall Cottages, Broighter Rd,
BT49 9GH. ☎ (050 47) 63488.
B&B s£12.50 d£25. Rooms 2, ensuite 1.
Open all year.

🆃 🅿 ✿ ♣ 🌛 🛆 🕮 ✎ ♪ ↑ ∪

B&B = bed and breakfast   s = single   d = double   BB&M = bed, breakfast & evening meal

THE POPLARS
(Mrs H McCracken), 352 Seacoast Rd,
BT49 0LA. ☎ (050 47) 50360.
B&B s£15 d£28. BB&M s£22 d£44. Rooms
6, ensuite 2. High tea £8. Dinner £8.
Last orders 1600 hrs. Open all year.
On A2, 6½ m N of Limavady

WHITEHILL
(Mrs M McCormick), 70 Ballyquin Rd,
BT49 9EY. ☎ (050 47) 22306.
B&B s£14 d£28. Rooms 3, ensuite 1.
Open all year.
On B68, 1m S of Limavady

Hotels

BEECH HILL COUNTRY
HOUSE HOTEL ***
32 Ardmore Rd, BT47 3QP.
☎ (0504) 49279. Fax 45366.
B&B s£52.50 d£70. BB&M s£69.50 d£109.
Rooms 17, ensuite 17. Dinner £25.
Last orders 2145 hrs. Open all year.

BROOMHILL HOUSE HOTEL ***
Limavady Rd, BT47 1LT. ☎ (0504) 47995.
B&B s£45 d£60. BB&M s£60.75 d£91.50.
Rooms 42, ensuite 42. High tea £8.50.
Dinner £15.75. Last orders 2130 hrs.
Open all year.

EVERGLADES ***
Prehen Rd, BT47 2PA.
☎ (0504) 46722. Fax 49200.
B&B s£65 d£80. BB&M s£78.95 d£107.90.
Rooms 52, ensuite 52. High tea £8.50.
Dinner £13.95. Last orders 2130 hrs.
Open all year.

WATERFOOT HOTEL ***
Caw Roundabout, 14 Clooney Rd, BT47
1TB. ☎ (0504) 45500. Fax 311006.
B&B s£50 d£63. BB&M s£66 d£88.
Rooms 51, ensuite 51. Dinner £13.50.
Last orders 2215 hrs. Open all year.

WHITE HORSE HOTEL ***
68 Clooney Rd, Campsie, BT47 3PA.
☎ (0504) 860606. Fax 860371.
B&B s£44.25 d£49.50. BB&M s£54.25
d£69.50. Rooms 43, ensuite 43. High tea
£7.50. Dinner £10. Last orders 2215 hrs.
Open all year.

Guesthouses

CLARENCE HOUSE (B)
(Mrs E Slevin), 15 Northland Rd, BT48 7HY.
☎ (0504) 265342.
B&B s£15 d£30. Rooms 8, ensuite 4.
High tea £12. Open all year.

Facilities are liable to change. Check prices when you book. Key to symbols is on the back flap.

Bed & Breakfast

ABODE
(Mr & Mrs N Dunn), 21 Dunnwood Park,
Victoria Rd, BT47 2NN. ☎ (0504) 44564.
B&B s£10 d£20. BB&M s£14 d£28. Rooms
4. Open all year.

ARDOWEN HOUSE
(Mrs C Stevin), 13 Northland Rd,
BT48 7HY.
☎ (0504) 264950.
B&B s£20 d£40. Rooms 3, ensuite 3.
Open all year.

BRAEHEAD HOUSE
(Mrs M McKean), 22 Braehead Rd,
BT48 9XE. ☎ (0504) 263195.
B&B s£13.50 d£25. Rooms 3.
Open all year.

ELAGH HALL
(Mrs E Buchanan), Buncrana Rd,
BT48 8LU. ☎ (0504) 263116.
B&B s£15 d£30. Rooms 3, ensuite 2.
Open all year.
On A2, 2m NW of Londonderry

FAIRLEE
(Mrs M Cassidy), 86 Duncreggan Rd,
BT48 0AA. ☎ (0504) 268943/354285.
B&B s£13 d£26. Rooms 8, ensuite 2.
Open all year.

FLORENCE HOUSE
(Mr & Mrs McGinley), 16 Northland Rd,
BT48 7JD. ☎ (0504) 268093.
B&B s£13 d£26. Rooms 5. Open all year.

GROARTY HOUSE
(Mr J Hyndman), 62 Groarty Rd, BT48 0JY.
☎ (0504) 261403.
B&B s£13 d£26. Rooms 3. Open all year.

KILLENAN HOUSE
(Mrs A Campbell), 40 Killenan Rd,
Drumahoe, BT47 3NG. ☎ (0504) 301710.
B&B s£13 d£26. BB&M s£19 d£38.
Rooms 3. High tea £6. Dinner £8.
Last orders 1500 hrs. Open all year.
Off B118, 5m SE of Londonderry

MAGEE COLLEGE
26 Northland Rd, BT48 7JL.
☎ (0504) 265621 or
(0265) 44141 (ext 4567).
Fax (0265) 40903.
B&B s£16.02 d£23.82. BB&M s£22.22
d£36.22. Rooms 58. Dinner £6.20.
Last orders 1800 hrs. Open Jul-Sept.

NO. 10
(Gerry & Grace McGoldrick), 10 Crawford
Square, BT48 7HR. ☎ (0504) 265000.
B&B s£14 d£29. Rooms 5. Open all year.

OAKGROVE HOUSE
(Mrs M Holmes), 3 Columba Terrace,
Waterside, BT47 1JT. ☎ (0504) 44269.
B&B s£12 d£24 . BB&M s£17 d£34.
Rooms 3. Dinner £5. Last orders 1800 hrs.
Open all year.

Ⓣ Ⓟ 🛏 [OAP] �____.

Mrs J PYNE
36 Great James St, BT48 7DB.
☎ (0504) 269691.
B&B s£14 d£28. Rooms 7, ensuite 1.
Open all year.

Ⓟ ♨ ✻ 🛏 🐎 �____ 🖵 ⅍ ♪ ↾ ∪ ♦

RASPBERRY HILL HEALTH FARM
(Mr & Mrs Danton), 29 Bond's Glen Rd,
Dunamanagh, BT47 3ST.
☎ (0504) 398000. Fax 398000.
6 day course
B&B s£225 d£360. Rooms 7, ensuite 7.
Open Jan-Nov.

Ⓟ ✻ ♣ ᴗ゙ [OAP] �____ ⅍ 🐿 ♦ ⚘ ⚘ ♪ ↾ ∪ ♦ ⇶

ROBIN HILL
(Mr & Mrs M Muir), 103 Chapel Rd,
BT47 2BG. ☎ (0504) 42776.
B&B s£13 d£26. BB&M s£19 d£38. Rooms
3. High tea £5. Dinner £6. Open all year.

Ⓟ ♨ ✻ ᴗ゙ 🛏 [OAP] �____ 🖵 ⅍ ♪ ↾ ∪ ⟋ ♦ ⇶

TULLY FARM
(Mrs E Henderson), 109 Victoria Rd, New
Buildings, BT47 2RN. ☎ (0504) 42832.
B&B s£12 d£24. Rooms 5, ensuite 1.
Open all year.
On A5, S of Londonderry

Ⓟ ✻ ♣ ᴗ゙ 🛏 �____ ⅍ ♪ ↾ ∪

Mrs I WILEY
153 Culmore Rd, BT48 8JH.
☎ (0504) 352932.
B&B s£10 d£20. BB&M s£13 d£26.
Rooms 3. Open all year.

Ⓟ ♣ ᴗ゙ 🛏 [OAP] �____ 🖵 ⅍ ♪ ↾ ∪ ⟋ ♦ ⇶

YMCA
Inter Point, 51 Glenshane Rd, Drumahoe
Rd, BT47 3SF.
☎ (0504) 301662. Fax 301662.
B&B s£8.50. Open all year.

Ⓟ ✻ ♣ ᴗ゙ ⚘ ♪ ↾ ♀

MAGHERA

Bed & Breakfast

SPERRIN-VIEW
(Mrs B Crockett), 110a Drumbolg Rd,
Upperlands, BT46 5UX. ☎ (0266) 822374.
B&B s£12.50 d£25. BB&M s£19.50 d£39.
Rooms 1. High tea £5. Dinner £7.50.
Open all year.

Ⓟ ✻ ♣ ᴗ゙ ᴗ゙ 🛏 �____ 🖵 ⅃ ⅍ ♪ ↾ ∪ ⟋ ♦ ⇶

MAGHERAFELT

Guesthouses

LAUREL VILLA   (B)
(Mrs M Kielt), 60 Church St, BT45 6AW.
☎ (0648) 32238.
B&B s£15 d£30. BB&M s£22 d£44.
Rooms 5, ensuite 1. Open all year.

Ⓣ Ⓟ ♨ ✻ ᴗ゙ �____ ⅍ ♪ ↾ ∪ ⟋ ♦ ⇶

Facilities are liable to change. Check prices when you book. Key to symbols is on the back flap.

Bed & Breakfast

INVERLAKE HOUSE
2 Ballyneill Rd, Ballyronan BT65 6JE.
☎ (0648) 418500/418452.
B&B s£11 d£22. Rooms 4. Open all year.

🅿 ❀ ♣ 🐾 ⛲ [OAP] ⟰ ⚡ ♪ ⌐ ↗ ⚓ ⚲

Hotels

EDGEWATER HOTEL **
88 Strand Rd, BT55 7LZ.
☎ (0265) 833314. Fax 832224.
B&B s£55 d£80. BB&M s£63 d£100.
Rooms 31, ensuite 31. High tea £8. Dinner
£15. Last orders 2130 hrs. Open all year.

🆃 🅿 🐾 🍴 ⛲ [OAP] ⟰ ⌐ 📞 ✉ ♦ ♪ ⌐ ∪ ⚲ ⚓
🆓

WINDSOR HOTEL *
8 The Promenade, BT55 7AD.
☎ (0265) 832523. Fax 832649.
B&B s£28 d£52. BB&M s£33 d£62. Rooms
24, ensuite 14. High tea £5. Dinner £10.
Last orders 2100 hrs. Open all year.

🆃 🅿 🐾 🍴 ⛲ [OAP] ⟰ ⌐ ♦ ♪ ⌐ ∪ ⚲ ⚓ 🆓

Guesthouses

LIS-NA-RHIN (A)
(Mr & Mrs Montgomery), 6 Victoria
Terrace, BT55 7BA. ☎ (0265) 833522.
B&B s£20 d£39. BB&M s£30 d£58. Rooms
9, ensuite 4. High tea £6. Dinner £11.50.
Open all year.

🅿 🐾 ⛲ ⟰ ⚡ ♪ ⌐ ∪ ⚓ ⚲

OREGON   (A)
(Mrs V Anderson), 168 Station Rd,
BT55 7PU. ☎ (0265) 832826.
B&B s£25 d£35. BB&M s£35 d£55.
Rooms 9, ensuite 8. Dinner £10.
Last orders 1500 hrs. Open Feb-Nov.
On B185, SE of Portstewart

🅿 ❀ ♣ 🐾 ⛲ ⟰ ⌐ ⚡ ✉ ♪ ⌐ ∪ ⚓ ⚲ ◐ ⚲

GORSE BANK   (B)
(Mrs M Austin), 36 Station Rd, BT55 7DA.
☎ (0265) 833347.
B&B s£16 d£32. BB&M s£24 d£48. Rooms
6, ensuite 2. High tea £7. Dinner £8.
Last orders 1200 hrs. Open all year.

🆃 🅿 🏠 ❀ 🐾 ⛄ ⛲ [OAP] ⟰ ⟰ ⌐ ⚡ ♪ ⌐ ⚓ ⚲ ⚲

MULROY GUEST HOUSE   (B)
(Mr R Perry), 8 Atlantic Circle, BT55 7BD.
☎ (0265) 832293.
B&B s£16 d£32. BB&M s£22 d£44.
Rooms 7. Dinner £6. Last orders 1600 hrs.
Open all year.

❀ 🐾 ⛄ [OAP] ⟰ ⚡ ⚲ 🆓

Bed & Breakfast

ASHLEIGH
(Mrs M Gordon), 164 Station Rd,
BT55 7PU. ☎ (0265) 834452.
B&B s£20 d£30. BB&M s£30 d£50.
Rooms 4, ensuite 4. Dinner £10.
Last orders 1300 hrs. Open all year.
On B185

🅿 ❀ ♣ 🐾 [OAP] ⟰ ⌐ ⚡ ♪ ⌐ ∪ ⚲

Facilities are liable to change. Check prices when you book. Key to symbols is on the back flap.

117

CHEZ NOUS
(Mrs T Nicholl), 1 Victoria Terrace,
BT55 7BA. ☎ (0265) 832608.
B&B s£13.50 d£27. Rooms 3.
Open all year.

🅿 🎏 ✿ ♣ 🕎 [OAP] 🎢 ♪ ⌐ △⇄å

CRAIGMORE
(Mr J Kelly), 26 The Promenade, BT55 7AE.
☎ (0265) 832120.
B&B s£13 d£26. BB&M s£17.50 d£35.
Rooms 13, ensuite 1. Open Jan-mid Dec.

🅿 🎏 ✿ ♣ 🔥 🕎 [OAP] 🎢 ⌂ ♪ ⌐ ∪ ✓ △⇄å

HEBRON
(Mrs M Lutton), 37 Coleraine Rd,
BT55 7HP. ☎ (0265) 832225.
B&B s£13.50 d£27. BB&M s£18 d£43.
Rooms 4, ensuite 1. High tea £5.
Dinner £8. Open all year.

🅿 ✿ ♣ 🔥 🕎 [OAP] 🎢 ⌂ ⅙ ♪ ⌐ ∪ ✓ △⇄å

HILLVIEW
(Mrs M McConaghie), 73 Station Rd,
BT55 7HH. ☎ (0265) 833957.
B&B s£18 d£28. Rooms 2. Open Mar-Sept.

🅿 ✿ ♣ [OAP] 🐕 🎢 ⅙ ⌐ å

LOW SOUNDS
(Mrs I Ritchie), 5 Burnside Rd, BT55 7NS.
☎ (0265) 833863.
B&B s£17 d£30. Rooms 3. Open all year.

[T] 🅿 ✿ 🔥 🕎 🎢 ⌂ ⅙ å

MAIRE'S
(Mrs T McClarnon), 75 The Promenade,
BT55 7AF. ☎ (0265) 832067.
B&B s£13 d£25. Rooms 7. Open all year.

🔥 🕎 🎢 ⅙ ♪ ⌐ ∪ △å

MOUNT ORIEL
(Mrs B Laughlin), 74 The Promenade,
BT55 7AF. ☎ (0265) 832556.
B&B s£13 d£25. Rooms 5. Open Jun-Aug.

🎏 🔥 🎢 ⅙ å

ROCKHAVEN
(Mrs F Mann), 17 Portrush Rd, BT55 7DB.
☎ (0265) 833846.
B&B s£15 d£33. BB&M s£22 d£43. Rooms
7, ensuite 6. High tea £10. Dinner £14.
Open all year.

🅿 ✿ ♣ 🔥 🕎 🎢 ⌂ ♪ ⌐ ⇄å

SALEM
(Mr & Mrs A Craig), 5 Atlantic Circle,
BT55 7BD. ☎ (0265) 834584.
B&B s£12 d£24. BB&M s£16 d£32.
Rooms 5, ensuite 1. High tea £4.
Dinner £4. Last orders 1200 hrs.
Open all year.

🔥 🕎 [i] [OAP] 🎢 ⅙ ♪ ⌐ ∪ ✓ △⇄å

STRANDEEN
(Mrs E Caskey), 63 Strand Rd, BT55 7LU.
☎ (0265) 833159.
B&B s£17.50 d£35. BB&M s£25 d£50.
Rooms 3, ensuite 3. Dinner £7.50.
Open all year.

🅿 ✿ 🔥 🕎 ⌂ ⅙ ♪ ⌐ ∪ ✓ △⇄å

WANDERIN HEIGHTS
(Mr & Mrs E Robinson), 12 High Rd,
BT55 7BG. ☎ (0265) 833250.
B&B s£14 d£28. BB&M s£20 d£40.
Rooms 6. Open all year.

🔥 🕎 [OAP] 🕎 ⅙ ♪ ⌐ ∪ å

B&B = bed and breakfast   s = single   d = double   BB&M = bed, breakfast & evening meal

County Tyrone

AUGHER

Guesthouses

BEECH LODGE   (B)
(Mr & Mrs I Curran), 43 Glenhoy Rd,
BT77 0DG. ☎ (066 25) 48106.
B&B s£13 d£26. BB&M s£19.50 d£39.
Rooms 4. High tea £6.50. Open all year.

🅣 ✿ ♣ �►ℳ ☍ ⊞ ╳ ♪ ▶ ✓

AUGHNACLOY

Bed & Breakfast

GARVEY LODGE
(Mrs I McClements), 62 Favour Royal Rd,
BT69 6BR. ☎ (066 252) 239.
B&B s£12 d£24. BB&M s£18 d£36.
Rooms 2. High tea £5. Dinner £6.
Last orders 1900 hrs. Open all year.

🅿 ✿ ♣ ☍ ⊞ ℳ ╳ ♪ ▶ ∪ ✓ ☆

BALLYGAWLEY

Bed & Breakfast

THE GRANGE
(Mrs S Lyttle), 15 Grange Rd, BT70 2HD.
☎ (066 25) 68053.
B&B s£15 d£30. BB&M s£22.50 d£43.50.
Rooms 3, ensuite 3. High tea £7.50.
Dinner £8.75. Open Jan-Nov.
Ballygawley roundabout

🅿 🏠 ✿ ♣ ☍ ℳ ╳ ♪

HILLCREST HOUSE
(Mrs N McGinley), 135 Roscavey Rd,
BT70 2EQ. ☎ (066 25) 68088.
B&B s£15 d£30. Rooms 2, ensuite 1.
Open all year.

🅿 ✿ ♣ ☽ ☍ ⊞ ℳ ☍ ╳ ♦ ▶ ∪ ⊞

BENBURB

Bed & Breakfast

BENBURB CENTRE
10 Main St, BT71 7LA. ☎ (0861) 548170.
B&B s£12 d£20. BB&M s£15.50 d£27.
Rooms 33, ensuite 1. High tea £3.50.
Dinner £5. Open all year.

🅿 🏠 ✿ ♣ ☽ ☍ ⊞ ℳ ╳ ♪ ▶ ∪ ✓ ⬖ ☆ ♨ ☆

CALEDON

Bed & Breakfast

MODEL FARM
(Mr & Mrs J Agnew), 70 Derrycourtney
Rd, Ramakitt, Caledon. ☎ (0861) 568210.
B&B s£12 d£20. Rooms 2. Open all year.

🅿 🏠 ✿ ♣ ☍ ℳ ☍ ╳ ♪ ▶ ☆

TANNAGHLANE HOUSE
(Mrs E Reid), 15 Tannaghlane Rd,
BT68 4XU. ☎ (0861) 568247.
B&B s£15 d£26. BB&M s£25 d£40.
Rooms 1, ensuite 1. High tea £6.
Dinner £10.
Open all year.
Off B45, 1½ m SW of Caledon

🅿 🏠 ✿ ♣ ☽ ℳ ☍ ╳ ♪ ▶ ☆

Facilities are liable to change. Check prices when you book. Key to symbols is on the back flap.

CASTLEDERG

Guesthouses

ARDNAVEIGH   (B)
(Mr & Mrs H Johnston), 39 Corgary Rd,
BT81 7YF. ☎ (066 26) 71209 Fax 71209.
B&B s£30 d£50. Rooms 3, ensuite 3.
Open May-Sept.

DERG ARMS   (B)
(Mr & Mrs S Walls), 43 Main St,
BT81 7AS. ☎ (066 26) 71644.
B&B s£14.50 d£29. BB&M s£22.50 d£35.
Rooms 6, ensuite 6. High tea £6. Dinner £6.
Last orders 2100 hrs. Open all year.

CLOGHER

Bed & Breakfast

TIMPANY MANOR
(Mrs M McFarland), 53 Ballagh Rd,
BT76 0LB. ☎ (036 55) 21285.
B&B s£14 d£26. BB&M s£22 d£42.
Rooms 3. High tea £8. Dinner £8.
Last orders 2200 hrs. Open all year.

COALISLAND

Bed & Breakfast

O'CEANAGHOHAOHA
(Mr & Mrs P Hughes), 117 Moor Rd,
Shanless, Stewartstown, BT71 5QD.
☎ (086 87) 40403.
B&B s£11 d£22. Rooms 3, ensuite 1.
Open all year.

AVENDALE
(Mrs M Wallace), 51 Reenadeery Rd,
Coalisland. ☎ (086 87) 48805.
B&B s£15 d£30. Rooms 3. Open all year.

COOKSTOWN

Hotels

GLENAVON HOUSE HOTEL   ***
52 Drum Rd, BT80 8JQ.
☎ (064 87) 64949. Fax 64396.
B&B s£45 d£60. BB&M s£55 d£70. Rooms
53, ensuite 53. High tea £8. Dinner £10.
Last orders 2200 hrs. Open all year.

GREENVALE HOTEL   *
57 Drum Rd, BT80 8QS.
☎ (064 87) 62243/65196. Fax 65539.
B&B s£27.50 d£45. BB&M s£40 d£70.
Rooms 12, ensuite 12. High tea £10.
Dinner £15. Last orders 2200 hrs.
Open all year.

B&B = bed and breakfast   s = single   d = double   BB&M = bed, breakfast & evening meal

ROYAL HOTEL   *
64 Coagh St, BT80 8NG.
☎ (064 87) 62224. Fax 62224.
B&B s£23 d£46. BB&M s£32.50 d£65.
Rooms 10, ensuite 10. High tea £6. Dinner
£9.50. Last orders 2130 hrs. Open all year.

🅿️ ❄ ♣ 💡 ⛄ 🎦 ⬜ 📞 🎵 🍴 ∪ ⚓ 🍴 🕯 ♿

Guesthouses

EDERGOLE   (A)
(Mrs M Short), 70 Moneymore Rd,
BT80 8RJ. ☎ (064 87) 62924. Fax 65572.
B&B s£17 d£34. BB&M s£22 d£44. Rooms
4, ensuite 4. Dinner £5. Open all year.

🆃 🅿️ ❄ ♣ ⛄ 🆗 🐴 🎦 ⬜ 📞 ✂ 🎵 🍴 ∪ ✓ ⚓ ⚡

Bed & Breakfast

CENTRAL INN
(Mr H Quinn), 27 William St, BT80 8AX.
☎ (064 87) 62255.
B&B s£12.50 d£25. Rooms 5, ensuite 2.
Open all year.

🅿️ 💡 ⛄ 🎦 🎵 🍴 ∪ 🍴 ♿

THE FARMHOUSE
(Mr & Mrs R McKeown), 23 Drumconvis
Rd, BT80 0HD. ☎ (064 87) 37301.
B&B s£12 d£23. BB&M s£17 d£32.
Rooms 2, ensuite 1. High tea £5. Dinner £6.
Last orders 1930 hrs. Open all year.

🅿️ 🏠 ❄ ♣ 🎿 ⛄ 🐴 🎦 ✂ 🎵 🍴 ✓

Mrs F McCORD
51 Sandholes Rd, BT80 9AT.
☎ (064 87) 62668.
B&B s£12 d£24. BB&M s£20 d£40.
Rooms 3. High tea £10. Dinner £12.
Open all year.

🅿️ ❄ ♣ 🎿 ⛄ 🆗 🎦 ⬜ 📞 ✂ 🎵 🍴

THE PIPER'S CAVE
(Mrs E Warnock), 38 Cady Rd, BT80 9BD.
☎ (064 87) 63615.
B&B s£13.50 d£27. Rooms 3.
Open all year.
On A29, 4m S of Cookstown

🅿️ ❄ ♣ ⛄ 🆗 🎦 ✂ 🎵 🍴

Bed & Breakfast

CLANNMORE
(Mr & Mrs S Grimes), 6 Church View,
BT70 3EY. ☎ (086 87) 61410.
B&B s£15 d£28. Rooms 3. Open all year.

❄ ♣ ⛄ 🎦 ✂ 🎵 🍴 ✓ ⚓

IVY COTTAGE
(Mrs M Thornton), 9 Main St, BT70 3ES.
Tel (086 87) 67832.
B&B s£15 d£25. BB&M s£22 d£32.50.
Rooms 3. High tea £6.50. Dinner £7.
Last orders 2100 hrs. Open all year.

🅿️ 🏠 ❄ 🎿 ⛄ 🆗 🎦 ✂ 🎵 🍴 ∪ ⚓ ⚡

Bed & Breakfast

COMMERCIAL INN
(Mr F McCaffrey), 48 Main St, BT78 3AB.
☎ (0662) 898219.
B&B s£12 d£20. Rooms 4. High tea £10.
Dinner £10. Open all year.

🅿️ 💡 ⛄ 🎦 ✂ ♿

Facilities are liable to change. Check prices when you book. Key to symbols is on the back flap.

OAKLAND HOUSE
(Mrs M Mills), 19 Holme Rd, Greenan.
☎ (0662) 898305.
B&B s£12 d£24. Rooms 3. Open Jun-Sept.

🅿 ❋ 🎔 ⅄ ∪

DUNGANNON

Hotels

INN ON THE PARK HOTEL **
Moy Rd, BT71 6BS.
☎ (086 87) 25151. Fax 24953.
B&B s£37.50 d£55. BB&M s£52.50 d£85.
Rooms 14, ensuite 14. High tea £6. Dinner
£15. Last orders 2130 hrs. Open all year.

Ⓣ 🅿 ❋ ♣ 🍷 🐎 🐴 🎔 ▢ ✆ ⚲ ⚓ ┠ ∪ ⚓ ⚐ 🆔

Guesthouses

CREEVAGH LODGE   (A)
(Mr & Mrs G Nelson), Carland, BT70 3LQ.
☎ (086 87) 61342.
B&B s£14 d£26. BB&M s£22 d£42. Rooms
11, ensuite 3. High tea £6. Dinner £8.
Last orders 1930 hrs. Open all year.
Off A29, 3m N of Dungannon

🅿 ⛺ ❋ ♣ ☀ 🐎 🐴 🎔 ▢ ⅄

GRANGE LODGE   (B)
(Mrs N Brown), 7 Grange Rd, BT71 1EJ.
Tel (086 87) 84212/22458. Fax 23891.
B&B s£35 d£56. BB&M s£52 d£90.
Rooms 4, ensuite 4. Dinner £17.
Last orders 1200 hrs. Open all year.
1m S of M1, junction 15

Ⓣ ⛺ ❋ ♣ 🎔 ▢ ⅄ ⚲ ⚓ ┠ ∪ ⚐ 🆔

Bed & Breakfast

FARM BUNGALOW
(Miss M Currie), 225 Ballynakelly Rd,
Cohannnon, BT71 6HJ. ☎ (086 87) 23156.
B&B s£14 d£26. BB&M s£22 d£42.
Rooms 2. High tea £10. Open all year.
On A45, 5m E of Dungannon

🅿 ❋ ♣ 🐎 ᴅᴀᴘ 🎔 ⅄ ┠ ∪

SECOND CHOICE
(Mr J McGrath), 63 Old Caulfield Rd,
BT70 3NG. ☎ (086 87) 67774.
B&B s£15 d£28. Rooms 3. Open all year.

🅿 ❋ ♣ ☀ 🐎 🎔 ⅄ ⚓ ┠ ∪ ⚋ ⚐ ⚓

THE TOWN HOUSE
(Mr & Mrs Cochrane), 32 Northland Row,
BT71 6AP. ☎ (086 87) 23975.
B&B s£12 d£24. Rooms 4. Open all year.

🅿 ❋ 🐎 🎔 ▢ ⅄ ⚓ ┠ ∪ ⚋ ⚐ ⚓

FIVEMILETOWN

Hotels

VALLEY HOTEL **
60 Main St, BT75 0PW.
☎ (036 55) 21505. Fax 21688.
B&B s£30 d£56. Rooms 22, ensuite 22.
High tea £5.50. Dinner £12.50.
Last orders 2300 hrs. Open all year.

🅿 ❋ ♣ ☀ 🐎 🐴 ⅈ ᴅᴀᴘ 🐴 🎔 ▢ ✆ ⚓ ┠ ∪ ⚋ ⚐
⛾ 🜂 🆔

Facilities are liable to change. Check prices when you book. Key to symbols is on the back flap.

FOURWAYS HOTEL *
41 Main St, BT75 0LE.
☎ (036 55) 21260/21374.
B&B s£22 d£38. Rooms 10, ensuite 10.
High tea £7. Dinner £9.50.
Last orders 2130 hrs. Open all year.

Ⓣ 🅿 ⛵ OAP 🛏 💻 🗗 🕻 🍴 ⋃ ⟋ ♨ ⚓ ⚘

Guesthouses

AL-DI-GWYN LODGE   (A)
(Mrs V Gilmore), 103 Clabby Rd,
BT75 0QY. ☎ (036 55) 21298.
B&B s£17 d£34. BB&M s£25 d£50.
Rooms 4, ensuite 4. Dinner £8.
Last orders 1800 hrs. Open all year.
On B107, 2m N of Fivemiletown

🅿 ✻ ♣ ⚡ ⛵ OAP 💻 ✂ 🍴 ⟋

Bed & Breakfast

THE VALLEY VILLA
(Ms G Malone), 92 Colebrooke Rd,
Corcreevy, BT75 0SA. ☎ (036 55) 21553.
B&B s£12.50 d£25. Rooms 3.
Open all year.

🅿 ✻ ♣ ⚡ ⛵ 💻 ⋃ ♨ ⚘

GORTIN

Bed & Breakfast

CULLVAHULLION
(Mrs M Kelly), 71 Culvahullion Rd,
BT79 8QE. ☎ (066 26) 48919.
B&B s£12 d£24. Rooms 3. Open all year.
1½ m N of Gortin

✻ ♣ ⚡ ⛵ 💻 ✂ ⚘

MOY

Guesthouses

MULEANY HOUSE   (A)
(Mr & Mrs B Mullen), 86 Gorestown Rd,
BT71 7EX. ☎ (086 87) 84183.
B&B s£16 d£26. BB&M s£23 d£40.
Rooms 9, ensuite 9. Dinner £9.50.
Last orders 2000 hrs. Open all year.
1m W of Moy

🅿 ✻ ♣ ⛵ OAP 💻 ✂ ⚓ ⚲ 🍴 ⟋ ⋃ ▦

Bed & Breakfast

CHARLEMONT HOUSE
(Mr & Mrs L McNeice), 4 The Square,
BT71 7SG. ☎ (086 87) 84755/84895.
B&B s£15 d£30. BB&M s£20 d£35.
Rooms 3. Open all year.

🅿 🐎 ✻ ♣ ⚡ ⛵ OAP 🐴 💻 🗗 ✂ 🍴 ⟋ ⋃ ⟋ ♨
♨ ⚘ ▦

DEAL HOUSE
(Ann Hobson), 22 Charlemont St, BT71 1SL.
☎ (08687) 84601.
B&B s£16 d£30. BB&M s£24 d£38.
Rooms 5. High tea £7. Dinner £8.
Open all year.

🅿 🐎 ✻ ♣ ⛵ 💻 🗗 🍴 ⟋ ⋃ ⚓ ⚘

TOMNEY'S INN
(Mr D Tomney), 9 The Square, BT71 7SG.
☎ (086 87) 84895/84755.
B&B s£12.50 d£25. BB&M s£17.50 d£30.
Rooms 3. Open all year.

🅿 🐎 ✻ ♣ ⚡ 🍷 ⛵ OAP 🐴 💻 🗗 ✂ 🍴 ⟋ ⋃ ⟋
♨ ♨ ⚓ ⚘

B&B = bed and breakfast   s = single   d = double   BB&M = bed, breakfast & evening meal

NEWTOWNSTEWART

Hotels

HUNTING LODGE   *
Letterbin Rd, Baronscourt, BT78 4HR.
☎ (066 26) 61679. Fax 61900.
B&B s£25 d£50. Rooms 16, ensuite 16.
Dinner £12.95. Last orders 2130 hrs.
Open all year.

Bed & Breakfast

ANGLER'S REST
(Mr & Mrs D Campbell), 12 Killymore Rd,
BT78 4DT. ☎ (066 26) 61167/61543.
B&B s£12 d£24. BB&M s£18 d£36.
Rooms 2, ensuite 2. High tea £6. Dinner £6.
Last orders 2000 hrs. Open all year.

CROSH LODGE
(Mrs E Beattie), 22 Plumbridge Rd,
BT78 4DA. ☎ (066 26) 61421.
B&B s£12.50 d£25. BB&M s£19 d£38.
Rooms 2, ensuite 1. High tea £6.50. Dinner
£6.50. Last orders 2000 hrs. Open all year.

DEER PARK HOUSE
(Mrs N Gallagher), 14 Baronscourt Rd,
BT78 4EX. ☎ (066 26) 61083/61565.
B&B s£15 d£30. BB&M s£21 d£42.
Rooms 4. High tea £7. Last orders 2000 hrs.
Open all year.

WOODBROOK FARM
(Mrs I McFarland), 21 Killymore Rd,
BT78 4QT. ☎ (066 26) 61432.
B&B s£12.50 d£25. BB&M s£20 d£40.
Rooms 2, ensuite 1. High tea £6. Dinner
£8. Last orders 1800 hrs. Open all year.

OMAGH

Hotels

ROYAL ARMS HOTEL   **
51 High St, BT78 1BA.
☎ (0662) 243262/3. Fax 245011.
B&B s£34.50 d£64. BB&M s£47 d£89.
Rooms 21, ensuite 21. High tea £7.
Dinner £12.50. Last orders 2130 hrs.
Open all year.

SILVERBIRCH HOTEL   *
5 Gortin Rd, BT79 7DH.
☎ (0662) 242520/243360. Fax 249061.
B&B s£29 d£53. BB&M s£39.50 d£74.
Rooms 29, ensuite 24. Dinner £10.50.
Last orders 2130 hrs. Open all year.

Facilities are liable to change. Check prices when you book. Key to symbols is on the back flap.

125

Guesthouses

GREENMOUNT LODGE   (A)
(Mrs F Reid), 58 Greenmount Rd,
Gortaclare, BT79 0YE. ☎ (0662) 841325.
B&B s£16.50 d£30. BB&M s£27 d£50.
Rooms 8, ensuite 8. Dinner £15.
Last orders 1900 hrs. Open all year.
9m SW of Omagh

🅣 🅟 ✣ ♣ ➳ 🛏 ☐ ✂ ♪ ⌐ ∪ ✓ ⬙ ⚡ 🍴 ◐

Bed & Breakfast

ARDMORE
(Mrs I McCann), 12 Tamlaght Rd,
BT78 5AW. ☎ (0662) 243381.
B&B s£14 d£24. Rooms 3. Open all year.

🅟 ✣ ♣ 🛏 ✂

BANKHEAD
(Mrs S Clements), 9 Lissan Rd, BT78 1TX.
☎ (0662) 245592.
B&B s£12 d£24. Rooms 3. Open all year.

🅟 ✣ ♣ ➳ ➳ 🛏 ⌐

BLESSINGTON
(Mrs R McAskie), 35a Dunteige Rd,
Mountjoy, BT78 5PB. ☎ (0662) 243578.
B&B s£12.50 d£25. Rooms 5, ensuite 1.
Open all year.

✣ ♣ ➳ ➳ 🛏 ✂ ♪ ⌐ ♰

BRIDIES
(Mrs B Cuddihy), 1 Georgian Villas,
Hospital Rd, BT79 0AT. ☎ (0662) 245254.
B&B s£15 d£30. BB&M s£21 d£42.
Rooms 3. High tea £4. Dinner £6.
Open all year.

🅟 🏨 ✣ ♣ ➳ 🛏 ✂

BURN VIEW
(Mrs E McGrath), 16 Carnoney Rd,
Knockmoyle, BT79 7TF. ☎ (0662) 247661.
B&B s£12 d£24. Rooms 3. Open all year.

🅟 ♣ ➳ ➳ 🛏 ✂ ♰ Ⓔ

CAMPHILL FARM
(Mrs I Fulton), 5 Mellon Rd, Mountjoy,
BT78 5QU. ☎ (0662) 245400.
B&B s£14 d£28. Rooms 3. Open Jan-Dec.

🅟 ✣ ♣ ➳ ➳ 🛏 ✂ ♰

Mr & Mrs B CONWAY
254 Glenelly Rd, Cranagh, BT79 8LS.
☎ (066 26) 48334.
B&B s£13.50 d£27. Rooms 2.
Open all year.
On B47, 8m E of Plumbridge

🅟 ✣ ♣ ➳ ➳ 🛏 ✂ ♰

DALEVIEW
(Mrs I Johnston), 96 Beltany Rd, BT78 5QT.
☎ (0662) 241182.
B&B s£12 d£24. Rooms 3. Open all year.

🅟 ✣ ♣ ➳ ➳ 🛏 ✂ ♰

HEATHERLEA
(Mr & Mrs J Donaghy), 222 Barony Rd,
Creggan, BT79 9AQ. ☎ (066 27) 61555.
B&B s£11 d£22. Rooms 2. Open all year.

🅟 ✣ ♣ ➳ ➳ 🛏 ✂ ♪ ⌐ ∪ ✓

HILLCREST FARM
(Mrs A McFarland), Lislap, BT79 7UE.
☎ (066 26) 48284.
B&B s£11.50 d£21. BB&M s£16 d£30.
Rooms 2. Dinner £5. Last orders 1800 hrs.
Open Jan-Nov.
7 m NW of Omagh

🅟 ✣ ♣ ➳ ➳ 🛏 ✂ ✓ ♰

Facilities are liable to change. Check prices when you book. Key to symbols is on the back flap.

127

HILLTOP
(Mrs M O'Hagan), 19 Sperrin View,
BT78 5BJ. ☎ (0662) 241827.
B&B s£13 d£25. BB&M s£20 d£40.
Rooms 3, ensuite 1. High tea £12.
Dinner £10. Last orders 2000 hrs.
Open all year.

🅿 ❄ ♣ ⚶ ఠ ⊼ ▥ ◻ ♪ ∪

LETFERN
(Miss J Patterson), 118 Letfern Rd,
Seskinore, BT78 1UL. ☎ (0662) 841324.
B&B s£12 d£24. Rooms 4. Open all year.

🅿 ♣ ఠ ▥ ♪ ↑ ∪ ✓

MON ABRI
(Mrs I McLaren),
14 Moylagh Rd, Beragh, BT79 0RT.
☎ (066 27) 58224.
B&B s£12 d£22. BB&M s£18.50 d£35.
Rooms 2. High tea £5. Dinner £6.50.
Last orders 2100 hrs. Open all year.

🆃 🅿 🏠 ❄ ♣ ⚶ ఠ [OAP] ▥ ⊁ ♪ ↑ ∪ △ ⚴ ⚐
🌀

RYLANDS
(Mrs W Marshall), 31 Loughmuck Rd,
BT78 1SE. ☎ (0662) 242557.
B&B s£12.50 d£25. BB&M s£15 d£30.
Rooms 2. High tea £15. Dinner £15.
Open all year.

🅿 ♣ ఠ ▥ ♪

Bed & Breakfast

MOURNE GROVE FARM
(Mr & Mrs D Clarke), 30 Liskey Rd, Berney,
BT82 8NR. ☎ (066 26) 58957.
B&B s£18 d£36. Rooms 2, ensuite 1.
Open all year.

🅿 ❄ ♣ ⚶ ఠ ▥ ⊁ ♪ ↑ ∪

STRABANE

Hotels

FIR TREES LODGE HOTEL   **
Melmount Rd, BT82 9JT.
☎ (0504) 382382. Fax 885932.
B&B s£44 d£62. BB&M s£55 d£84.
Rooms 26, ensuite 26. High tea £7.50.
Dinner £11. Last orders 2130 hrs.
Open all year.

🆃 🅿 ❄ ♣ ⚶ ▼ ఠ [OAP] ▥ ◻ ☎ ⊁ ♪ ↑ ∪ ✓
⚴ ⚐ ⊞

Bed & Breakfast

Mrs J BALLANTINE
38 Leckpatrick Rd, Artigarvan, BT82 0HB.
☎ (0504) 882714.
B&B s£12 d£24. BB&M s£18 d£36. Rooms
3. High tea £6. Dinner £6. Open all year.
Off B49, 3m NE of Strabane

🅿 ❄ ♣ ⚶ ఠ ▥ ⊁ ↑ ⚴

BOWLING GREEN HOUSE
(Mr T Casey), 6 Bowling Green, BT82 8AS.
☎ (0504) 884787.
B&B s£14 d£25. Rooms 3. Open all year.

🅿 ఠ [OAP] ▥ ◻ ⊁ ♪ ↑

Facilities are liable to change. Check prices when you book. Key to symbols is on the back flap.

BROOK HOUSE.
(Mrs M O'Connor), 53 Brook Rd,
BT82 0RX. ☎ (0504) 398436.
B&B s£12 d£28. Rooms 2. Open all year.

🅿 ❄ ♣ ☡ ▥ ⅄ ♩ ⚑

MULVIN LODGE
(Mrs A Smith), 117 Mulvin Rd, BT82 9JR.
☎ (066 26) 58269.
B&B s£14 d£28. Rooms 2. Open all year.

🆃 🅿 ❄ ♣ ☀ ☡ ⅄ ♩ ⚑ ∪ ✓ ⛰ ⚓

TRILLICK

Bed & Breakfast

TOWNVIEW HOUSE
(Mr & Mrs R Stronge), 21 Girgadis Rd,
Annahill, BT78 3NX. ☎ (036 555) 227.
B&B s£11 d£22. Rooms 3. Open all year.

🅿 ♣ ☀ ☡ 🐎 ⅄ ♩ ⚑ ∪ ✓

B&B = bed and breakfast   s = single   d = double   BB&M = bed, breakfast & evening meal

Unclassified hotels

Some hotels in Northern Ireland do not appear in the main listings of this guide. This is because at the time of going to press they did not satisfy the criteria of the Board's classification scheme *or* do not meet the minimum standards for hotels as set out in the Tourism (Northern Ireland) Order 1992. The list includes hotels which, at the time of inspection, did not meet the requirements of the particular star rating within the scheme for which they had applied.

Arkeen Hotel Newcastle, Co Down - (039 67) 23473.
Avoca Hotel Newcastle, Co Down - (039 67) 22253.
Bay Hotel Cushendun, Co Antrim - (026 674) 267.
Carlingford Bay Hotel Warrenpoint, Co Down - (069 37) 73521.
Carnwood Lodge Hotel Keady, Co Armagh - (0861) 538935.
Carrybridge Hotel Lisbellaw, Co Fermanagh - (0365) 87148.
Cranfield House Hotel Kilkeel, Co Down - (069 37) 62327.
Curran Court Hotel Larne, Co Antrim - (0574) 275505.
Downshire Arms Hotel Banbridge, Co Down - (082 06) 62343.
Drummond Hotel Limavady, Co Londonderry - (050 47) 22121.
Drumsill House Hotel Armagh, Co Armagh - (0861) 522009.
Dunallan Hotel Donaghadee, Co Down - (0247) 883569.
Forte Crest Hotel Belfast - (0232) 612101.
Golf Links Hotel Portrush, Co Antrim - (0265) 823539.
Gosford House Hotel Markethill, Co Armagh - (0861) 551676.
Halfway House Hotel Ballygalley, Co Antrim - (0574) 583265.
Imperial Hotel Garvagh, Co Londonderry - (026 65) 58218.
Kilwaughter House Hotel Larne, Co Antrim - (0574) 272591.
Kirkistown Castle Hotel Cloughey, Co Down - (024 77) 72233.
Langholm Hotel Portrush, Co Antrim - (0265) 822293.
Leighinmohr Hotel Ballymena, Co Antrim - (0266) 652313.
McGlennon's Hotel Newcastle, Co Down - (039 67) 22415
Manor Hotel Ballymoney, Co Antrim - (026 56) 63208.
Parador Hotel Belfast - (0232) 643160.
Portmore Bay Hotel Portstewart, Co Londonderry - (0265) 832688.
Royal Court Hotel Portrush, Co Antrim - (0265) 822236.
York Hotel Belfast - (0232) 329304.

Hostels

The hostels listed here offer convenient low-cost accommodation for visitors on a limited budget.

The majority of these are likely to be young people under 25 but tourists of any age are welcome.

Entries include the hostels of the Northern Ireland Association of Youth Hostels (YHANI), independent hostels and also some school accommodation. All of them have been inspected by the Northern Ireland Tourist Board under new legislation regulating overnight accommodation in Northern Ireland. Facilities at some places are more comprehensive than at others, so check carefully when booking that the hostel meets your requirements.

Other places, not included in this section, that provide low-cost B&B accommodation are: Queen's University, Stranmillis College and the YWCA (all Belfast - see page 27), and University of Ulster campuses at Jordanstown near Belfast (page 50), Coleraine (page 110) and Londonderry (Magee College) (page 114).

Hostels which are open all or most of the year for backpackers and individual visitors appear in heavy type.

BELFAST

BELFAST INTERNATIONAL YOUTH HOSTEL - *opens March 1994*
22 Donegall Rd, Belfast BT12 5JN.

Big new central youth hostel (YHANI) near Queen's University, Ulster Museum and Botanic Rail Station. 126 beds. Family rooms. Meals. From £8. Open all year 24 hours. ☎ (0232) 324733 for details.

Visiting Belfast before spring 1994?
The old (present) youth hostel is on the A24 (Newcastle road) three miles south of city centre (buses 84, 79 & 38). ☎ (0232) 647865. Meals. From £5.95. Hostellers staying here can leave rucksacks at YHANI office in Belfast.

HUNTERHOUSE COLLEGE
Upper Lisburn Rd, Belfast BT10 0LE.
☎ (0232) 61229, fax 629790.
On south side of city, 4$^1/_2$ miles from city centre. On main Belfast-Lisburn bus route (bus stop nearby), Finaghy Halt (rail) 1 mile. Tennis, gym. 130 beds. Meals. From £12.50 (full board). Open 1 July-24 Aug only.

County ANTRIM

LARNE YOUTH HOSTEL
210 Coast Rd, Ballygalley BT40 2QQ.
☎ (0574) 583377.
Chalet-style hostel (YHANI) on Antrim coast road 4 miles north of Larne ferry terminal, on coastal bus route from Larne. Ulster Way 2 miles east. Fine views, walks. Golf, tennis, swimming nearby. 44 beds. Meals. From £5.95. Open March-mid-Dec.

Beds = approx number of bedspaces

CASTLE HOSTEL
62 Quay Rd, Ballycastle, BT54 6BH.
☎ (026 57) 62337.
Terraced house in resort town. Sea views.
Bus stop 50 yd. Horse-riding, golf, boat
hire nearby, diving off Rathlin Island.
Convenient for Ulster Way walkers. 22
beds. From £5. Open all year.

CUSHENDALL YOUTH HOSTEL
42 Layde Rd, Cushendall BT44 0NQ.
☎ (026 67) 71344.
Hostel (YHANI) 1 mile north of
Cushendall village in the glens. On
Cushendall-Ballycastle bus route, bus stop
1/2 mile. Near Ulster Way. Swimming, golf
nearby. 54 beds. Breakfast. From £5.95.
Open March-mid-Dec.

McCOOL'S INDEPENDENT YOUTH
HOSTEL
5 Causeway View Terrace, Portrush
BT56 8AT. ☎ (0265) 824845.
House in terrace with views of Causeway.
On Belfast-Londonderry bus and rail
routes (Portrush bus/ rail station 1/2 mile).
Coastal bus to Belfast, also bus to Dublin.
Horse-riding, golf, boat hire nearby. Near
Ulster Way. 14 beds. From £6. Open all
year.

NORTHERN IRELAND HOTEL
& CATERING COLLEGE
Ballywillan Rd, Portrush BT56 8JL.
☎ (0265) 824020, fax 824733.
Halls of residence. Playing fields, gym. On
Belfast-Londonderry bus/rail routes, bus
stop 1/2 mile, Portrush rail station 1 mile.
Near Ulster Way. 72 beds. Family rooms.
Meals. From £10. Open June-Aug only.

WHITEPARK BAY YOUTH HOSTEL
157 Whitepark Rd, Ballintoy BT54 6NH.
☎ (026 57) 31745.
Hostel (YHANI) 6 miles west of
Ballycastle. Bus stop 200yd. Near Giant's
Causeway and Carrick-a-rede rope bridge.
Coastal paths. Popular with Ulster Way
walkers. 44 beds. From £5.95. Open
March-mid-Dec.

County ARMAGH

THE ROYAL SCHOOL
College Hill, Armagh BT61 9DH.
☎ (0861) 522807/523196.
School (1775) in Armagh city. Sports hall,
tennis, squash. 72 beds. Open July/Aug
only. Groups only.

County DOWN

CASTLEWELLAN CASTLE CHRISTIAN
CONFERENCE CENTRE
Castlewellan BT31 9BU.
☎ (039 67) 78733.
In Castlewellan Forest Park. On
Newcastle-Castlewellan bus route, bus
stop near park gate, 1/2 mile from Centre.
Games room. Pony-trekking nearby. 120
beds. Family rooms. Groups only. Open
all year except Christmas.

FRIENDS SCHOOL
6 Magheralave Rd, Lisburn BT28 3BH.
☎ (0846) 662156, fax 672134.
Near Lisburn rail station. Town centre/bus
station 1/2 mile. Indoor swimming pool,
games room. 95 beds. Meals. From
£13.50 (£7 self-catering). Open during
school holidays only - July, Aug, Easter,
Christmas.

Beds = approx number of bedspaces

HOSTELS

NEWCASTLE YOUTH HOSTEL
30 Downs Rd, Newcastle BT33 0AG.
☎ (039 67) 22133.
Hostel (YHANI) in resort town in foothills of Mourne mountains. Nature reserve, forest parks and Ulster Way route nearby. Coastal walks. Bus station 50yd. 50 beds. Meals. From £5.95. Open March-mid-Dec.

ULSTER FOLK & TRANSPORT MUSEUM
Educational Residential Centre
Cultra, Holywood BT18 0EU.
☎ (0232) 428428, fax 428728.
In grounds of Ulster Folk & Transport Museum. Price includes entry to all exhibits. On Belfast-Bangor bus/train routes, bus stop nearby, Cultra Halt ¹/₂ mile. Near Ulster Way. 76 beds. Family rooms. Meals. From £10/12. Groups only. Open all year.

County FERMANAGH

CASTLE ARCHDALE YOUTH HOSTEL
Lisnarick BT94 1PP.
☎ (036 56) 28118.
Converted 17th-century stables in Castle Archdale Country Park, on lough shore (YHANI). Nature trails, horse-riding, canoeing, ferry to White Island in summer. Marina 100yd. On Enniskillen-Kesh bus route (bus stop is 1 mile from hostel). 54 beds. Meals. Family rooms. From £5.95. Open March-mid-Dec.

LAKELAND CANOE CENTRE
Castle Island, Enniskillen BT74 7BA.
☎ (0365) 324250, fax 323319.
Chalet accommodation, ¹/₂ mile west of Enniskillen town centre and bus station. Archery, canoeing, caving, jet-skiing, windsurfing, sailing, water-biking. Bicycle hire. Summer camps. 36 beds. Meals. From £9 (B&B £10.50). Open all year.

LOUGH MELVIN HOLIDAY CENTRE
Garrison BT93 3FG.
☎ (036 56) 58142/58143.
In Garrison village, 4 miles north of Belleek on shores of Lough Melvin. On Enniskillen-Belleek bus route (bus goes via Garrison Tues & Thurs only). Fishing, boating, wind-surfing, bicycle hire. Pony-trekking. Camping/caravan site adjacent. 48 beds. Family rooms. Meals. From £10. Open all year.

PORTORA ROYAL SCHOOL
Derrygonnelly Rd, Enniskillen BT74 7AJ.
☎ (0365) 322658.
School on outskirts of Enniskillen. Outdoor heated swimming pool, hard tennis courts, squash courts, gym. 60 beds. From £35 per person per week. Groups only. Open 9 July-20 Aug.

THE SHARE CENTRE
Smith's Strand, Lisnaskea BT92 0EQ.
☎ (036 57) 22122, fax 21893.
Hostel and self-catering chalets. On Belfast-Enniskillen bus route, 4 miles south of Lisnaskea. Near Ulster Way. Motor sports, water sports, archery, walking, bicycle hire. Viking longship cruises. Tepee campsite. Indoor leisure complex with swimming pool. 116 beds. Meals. Variable rates. Suitable for disabled visitors/groups. Open all year.

Beds = approx number of bedspaces

WILLOW PATTERN COMPLEX
89 Crevenish Rd, Kesh BT93 1RQ.
☎ (036 56) 31012.
Dormitory accommodation, 12 miles
north-west of Enniskillen. On Enniskillen-
Kesh bus route, bus stop 2½ miles. Putting
green, tennis, fishing, boating, golf nearby.
Shop and restaurant on site. 42 beds.
Meals by arrangement. From £3.50. Open
all year.

County LONDONDERRY

CAUSEWAY COAST INDEPENDENT HOSTEL
4 Victoria Terrace, Portstewart BT55 7BA.
☎ (0265) 833789.
Terraced house by seafront. On Coleraine-
Portstewart bus route. Coleraine rail
station 3 miles. Direct bus link to Giant's
Causeway from hostel. Near Ulster Way.
Golf, pony-trekking, sea-angling, bicycle
hire nearby. 30 beds. Family rooms. From
£5. Open all year.

COLERAINE ACADEMICAL INSTITUTION
Castlerock Rd, Coleraine BT51 3LA.
☎ (0265) 44331.
School on outskirts of market town. On
Coleraine-Castlerock bus route, bus stop
50yd. Tennis, running track, gym. Near
Ulster Way. 186 beds. Meals. From £4
self-catering, £12 full board. Open 24
July-14 Aug only.

COLERAINE HIGH SCHOOL
Lodge Rd, Coleraine BT52 1LZ.
☎ (0265) 43178, fax 51499.
One mile from town centre/Coleraine rail
station. On Coleraine-Ballymoney bus
route (bus stop 50yd). Tennis, running
track, hockey pitch, gym. Near Ulster

Way. Leisure centre nearby. 34 beds.
Meals by arrangement. From £6. Open
July/ Aug only.

DERRY CITY HOSTEL
4 Magazine St, Londonderry BT48 6HJ.
☎ (0504) 372273.
New hostel (YHANI) inside walled city,
near museums, galleries, theatres, shops
and all services. 132 beds. Meals. Family
rooms. From £7. Open all year.

INDEPENDENT HOSTEL
29 Aberfoyle Terrace, Strand Rd,
Londonderry BT48 7NA.
☎ (0504) 370011.
Terraced house close to Magee College
1 mile from Derry city centre. Bus stop
10yd, bus station 1 mile. Free transport
to/from rail station. Also on Londonderry-
Lough Swilly bus route. Traditional music
venues nearby. 6 beds. From £7. Open all
year.

County TYRONE

GLENHORDIAL HOSTEL
9a Waterworks Rd, Omagh BT79 7JS.
☎ (0662) 241973, fax 241973.
New hostel 2½ miles north-east of Omagh
centre and bus station. Backpackers
picked up from station by arrangement. 30
minutes' drive/bus from Ulster-American
Folk Park, Gortin Forest Park, Fermanagh
Lakes. 3 miles off Ulster Way route. 20
beds. From £6. Open all year.

Beds = approx number of bedspaces

Key to self-catering symbols

T Bookable through travel agents
Possibilité de réservation à l'agence de voyage
Reservierung über Reisebüros möglich

P Parking spaces
Parking
Parkmöglichkeit

Building of architectural/ historical interest
Bâtiment d'intérêt architectural/historique
Architecktonisch/ historisch interessantes Gebäude

Garden for guests' use
Jardin à l'usage des résidents
Garten steht den Gästen zur Verfügung

Children welcome
Les enfants sont bienvenus
Kinderfreundlich

Cots and/or high chairs
Lits et/ou chaises d'enfants
Kinderbetten und/oder Hochstühle

Baby sitting/listening service
Service de garde d'enfants/d'écoute
Baby-Sitting/- Lauschdienst

OAP Reduced rates for senior citizens
Réduction pour les retraités
Ermäßigungen für Senioren

Accessible to people with limited mobility
Accessible aux personnes dont la mobilité est limitée
Für gehbehinderte Besucher zugänglich

Dogs accepted
Les chiens sont admis à l'intérieur
Hunde im Haus gestattet

Central heating in unit
Chauffage central dans l'appartement
Wohneinheit mit Zentralheizung

M Gas/electricity charged by meter
Gaz/électricité tariffiés au compteur
Gas- u. Stromabrechnung nach Verbrauch

Clothes washing machine
Machine à laver le linge
Waschmaschine

Clothes drying facilities
Facilités pour le séchage du linge
Möglichkeit zum Wäschetrocknen

Ironing facilities
Facilités pour le repassage
Bügeleinrichtung

Refrigerator
Réfrigérateur
Kühlschrank

Radio

Television
Télévision
Fernsehgerät

Electric shaver point
Prises pour rasoir électrique
Anschluß für Trockenrasierer

Linen provided
Linge de maison fourni
Wäsche wird gestellt

Linen available for hire
Possibilités de location du linge de maison
Wäscheverleih

Telephone exclusively for guests' use
Usage du téléphone réservé aux résidents
Telefon nur für Gäste

Food shop
Magasin d'alimentation
Lebensmittelverkauf

Licensed bar
Vente de boissons alcoolisées
Bar mit Ausschanklizenz

X Café/restaurant
Café/restaurant
Café/Restaurant

Games room
Salle de jeux
Freizeitraum

Tennis courts
Courts de tennis
Tennisplätze

Outdoor swimming pool
Piscine découverte
Freibad

Indoor heated swimming pool
Piscine couverte chauffée
Beheiztes Hallenbad

Fishing arranged
Pêche
Angelmöglichkeit

Pony trekking/riding arranged
Promenades à poney/ équitation
Pony Trekking -reiten

Credit cards accepted
Cartes de crédit acceptées
Kreditkarten akzeptiert

Self-catering

More people than ever before are enjoying the freedom of a self-catering holiday in Northern Ireland, and there is a wide range of accommodation to choose from. There are chalets and houses on secluded estates, luxury apartments in lively coastal resorts, island cottages and mansion flats in beautiful surroundings, with plenty of leisure activities and places of interest nearby.

Self-catering accommodation which may be suitable for wheelchair users but has not yet been inspected under the National Accessible Scheme is indicated by &.

All establishments listed are regularly inspected by the Northern Ireland Tourist Board (NITB) and we have every reason to believe that the accommodation will meet your expectations. If there is any kind of problem please tell the owner or manager immediately so that it can be put right without delay. If thereafter you wish to bring the matter to the Board's attention write to: Director of Visitor & Industry Services, NITB, 59 North Street, Belfast BT1 1NB.

County Antrim

Ballintoy

BRAESIDE
127 Whitepark Rd, BT54 6LS.
☎ (026 57) 62921. *(Mrs M McCullough)*.
Cottage (2 bedrooms), £130 low season,
£160 high season, open Feb-Nov.

JURA
37 Harbour Rd, BT54 6NA.
☎ (0247) 853474. *(Mrs C Belford)*.
Bungalow, £150 low season, £200 high
season, open all year.

OLD WATCH HOUSE
33 Harbour Rd, BT54 6NA.
☎ (0960) 322300. *(Mrs Bertha Craig)*.
Cottage, £150 low season, £210 high
season, open all year.

Ballycastle

BALLINLEA MILL
34 Kilmahamogue Rd, BT54 6JJ.
☎ (026 57) 62287. *(Mr C Stewart-Moore)*.
Restored mill house (3 bedrooms, sleeps
8) £200 low season, £300 high season,
open all year. Paddock.

Prices given are the weekly rate

HILLTOP APARTMENTS
14 Clare Rd, BT54 6DB.
☎ (026 57) 63519.
2 apartments (1 bedroom), £150 low season, £200 high season, open all year.

Mrs M MULHOLLAND
47c Castle St, BT54 6AS.
☎ (026 57) 62080.
Apartment (sleeps 6), £190 low season, £220 high season, open June-Sept.

Mr A MULLAN
19 Ballynagard Rd, BT54 6PW. Bookings through: 18 Kensington Gardens, Belfast BT5 6NP. ☎ (0232) 795489.
Bungalow, £125 low season, £185 high season, open all year.

MURLOUGH LODGE
10 Murlough Rd. ☎ (026 57) 62270.
(*Mr P McCarry*).
Lodge (sleeps 6), £150 low season, £200 high season, open all year.

SILVERCLIFFS HOLIDAY VILLAGE
21 Clare Rd, BT54 5DB. ☎ (026 57) 62550. Fax 62259. (*Mrs Hagan*).
19 caravans, 25 apartments, 2 chalets: £105/155 low season, £270/355 high season. Caravans, open Mar-Oct. Others open Jan-Dec. Indoor heated pool.

Ballymena

LURE COTTAGE at CLEGGAN LODGE
Broughshane BT43 7JW.
☎ (0266) 862222. Fax 862000.
Remote converted 19th-century shepherd's cottage. 3 bedrooms (sleeps 6), £250 high season, £120 low season, open all year. Open fire, spring water, pheasant/rough shooting.

MANN'S COTTAGE at CLEGGAN LODGE
Broughshane BT43 7JW.
☎ (0266) 862222. Fax 862000.
Restored 19th-century farmhouse. 3 bedrooms (sleeps 6), annex (sleeps 4), £400 high season, £250 low season, open all year. Open fires, spring water, bicycles, pheasant/rough shooting.

MEWS COTTAGES
Galgorm Manor, BT42 1EA.
☎ (0266) 881001. Fax 880080.
6 cottages (1/2 bedrooms), £175 low season, 220 high season, open all year.

HOME FARM
34 Caherty Rd, Broughshane BT42 4??.
☎ (0266) 861564.
(*Mrs Taggart*).
Cottage (sleeps 4), £230 low season, £290 high season, open all year.

Prices given are the weekly rate

Bushmills

21 BUSHFORD
Dunluce Rd, BT57 8AQ.
☎ (0266) 41547. *(Mrs M Boyce).*
Apartment (ground floor), (sleeps 4/6),
£125 low season, £175 high season, open
all year.

CRAIG COTTAGE
51 Carnbore Rd, BT57 8YF.
☎ (026 57) 31547 after 6 pm.
(Mr W J Dunlop).
£175 low season, £250 high season, open
April-Nov.

H & D DUNLOP
38 Castlecat Rd, BT57 8TN.
☎ (026 57) 31252.
Detached house (sleeps 8), £250, open all
year.

HILLVIEW
50 Carnbore Rd, BT57 8YF. ☎ (026 57)
31547 after 6 pm. *(Mrs M Dunlop).*
House (3 bedrooms), £175 low season,
£250 high season, open May-Nov. Golf,
fishing, pony trekking nearby.

**GIANT'S CAUSEWAY HOLIDAY
    COTTAGES**
71 Causeway Rd, BT57 8SX. ☎ (026 57)
31673. Fax 32533. *(Ms A Millar).*
8 cottages, £200 low season, £360 high
season, open all year. Bicycle hire.

JASMINE COTTAGE
11 Ballyclough Rd, BT57 8TU.
☎ (081 693) 2494.
Fax 2494. *(Mr A Crawford).*
Traditional style cottage (new) (sleeps 4/6),
£110 low season, £270 high season, open
all year.

ROSE COTTAGE
8 Ballyclough Cottages, BT57 8XA.
☎ (026 57) 31592 after 6 pm. *(Mrs R
Campbell).*
Cottage (2 bedrooms, sleeps 4/6), £120
low season, £280 high season, open all
year.

WALKMILLS
28a Priestland Rd, BT57 8XB.
☎ (026 57) 31261. *(Mr D Adams).*
Cottage, £200 low season, £275 high
season, open all year.

Carnlough

MRS M KANE
44 High St, BT44 0EA. ☎ (0232) 746169.
Terrace house (2 bedrooms), £115 low
season, £145 high season, open all year.

Cushendall

PORTNAGOLAN HOUSE
17 Layde Rd, BT44 0NQ.
☎ (026 67) 71239. *(Mrs L Dobbs).*
Flat (2 bedrooms), £135 low season, £160
high season, open all year.

Prices given are the weekly rate

THORNLEA HOTEL
6 Coast Rd, BT44 0RU. ☎ (026 67) 71223.
Fax 71362.
4 apartments, £90/125 (sleeps 2/3),
£175/250 (sleeps 4/6), open all year.

Cushendun

ASH COTTAGE
30 Glendun Rd, BT44 0PX. ☎ (0247)
463249. *(Mr D McKenna).*
Bungalow, £190 low season, £240 high
season, open Jan-Nov.

Mrs W McKAY
107a Knocknacarry Rd, BT44 0NT.
☎ (026 674) 513.
Apartment, £125 low season, £170 high
season, open all year.

TYBANN HOUSE APARTMENTS
51 Glendun Rd, BT44 0PY.
☎ (026 674) 289. *(Mrs M McNeill).*
4 apartments and 2 houses, £120/190 low
season, £190/240 high season, open all
year.

Glenarm

BRIARFIELD
65 Dickeystown Rd, BT44 0BA.
☎ (0574) 841296. *(Mrs C Matthews).*
Cottage-style farmhouse, (sleeps 4), £110
low season, £210 high season, open all
year.

UPPER BRIARFIELD
67 Dickeystown Rd, BT44 0BA.
☎ (0574) 841296. *(Mrs C Matthews).*
Country house, £100 low season, £110
high season, open all year.

Portballintrae

ATLANTIC HOUSE APARTMENTS
55 Beach Rd, BT57 8RT. ☎ (026 57)
31453. Fax 32360. *(Mr S Sweeney).*
Town house, 6 flats (sleeps 4/6), £120 low
season, £265 high season, open all year.

GLENVILLE
Bayhead Rd, BT57 8SB. ☎ (026 57) 31453.
Fax 32360. *(Mr S Sweeney).*
6 apartments, sleeps 5-6, £250, open all
year.

RUNKERRY VIEW
11 Benbane Park, BT57 8SB.
☎ (0265) 57445. Fax 55290.
(Mr & Mrs A Kennedy).
Chalet bungalow with patio (2 bedrooms,
sleeps 4/5), £125 low season, £295 high
season, open all year.

Prices given are the weekly rate

THE OLD BARN
6a Seaport Avenue, BT57 8SB. ☎ (026 57) 31453. Fax 32360. *(Mr S Sweeney).* Converted 18th-century coach house (3 bedrooms), £150 low season, £325 high season, open all year.

STRANDVIEW
7 Bushfoot Drive, BT57 8YW. ☎ (0265) 43057. *(Mrs A Wilson).* House (sleeps 5), £135 low season, £290 high season, open all year.

STRAWBRIDGE HOUSE
39 Bushfoot Rd, Bushmills, BT57 8RR. ☎ (026 57) 31215. *(Lady Macnaghten).* Restored historic farmhouse overlooking sea, divided into 2 houses, each with 3 bedrooms (sleeps 5/6), from £170 to £375, open all year. Golf. 300 yds from 1¹/₂ miles of private salmon fishing.

Portrush

ASHLEA COTTAGES
39 Magheraboy Rd, BT56 8MX. ☎ (0265) 824057/822779. *(Mr & Mrs T Houston).* 5 cottages (sleep 4/6), £120 low season, £260 high season, open all year. 2 chalets (sleeps 8), £200 low season, £350 high season, open all year.

BALLINAHONE
160 Causeway St, BT56 8JE. ☎ (064 87) 37160. *(Mrs M Wright).* House (sleeps 5/7), £150 low season, £170 high season, open June-Sept.

BEACH HEAD
25 Kerr St, BT66 8DG. ☎ (0265) 823666. *(Mr & Mrs G McClay).* Terrace house, £120/150 low season, £300 high season, open June-Sept.

CRAIGVARA COTTAGE
6 Craigvara, BT56 8AJ. ☎ (026 56) 62329. *(Mrs K Connolly).* House (sleeps 6), £85 low season, £200 high season, open all year.

Mr J DIXON
105 Golf Terrace, BT56 8DZ. ☎ (0265) 848421. 3 apartments (sleeps 4), £40 low season, £140 high season, open April-Sept.

JACARANDA HOUSE
Golden Triangle Apartments, 58 Dhu Varren, BT56 8EW. ☎ (0265) 822410. *(Mr G Neill).* 3 apartments (sleeps 6/7), £90 low season, £220 high season, open June-Sept.

Mr & Mrs J MILLIKEN
33 Glen Crescent, BT56 8LL. ☎ (0265) 823823. Bungalow (sleeps 6), £175 low season, £275 high season, open all year.

Prices given are the weekly rate

O'NEILL'S CAUSEWAY COAST APARTMENTS
36 Ballyreagh Rd, BT56 8LR.
☎ (0265) 822435. Fax 824495.
20 apartments (3 bedrooms, sleeps 8),
£250 low season, £350 high season, open
all year.

RAWHITA
20 Mark St, BT56 8BT. ☎ (0265) 823666.
(Mr & Mrs McClay).
Terrace house (sleeps 14), £120/150 low
season, £300 high season.

SEAVIEW
16 Ballyreagh Rd, BT56 8LR.
☎ (0265) 52153. *(Mrs B MacAfee)*.
Bungalow (5 bedrooms), £160 low
season, £220 high season, open June-Sept.

Mrs E STRINGER
Flats 3/4 10 Mount Royal, BT56 8DA.
☎ (0265) 822314.
2 flats. £130 low season, £180 high
season, open June-Sept.

TARA APARTMENTS
1/4 Dhu Varren Park, BT56 8EL.
☎ (084 94) 28526. *(Mrs T Harbison)*.
6 flats (sleeps 4/6), £175 low season, £210
high season, open June-Sept.

(1 Dhu Varren Park)

(4 Dhu Varren Park)

Waterfoot

RED BAY HOUSE
233 Garron Rd, BT44 0RB.
☎ (026 67) 71396. *(Mrs McKillop)*.
Cottage (sleeps 6), £200 low season, £250
high season, open all year.

County Armagh

Armagh

THE CHALET
Dean's Hill, 34 College Hill, BT61 9DF.
☎ (0861) 522099. *(Mrs M Armstrong)*.
Chalet in courtyard of Georgian house,
£60 low season, £80 high season, open all
year.

Forkhill

BENBREE
67 Carrive Rd, BT35 9TE.
☎ (0693) 888394. *(Mrs B Watters)*.
House, 3 bedrooms, £120 low season,
£160 high season, open all year.

Mrs L McCREESH
139 Longfield Rd, BT35 9SD.
☎ (0693) 888314.
Cottage (sleeps 5), £80 low season, £90
high season, open all year.

Prices given are the weekly rate

Mrs M McDONNELL
15 Forest Rd, Longfield, BT35 9SA.
☎ (0693) 65791.
Cottage (sleeps 5), £100 low season, £130 high season, open all year.

County Down

Annalong

BINNIAN REST
80 Brackenagh West Rd, Ballymartin.
BT34 4PP.
☎ (069 37) 63341. *(Mr & Mrs R Gracey).*
Cottage (sleeps 4), £160 low season, £180 high season, open all year.

MANX VIEW
257 Kilkeel Rd, BT34 4TW.
☎ (069 37) 63222. *(Miss M Bingham).*
Cottage (sleeps 3), £160 low season, £180 high season, open all year.

MOURNE COTTAGE
80 Brackenagh West Rd, Ballymartin,
BT34 4PP.
☎ (069 37) 63341. *(Mr R Gracey).*
Traditional cottage (2 bedrooms), £150 low season, £170 high season, open all year.

Bangor

INNISFREE
82 Dufferin Avenue, BT20 3AD.
☎ (0247) 472128. *(Mrs J Martin).*
1 flat (sleeps 5/6), £150 low season, £200 high season; 1 flat (sleeps 3), £150/200, open all year.

Mrs A THOMPSON
7 Albert St, BT20 5ES. ☎ (0247) 461423.
Town house (4 bedrooms, sleeps 6/8), £200 low season, £220 high season, open all year.

MRS A THOMPSON
1 Alfred St, BT20 5DH. ☎ (0247) 461423.
House, £175 low season, £200 high season, open all year.

Castlewellan

WILD FOREST COTTAGE
28 Ballyhafrey Rd, BT34 0PS. ☎ (039 67) 68451. Fax 67041(Glassdrumman Lodge).
(Mrs J Hall).
Cottage (sleeps 8), £250 low season, £500 high season, open all year.

Craigavad

EDMORE COTTAGE
38 Ballygrainey Rd, BT18 0HE. ☎ (0232) 423159. *(Mr & Mrs W Henderson).*
Cottage (2 bedrooms, sleeps 5), £225, open all year.

Prices given are the weekly rate

Downpatrick

THE BARN
53 Killyleagh Rd, Crossgar, BT30 9EE.
☎ (0396) 830792. *(Mrs M Davison).*
Flat (sleeps 6), £140 low season, £150
high season, open all year.

[icons]

Dundrum

MURLOUGH HOLIDAY COTTAGES
Widows Row, South Promenade, BT33
0NG. *(National Trust).* ☎ (0238) 510721
or NT central reservations (0225) 704545.
2 cottages, £135 low season, £260 high
season, open all year.

[icons]

Groomsport

EVETIDE
13 Sandeel Lane, Orlock, BT19 2LP.
☎ (0232) 798247/(0247) 883511.
(Mrs H Crowe).
House (3 bedrooms), £100 low season,
£150 high season, open all year.

[icons]

Kilkeel

CRANFIELD CHALETS
Cranfield Rd, BT34 4LJ.
☎ (069 37) 62745/64518. Fax 63022.
(W & R Coulter).
6 bungalows (2 bedrooms), £125 low
season, £170 high season, open all year.

[icons]

HILLVIEW
18 Bog Rd, Attical BT34 0JY.
☎ (069 37) 64269. *(Mrs M Trainor).*
Ground floor apartment (2 bedrooms,
sleeps 8) in heart of Mournes, £100 low
season, £200 high season, open all year.

[icons]

JIRAH
91 Greencastle Rd, BT34 4JL. ☎ (0238)
561885. *(Mr & Mrs B Henderson).*
Large bungalow (sleeps 12/13), £120 low
season, £140 high season, open all year.

[icons]

WYNCREST CHALET
30a Main Rd, Ballymartin, BT34 4NU.
☎ (069 37) 63012. *(Mrs J Adair).*
Chalet, £150 low season, £150 high
season, open April-Sept.

[icons]

Killinchy

AULDS CLOSE COTTAGES
17 Ballymacreely Rd, BT23 6RP.
☎ (0238) 541670. Fax (0247) 820085.
(Mrs R Morrison).
2 stone-built cottages, 1 (sleeps 2), 2
(sleeps 4/6), £130/200 low season,
£175/295 high season, open all year.

[icons]

ROCKLIN
5 Braddock Reach, Whiterock, BT23 6PY.
☎ (0396) 828901. Fax (0232) 642498,
(D N Lindsay).
Bungalow (3 bedrooms), £200 low
season, £300 high season, open all year.

[icons]

Prices given are the weekly rate

Killyleagh

DUFFERIN HOUSE
38 High St, BT30 9QF. (*Mr Crawford or Ms Stewart*). ☎ (0396) 828229.
3 apartments (sleeps 6/7). £130, open all year. Bicycle hire.

Kircubbin

BLOODYBURN COTTAGE
Nunsquarter, BT22 2RP. ☎ (024 77) 38379. Fax 38379. (*Mrs G Gilmore*).
Cottage (sleeps 2), £175, open all year.

Millisle

COACH HOUSE
Eastonville, 93 Donaghadee Rd, BT22 2BZ.
☎ (0247) 888910. (*Mrs E McDermott*).
Apartment in former coach house (1 bedroom, sleeps 2), £150 low season, £150 high season, open all year.

Newcastle

BEVERLEY ANNEX
72 Tullymore Rd, BT33 0JN.
☎ (039 67) 22018. (*Mrs McNeilly*).
Apartment (sleeps 4), £135 low season, £165 high season, open all year.

BEVERLEY COTTAGE
72 Tollymore Rd, BT33 0JN.
☎ (039 67) 22018. (*Mrs McNeilly*).
Stone built cottage (sleeps 4), £140 low season, £165 high season, open all year.

DIAMOND COTTAGE
110a Tullybrannigan Rd, BT33 0PW.
☎ (039 67) 22687. (*Brendan Downey*).
Flat (sleeps 4), £125 low season, £200 high season, open all year.

IVYDENE COTTAGE
112 Dundrum Rd, BT33 0LN.
☎ (039 67) 22009. (*Mr & Mrs Donnelly*).
Cottage (sleeps 7), £145 low season, £185 in high season, open all year.

THE MEWS
81 Burrenreagh Rd, Bryansford,
BT33 0PU. ☎ (039 67) 24698. Fax 24698.
(*Mrs M Railton*).
In historic country house, £160 low season, £180 high season, open all year.
Tennis courts.

Mrs C MURPHY
16 Marguerite Court. ☎ (039 67) 24253.
Modern town house (3/4 bedrooms), £160 low season, £240 high season, open all year.

Prices given are the weekly rate

Mrs M C MURRAY
136 Tullybrannigan Rd, BT33 0PW.
☎ (039 67) 22628.
Mobile home (sleeps 6), £75 low season,
£130 high season, open all year.

Mr M NUGENT
58 Main St, BT33 0AE.
☎ (039 67) 23492. Fax 23472.
2 units (sleep 4/5), £160 low season,
£280 high season.

Mr J NUGENT
85 Central Promenade, BT33 0HH.
☎ (039 67) 24647.
2 apartments (sleeps 4/5), £200/300,
open all year.

ROCKVILLE
165 Central Promenade, BT33 0EU.
☎ (0232) 642716. *(Mrs M Doherty).*
Apartment (sleeps 6), £200 low season,
£255 high season, open all year.

ROSE COTTAGE
46 Tollymore Rd, BT33 0JN.
☎ (039 67) 22018. *(Mrs E McNeilly).*
House (2 bedrooms, sleeps 6), £225 low
season, £300 high season, open all year.
Close to Mournes, beach and forest parks.

Miss P K SPEEDY
Widows Row, 161 South Promenade,
BT33 0HA. ☎ (039 67) 22642.
Cottage (historic interest), £185 low
season, £230 high season, open all year.

WAYSIDE
22 Dundrum Rd, BT33 0BG. ☎ (039 67)
23911. *(Mrs J Murray)*
Mobile home (sleeps 6), £40 low season,
£130 high season, open all year.

WYLLIE COTTAGE
17 Bryansford Village, BT33 0PT.
☎ (0238) 562800. *(Mr & Mrs Maguire).*
Cottage (3 bedrooms), £180 low season,
£240 high season, open all year.

Newry

FREEDUFF COTTAGE
43 Cregganduff Rd, Cullyhanna,
BT35 0NA. ☎ (0693) 861271.
(Ms M Quinn).
Bungalow (3 bedrooms), £100 low
season, £160 high season, open all year.

GRINAN LODGE
49 Greenan Rd, BT34 2PZ.
☎ (0693) 61992. *(Mrs Farrell).*
House (sleeps 6), £160 low season, £200
high season, open all year.

ROSE COTTAGE
4 Drumalt Rd, Silverbridge, BT35 9LQ.
☎ (0693) 861543. *(P Mackin).*
Cottage (2 bedrooms), £100 low season,
£140 high season, open all year.

Prices given are the weekly rate

Mrs C WRIGHT/Mrs A FEENAN
2 Archview Terrace, Craigmore,
BT35 7AF. ☎ (0693) 838484.
Cottage (sleeps 4), £120 low season, £140
high season, open all year.

Portaferry

CAMOMILE
9 Steel Dickson Avenue, BT22 1LG.
☎ (024 77) 28541. *(Mrs S Gargan)*.
Terrace cottage, £90 low season, £120
high season, open May-Sept.

Rathfriland

FORTH COTTAGE
67 Lisnacroppin Rd, BT34 5NZ.
☎ (0232) 666644. *(Mrs H Harper)*.
Cottage (2 bedrooms), £160 low season,
£220 high season, open all year.

Rostrevor

LECALE COTTAGES
125 Kilbroney Rd, BT34 3BW.
☎ (069 37) 38727. Fax 38965.
(Mr Baxter).
Cottages (sleep 6), £150, open all year.

Strangford

POTTER'S COTTAGE
Castle Ward, BT30 7LS. *(National Trust)*.
Stone cottage (1 bedroom, sleeps 4), £120
low season, £220 high season, open all
year.

TERENICHOL 1 & 2
Castle Ward, BT30 7LS. *(National Trust)*.
2 flats (sleeps 8), £150 low season, £365
high season, open all year.

*Bookings through National Trust,
Castleward ☎ (0396) 881204 or
NT Central Reservations (0225) 704545.*

County Fermanagh

Ballinamallard

SCHOOL HOUSE
31 Rossfad Rd, Whitehill, BT74 8AL.
☎ (0846) 675261/(0232) 614629.
(Mr & Mrs J Magee).
House (5 bedrooms), £150 low season,
£180 high season, open all year.

Prices given are the weekly rate

Belcoo

Mr & Mrs CATTERALL
Corralea Forest Lodge, Corralea,
BT93 5DZ. ☎ (036 586) 325.
6 bungalows (sleeps 4), £155 low season,
£210 high season, open March-Oct. Set in
50 acres of woodland.

G & B HOLIDAY HOMES
Forthill, BT94 1FY.
☎ (036 586) 261. *(G & B Ferguson).*
2 cottages (2 bedrooms), £175 low
season, £200 high season. Open all year.
Boat and engine for hire.

Belleek

CARLTON COTTAGES
Belleek, BT93 3FX. ☎ (036 56) 58181.
Fax 58181.
14 cottages, £225 low season, £395 high
season, open all year. Information centre.
Fishing on site, sea fishing trips, bicycle
hire.

CHIMNEY HOUSE
Drumnisaleen. ☎ (036 56) 58755.
(Mr McCafferty).
House (sleeps 6), £150 low season, £250
high season, open all year. Boat and pony
free of charge.

GIL-MAR LODGE
2 Cliff Rd, BT93 3FY. ☎ (0232) 705112.
(Mr W J Gilmartin).
House (4 bedrooms, sleeping 7) £150 low
season, £250 high season, open all year.

GLENROSS
454 Boa Island Rd, Ross Harbour, Leggs,
BT93 2AD. ☎ (0846) 683656.
(Ms C Hamilton).
Bungalow (sleeps 8), £230 low season,
£300 high season, open all year. Private
jetty and beach.

THE BUNGALOW
Rosscor Bridge Rd, Tawnynoran, Rosscor,
BT93 3DB. ☎ (0923) 265759.
(Mr & Mrs P Irving).
Bungalow (2 bedrooms), £160 low
season, £190 high season, open all year.

LOUGH ERNE COTTAGES
Bolusty, Rosscor, BT74 7BW.
☎ (0365) 322608/(036 565) 305.
Fax 322967. *(Mr Richardson).*
3 modern bungalows, (1-3 bedrooms),
£140/210 low season, £250/350 high
season; penthouse £290 low season, £400
high season, open Feb-Dec.

Prices given are the weekly rate

Mrs B McAULEY
Meadow Brook, Laughill, BT93 3DH.
☎ (010 353) 725 1248.
Bungalow, £150 low season, £215 high
season, open all year.

Derrygonnelly

BLANEY BAY and INNISH BEG
COTTAGES
Innishbeg, Blaney, BT93 7EP.
☎ (036 564) 525. (Mrs G Tottenham).
2 cottages (sleeps 10), £130/150 low
season, £220/270 high season, open all
year. Rowing boat, private shore.

ROCKFAD
25 Doagh Rd, BT93 6HW.
☎ (036 564) 276. (Mr G Ferguson).
House, £150 low season, £250 high
season, open all year.

Enniskillen

COACH HOUSE
80 Irvinestown Rd, BT74 6DN.
☎ (0365) 325789. (Mrs R Wilkinson).
House (2 bedrooms), £170 low season,
£220 high season, open all year. Boat
available.

CORVILLA COTTAGE
Corravehy, Kinawley, BT92 4AF.
☎ (036 57) 48311. (Mr R Martin).
Cottages (2 bedroom), £150 low season,
£195 high season, open all year.

THE COTTAGE
Killyreagh, Tamlaght, BT74 7HA.
☎ (0365) 87221. (Lord A Hamilton).
Cottage (sleeps 7), £150 low season, £275
high season, open all year.

THE DIAMOND HOUSE
Derrymacausey, Derrylin, BT92 9NU.
☎ (0365) 748274. (Mary McDaid).
Farmhouse (3 bedrooms), £150 low
season, £250 high season, open all year.

DRUMCOO LODGE
30 Cherryville, Carnagrade Rd, BT74 4FY.
☎ (0365) 326672. (Mrs H Farrell).
Bungalow (sleeps 5), £200 low season,
£240 high season, open all year. Tackle
and bait storage.

DRUMCOO WORK CENTRE
3 Devenish Crescent, Silverhill, BT74 5JP.
☎ (0365) 324339.
Bungalow (4 bedrooms), (sleeps 8), £35,
open all year. Adapted for disabled
people.

Prices given are the weekly rate

ELY ISLAND CHALETS
Ely Island, BT93 7EG. ☎ (0365) 341777.
Fax 341328. *(Mr C Plunket).*
10 log cabins (3 bedrooms), £250 low
season, £350 high season, open all year.
Rainbow trout fishing on private lake.
Boat and engine included. Jetty and
slipway. Walks in 277-acre estate.

THE OLD SCHOOL
Ballycassidy, BT94 2LY.
☎ (0365) 323030. *(Mr A Johnston).*
Cottage (2 bedrooms, sleeps 4), £120 low
season, £160 high season. Boat for hire.
Clay pigeon shooting. Open all year.

KILLYHEVLIN CHALETS
Dublin Rd, BT74 4AU.
☎ (0365) 323481. Fax 324726.
13 chalets (2 bedrooms), £260 low
season, £330 high season, open all year.

LARAGH
Ballycassidy, BT74 2JT. ☎ (0365) 323838.
(Mrs E West).
Bungalow, (4 bedrooms, sleeps 6), £160/
190, open all year. Boating, forest parks.

MANOR HOUSE CHALETS
Rockfield, Killadeas, BT94 1NY.
☎ (036 56) 28100. Fax 28000.
12 chalets (2 bedrooms), £275 low
season, £325 high season, open all year.
Boats and cruisers for hire. Pitch & putt,
bicycle hire, barbecue site.

Mr & Mrs D ROLSTON
16 Mullinaskea Rd, Garvery, BT74 4QR.
☎ (0365) 323246.
Large bungalow on farm, £185 low
season, £200 high season, open all year.

ROSS HOUSE
Corragole, Kinawley, BT92 9DW.
☎ (036 57) 48518. *(Mrs Finlay).*
House (sleeps 7), £165 low
season, £200 high season, open all year.

Florencecourt

THE CHALET
Rossaa, BT92 1BR.
☎ (0365) 348317/322727 before 7 pm.
(Mrs A Reid).
Chalet (3 bedrooms), £130 low season,
£190 high season, open all year.

MELVIN COTTAGES
Garrison, BT93 4ET. ☎ (0365) 326747.
Fax 326145.
4 cottages (sleep 6/7), £150/210 low
season, £285 high season, open all year.

Prices given are the weekly rate

ROSE COTTAGE
Florence Court Demesne, BT92 1DB
(National Trust).
☎ (0365) 348249/348788 or NT central
reservations (0225) 704545.
Walled garden cottage (sleeps 4), £150
low season, £330 high season, open all
year.

Garrison

ROSSMORE HOUSE
Muckenagh, BT93 4FA.
☎ (036 56) 58476. *(B Flanagan).*
House (sleeps 8), £300 low season, £350
high season, open all year. Boat.

Irvinestown

WOODHILL HUNTING LODGE
Derrynanny, BT94 1QA.
☎ (036 56) 21863/21795.
(Thomas Dayne).
Two-storey house, £200 low season, £250
high season, open all year.

Kesh

CALDRAGH HOUSE
Dreenan, Boa Island, BT93 8AA.
☎ (0365) 631660. *(Mr & Mrs L Fivey).*
Two-storey detached house, £200 low
season, £260 high season, open all year.

THE VILLA & THE ANNEX
89 Crevenish Rd, Clareview, BT93 1RB.
☎ (036 56) 31012. *(Mrs E Baxter).*
2 chalets (sleep 4/5), £120/145 low
season, £175 high season, open all year.

THE COTTAGE
Manville House, Letter, BT93 2BF.
☎ (036 56) 31668. *(Mrs Graham).*
Cottage (2 bedrooms), £180 low season,
£190 high season, open all year.

ERNE SEE
Clonaweel, BT93 8DD.
☎ (036 56) 31771. *(Mrs H Johnston).*
(On A35, 3m W of Kesh).
Bungalow (3 bedrooms), £150 low
season, £175 high season, open all year.

FERMANAGH LAKELAND LODGES
Muckross Wood, Letter, BT93 2BF.
☎ (0232) 342872/(036 56) 31957.
(Mr R Beare).
12 chalets (sleeps 6/8), £250/350 low
season, £420 high season, open all year.
Boat for hire, bicycles, nature trails.

HAREVIEW COTTAGE
Boa Island, BT93 8AN.
☎ (036 56) 32070. *(Mr McCaffery).*
Bungalow (sleeps 6), £220 low season,
£250/325 high season, open all year.

Prices given are the weekly rate

LETTERKEEN
Boa Island Rd, BT93 1RF. ☎ (036 56)
32102. *(Mr & Mrs A Mahon).*
Cottage (3 bedrooms), £150 low season,
£190 high season, open April-Sept.

LUSTY BEG
Boa Island, BT93 8AD. ☎ (036 56) 32032.
Fax 32033.
Cabins (sleeps 4), £300 low season, £350
high season, open all year.

RAILWAY COTTAGE
Ederney Rd, BT93 1TF. ☎ (036 56) 31096.
(Mrs N Stronge).
Cottage (sleeps 4-6), £150 low season,
£170 high season, open all year.

Lisbellaw

ANNANDALE
Derryvullan Rd, Tamlaght, BT74 4LW.
☎ (0365) 87907/87270. *(Mrs E Johnston).*
House (sleeps 6), £200/280, weekends
£80, open all year.

BRIDGE HOUSE
Belle Isle Estate, BT94 5HG.
☎ (0365) 87231. Fax 87261.
(Sir B Mulholland).
House (3 bedrooms), £175/225 low
season, £310 high season, open all year.

THE GARDEN HOUSE
Belle Isle Estate, BT94 5HG.
☎ (0365) 87231. Fax 87261.
Modern single-storey house (3 bedrooms,
sleeps 6), £165/215 low season, £295
high season, open all year.

GLEN COTTAGE
Belle Isle Estate, BT94 5HG. ☎ (0365)
87231. Fax 87261. Cottage (2 bedrooms),
£110/160 low season, £195 high season,
open all year.

HAMILTON WING
Belle Isle Estate, BT94 5HG. ☎ (0365)
87231. Fax 87261. Self-contained wing of
listed mansion (5 bedrooms) from £800,
open all year.

WALLED GARDEN COTTAGE
Belle Isle Estate, BT94 5HG.
☎ (0365) 87231. Fax 87261. Traditional
cottage, £175/225 low season, £310 high
season, open all year.

RAMAS COTTAGE
4 Drumhirk Rd, Innishmore, BT94 5LD.
☎ (0365) 87183. *(Mrs R Dunn).*
Cottage (sleeps 4), £110/125 low season,
£140 high season, open all year.

RATHSIDE
Whinnigan Glebe, BT74 4NL.
☎ (0365) 87278. *(Mrs I Carrothers).*
House (3 bedrooms), £160, open June-
Sept.

Prices given are the weekly rate

Lisnaskea

CORRADILLAR
Corradillar Quay, BT92 0ES. ☎ (036 57)
21165 after 6 pm. *(Mr & Mrs Clifford)*.
Bungalow (2 bedrooms, sleeps 4/8), £150
low season, £200 high season, open all
year.

IDLEWILD
Derryad, BT92 0BX. ☎ 081-567 4487. Fax
567 4487. *(Mr E Dawson)*.
Lakeside villa (sleeps 10), £200/250 low
season, £350/400 high season, open all
year. Free use of boat and private jetty.

INNISFREE COTTAGE
Derryad, BT92 0BX. ☎ 081-567 4487.
Fax 567 4487. *(Dr W Dawson)*.
Lakeside cottage (sleeps 5), £160 low
season, £280 high season, open all year.
Free use of boat and private jetty.

KILMORE SOUTH HOLIDAY CHALETS
Kilmore, BT92 0DT. ☎ (0247) 472118.
(Mr G N Hopes).
6 chalets, £100 low season, £250 high
season, open Easter-Nov. Fishing boat for
hire. Games room, café and restaurant.

SHARE CENTRE
Smith's Strand, Shanaghy, BT92 0EQ.
☎ (036 57) 22122. Fax 21893.
16 chalets (sleeps 4/12), £200 low season,
£265 high season (for 8 berth), open all
year. Sports instruction for disabled.

Maguiresbridge

OLD SCHOOL HOUSE
Littlemount, BT94 4RS.
☎ (0365) 53709. *(Mrs D Kerr)*.
School house (sleeps 6), £170/200 low
season, £250 high season, open all year.

Newtownbutler

CLINCORICK
16 Clincorick Rd, BT92 6ET.
☎ (03657) 38696. *(Mr & Mrs McCabe)*.
Bungalow (3 bedrooms, sleeps 10), £115
low season, £160 high season, open all
year.

THREE OAKS HOUSE
Ports BT92 8DT. ☎ (036 57) 38456.
(Mr P V Clarke).
House (5 bedrooms), £160 low season,
£280 high season.

Tempo

DOON LODGE
Windyridge, Doon, Tempo, BT94 3GQ.
☎ (0365) 54282. *(Mr & Mrs E Campbell)*.
2 houses(2/3 bedrooms), £180 low
season, £200 high season, open all year.
Boat for hire. Barbecue.

Prices given are the weekly rate

County Londonderry

Bellaghy

LOUGH BEG COACH HOUSES
Ballyscullion Park, BT45 8NA.
☎ (0648) 386235. Fax 386416.
6 houses (each 3 bedrooms, sleeps 8), in courtyard of estate. £300 low season, £350 high season, open all year.

Castlerock

SEAVIEW
20 Bogtown Cottages, Ballywoolen Rd, BT51 4XE. ☎ (081 693) 2494. Fax 2494. *(Mr A Crawford).*
House (4 bedrooms), £140 low season, £250 high season, open all year.

Mr & Mrs J MOODY
229b Mussenden Rd, BT51 4TY.
☎ (0265) 848234.
Bungalow, £150 low season, £190 high season, open June-Sept.

Claudy

RIO GRANDE
207 Learmount Rd, Park, BT47 4DF.
☎ (050 47) 81210. *(Mrs McElhinney).*
Apartment (sleeps 6), £160, open June-Sept.

Eglinton

LONGFIELD FARM COTTAGES
140 Clooney Rd, BT47 3DX.
☎ (0504) 810952.
3 cottages (sleep 5), £150 low season, £220 high season, open all year.

Coleraine

BALLYVENNOY
80 Ringrash Rd, BT51 4LJ. ☎ (0265) 51367. *(Mr & Mrs W King).*
Cottages (sleeps 4/6), £145 low season, £165 high season, open all year.

BREEZEMOUNT HOUSE
26 Castlerock Rd, BT51 3HP. ☎ (0265) 44615. Fax 43641. *(Mr W Wallace).*
2 flats (1 bedroom), £150 low season, £200 high season, open all year.

Limavady

GOLDEN SANDS
Benone Avenue, Magilligan, BT49 0LQ.
☎ (050 47) 50324. Fax 50405.
(J & S Walls).
6 caravans (8 berths), £180/200 low season, £210/230 high season, open April-Oct.

Prices given are the weekly rate

WILLOW COTTAGE
141 Seacoast Rd, BT49 9EG.
☎ (050 47) 62574. *(Mrs H Smithson).*
Cottage (2 bedrooms), £125 low season,
£160 high season, open all year.

P ❋ 🏇 ▥ ▦ M ∥ ◢ 🗄 💻 ☉ 🛏 ♩ ∪

Portstewart

MR & MRS H McCORMICK
18 Seahaven Court, BT55 7DS.
☎ (0232) 761547.
Bungalow (sleeps 4), £240, open June-
Sept.

P ❋ 🏇 ▥ ◨ ∥ ◢ 🗄 📠 💻 ☉ 🛏

Mr & Mrs H McCORMICK
20 Strandview Avenue, BT55 7LL.
☎ (0232) 761547.
Bungalow (3 bedrooms - sleeps 6), £130
low season, £300 high season, open all
year.

P ❋ 🏇 ▥ ◨ ∥ ◢ 🗄 📠 💻 ☉ 🛏

ROCK CASTLE COTTAGES
Rock Castle, Berne Rd, BT55 7PB.
☎ (0265) 832271. Fax 53421. *(S Pollock).*
4 apartments (2 bedrooms), from £130
low season, £450 high season, open all
year. Outdoor swimming pool (unheated).

🆃 P 🏠 ❋ ▥ M ◢ 🗄 💻 ☉ 🛏 ∿ ♩ ∪

YORK
2 Station Rd, BT55 7DA. ☎ (0265)
833594. *(Mr & Mrs Henderson).*
8 apartments (sleeps 3), £210 low season,
£350 high season, open all year.

P 🏠 🏇 ▥ ▥ ◨ 💻 ☉ 🛏 🍴 📞 🍷 ✕ ◀ ♩ ∪

County Tyrone

Clogher

ASHFIELD PARK
8 Ashfield Rd, BT76 0HF. ☎ (066 25)
48684. *(Mr & Mrs W Beattie).*
Flat (ground floor, sleeps 6/8), £150 low
season, £175 high season, open all year.

P 🏠 ❋ 🏇 ▥ ➡ OAP 🐕 ▥ M ◨ ∥ ◢ 🗄 📠 💻
☉ 🛏 🍴 📞

Dungannon

Miss N BRADLEY
The Residence, 52 Trewmount Rd,
Killyman, BT71 6RL. ☎ (086 87) 23188.
Fax 071-235 8542.
House (3 bedrooms), £300, open all year.

P ❋ 🏇 ➡ ▥ ◨ ∥ ◢ 🗄 📠 💻 ☉ 🛏 🐾 ♩ ∪

MULEANY COTTAGE
86 Gorestown Rd, Moy BT71 7EX.
☎ (086 87) 84183. *(Mr & Mrs B Mullen).*
Cottage (2 bedrooms, sleeps 4/6), £150
low season, £175 high season, open all
year.

P ❋ 🏇 ▥ ➡ OAP ▥ M ◨ ∥ ◢ 🗄 📠 💻 ☉ 🛏
🍴 ◐ ♩ ∪ ♿

Fivemiletown

Capt R M LOWRY
Blessingbourne, BT75 0QS.
☎ (036 55) 21221.
2 apartments (2 bedrooms), £220 low
season, £250 high season, open all year.
Use of rowing boats on private lake.

P ❋ 🏇 ▥ ⅋ 🐕 ▥ M ◨ ∥ ◢ 🗄 💻 ☉ 🛏 📞 🍷
✕ ◀ ◐ ♩ ∪ ♿

Prices given are the weekly rate

Newtownstewart

BARONSCOURT COTTAGES
Golf Course Rd, BT78 4HU.
☎ (066 26) 61013/62021. Fax 61900.
(Mr & Mrs A K Scott).
9 cottages (2 and 3 bedrooms), £220 low
season, £250 high season, open all year.
Private lake. Golf, windsurfing, water
skiing, clay pigeon shooting.

FISHERMAN'S LODGE
33 Moyle Rd, BT78 4AP.
☎ (066 26) 61450. *(Mrs M Coulter).*
Lodge (sleeps 2), £50 low season, £75
high season, open all year.

Omagh

GORTIN GLEN COTTAGE
186 Glen Park Rd, Gortin, BT79 8PT.
☎ (0662) 249242. *(Ms D Brogan).*
Forester's cottage in Gortin Glen.
£100/150 low season, £200 high season,
open all year.

LISLAP COTTAGES
Gortin, Lisnaharney Rd, BT79 7UE.
☎ (066 26) 48108. *(F Sweeney).*
Cottages (1-2 bedrooms), some suitable
for disabled, £80/175 low season,
£140/275 high season, open all year.

Mrs R MITCHELL
11 Leardin Rd, Gortin, BT79 8QD.
☎ (0762) 326857.
Cottage, £150 low season, £200 high
season, open all year.

Stewartstown

ERIN DENE
98 Knockanroe Rd, BT71 5NA.
☎ (064 87) 62606. *(Mr & Mrs T Gibson).*
Modern bungalow, £280 low season.
£300 high season (including heating and
electric), open all year.

Key to camping & caravan symbols

Spaces for touring caravans
Les caravanes sont admises
Aufnahme von Wohnwagen

Spaces for motor caravans
Les camping-cars sont admis
Aufnahme von Wohnmobilen

Spaces for tents
Les tentes sont admises
Aufnahme von Zelten

Dogs admitted on lead
Les chiens sont admis en laisse
Hunde nur an der Leine

Showers
Douches
Duschen

Electric points for shavers
Prises électriques pour rasoirs
Elektroanschlüsse für Rasierapparate

Electricity supply to pitches
Prises électriques conjugués pour caravanes
Elektro-Gemein-schaftsanschluß für Wohnwagen

Gas cylinders for hire
Cartouches de gaz à louer
Austausch von Gaszylindern

Booking recommended in summer
Il est prudent de réserver l'été
Im sommer empfiehlt sich Voranmeldung

Café/restaurant
Café/restaurant
Café/Restaurant

Food shop/mobile shop
Magasin ou camion épicerie
Lebensmittelladen

Public telephone
Téléphone public
Öffentlicher Fernsprecher

Laundry facilities
Machine à laver
Waschmaschine

Lounge/television room
Salle de télévision
Fernsehraum

Games/sports area
Terrain réservé aux jeux et sports
Sportplatz

Children's playground
Terrain de jeux pour enfants
Kinderspielplatz

Facilities nearby

Indoor swimming pool
Piscine couverte
Hallenbad

Tennis courts
Courts de tennis
Tennisplätze

Golf

Riding/pony trekking
Equitation ou poney
Reiten/Pony-Trekking

Boating
Bateau ou voile
Bootfahren/Segeln

Sites graded by British Holiday & Home Parks Association/National Caravan Council
The more ticks the better!

Sites classés par la BHHPA/NCC. Le nombre de coches est proportionnel à la qualité des services et équipements offerts.

Von der BHHPA/NCC eingestufte Plätze. Je mehr Häkchen, desto besser!

Convenient to Ulster Way
Pratique pour faire l'Ulster Way
Idealer Ausgangspunkt für den Ulster Way.

The maximum speed limit for cars towing caravans or trailers on single carriageways in Northern Ireland is 50 mph, and on dual carriageways and motorways 60 mph.

158

Camping & Caravan Parks

The province is well provided with camping parks near points of entry. For visitors coming by ferry from Britain sites around Larne and Belfast ports are convenient for overnight stops. Kilbroney park in Rostrevor forest is popular with tourists travelling north from the Republic via Newry. Over in the west, the Fermanagh Lakeland has attractive parks easily accessible from south of the border, and caravanners entering from Donegal have a wide choice all along the Causeway Coast.

You can take your caravan to any of the forests listed, and most also accept campers. A permit for any period from two to 14 nights, with a maximum of seven nights at any one place, is available from the Forest Service and guarantees you a space at the forests of your choice. Contact: Forest Service, Belfast BT4 3SB. ☎ (0232) 524456.

Four of the forest parks – Glenariff, Castlewellan, Gosford and Tollymore - have facilities to accommodate caravans for up to 14 nights. If you want to do that please make a direct booking with the particular forest park. Contact addresses are given in the relevant entry.

Details of amenities and prices, where given, have been supplied by the owners and are subject to alteration. Not all site owners have supplied prices. The Northern Ireland Tourist Board has no control over caravan sites.

About a third of the parks listed are in public ownership, the others are privately run. Nearly all have mains water supply and flush toilets. Most parks are open April-October only. Outside this period check with individual sites. Overnight charges are based on two persons, car, and caravan or tent.

Sites around Belfast

BELVOIR FOREST
Central for Belfast and Lagan Valley. Forest walks. Off A504 (dual carriageway). Belfast city centre 3 miles. Contact Forest Service for details. ☎ (0232) 524456.

7 🚐 🚛 @ £3.50 per night. Prices under review.

DUNDONALD LEISURE PARK
110 Old Dundonald Rd.
☎ (0232) 482611.

20 🚐 🚛 10 ⛺

Opens late summer 1994.

JORDANSTOWN LOUGH SHORE PARK
Overlooking Belfast Lough. Close to leisure centre. Shore Rd, Newtownabbey. On A2, 5 miles north of Belfast. ☎ (0232) 863133/868751. Fax (0232) 365407 (Newtownabbey Borough Council).

6 🚐 🚛 @ £6 per night. Maximum stay 2 consecutive nights.

🐎 🏠 ☉ ♨ ⛲ ☎ ⛏ ∪ ⚓

County Antrim

Antrim

SIXMILEWATER CARAVAN PARK
Antrim Forum, Lough Rd. ☎ (0849)
463113. Fax 464469 (Antrim Borough
Council).

18 🚐🚏 @ £4 per night, electric hook-up
£2 per night.   10 ▲ @ £3.50 per night.
Refundable key deposit £10.

Ballintoy

LARRYBANE CAMPSITE
Interpretive centre, small aquarium.
¹/₂ mile from Carrick-a-rede rope bridge,
8 miles east of Giant's Causeway.
☎ (026 57) 62178/31159/32143 (National
Trust).

▲ one night only (dusk to 10 am). Carpark
£1.50, camping free. Minimal facilities.

Ballycastle

BALLYPATRICK FOREST PARK
Sheltered site, picnicking, forest drive,
walks, toilets, camping. On A2,
Ballycastle 6 miles.
Contact Forest Service for details.
☎ (0232) 524456. Camping (tents)
information: ☎ (026 57) 62301.

12 🚐🚏   10 ▲ @ £3.50 per night.
Prices under review.

HAYES CARAVAN PARK
76 Clare Rd. ☎ (026 57) 62905.

6 🚐🚏 @ £6/7 per night.

SILVER CLIFFS HOLIDAY VILLAGE
Overlooking sea, heated indoor swimming
pool, sauna. Bar and lounge facilities. 21
Clare Rd. ☎ (026 57) 62550 or (0960)
340200.

100 🚐🚏   60 ▲ @ £7/9 per night, electric
hook-up £1.50 per night.

WATERTOP OPEN FARM
118 Cushendall Rd. ☎ (026 57) 62576.

5 🚐 @ £6 per night   7 🚏▲ @ £5 per
night.

WHITEHALL CARAVAN PARK
13 Whitepark Rd. ☎ (026 57) 62077.

30 🚐   10 🚏   10 ▲ @ £5 per night.

Ballymoney

**DRUMAHEGLIS MARINA
& CARAVAN PARK**
On Lower Bann, water sports, fishing.
Glenstall Rd. ☎ (026 56) 66466/62280.
Fax 65150 (Ballymoney Borough
Council).

45 🚐🚏 @ £6.50 per night (includes
hook-up)   12 ▲ @ £4.50 per night.
Prices under review.

RIVERSIDE PARK
On parkland with riverside walks, trim trail, boating lake. Armour Avenue.
☎ (026 56) 64962/62280. Fax 65150 (Ballymoney Borough Council).

6 🚐 🚥 @ £6.50 per night.
Prices under review.

Carnlough

BAY VIEW CARAVAN PARK
89 Largy Rd. ☎ (0574) 885685.

4 🚐 8 🚥 @ £4 per night (includes hook-up) 4 ⛺ @ £3 per night.

RUBY HILL CARAVAN PARK
46 Largy Rd. ☎ (0574) 885692.

2 🚐 @ £5 per night 4 ⛺ @ £3 per night.

WHITEHILL CARAVAN PARK
30 Whitehill Rd. ☎ (0574) 885233.

3 ⛺ @ £3 per night.

Cushendall

CUSHENDALL CARAVAN PARK
62 Coast Rd. ☎ (026 67) 71699. Fax (026 57) 62515 (Moyle District Council).

20 🚐 🚥 @ £7.25 per night
6 ⛺ @ £4.40/£7.25 per night.

GLENVILLE CARAVAN PARK
20 Layde Rd. ☎ (026 67) 71520 or (0265) 832442.

6 🚐 🚥 @ £4/6 per night 6 ⛺ @ £2/4 per night.

LURIG CARAVAN PARK
Middlepark Rd. ☎ (026 67) 71267.

6 🚐 🚥 8 ⛺ (family) @ £5 per night.

Cushendun

CUSHENDUN CARAVAN PARK
14 Glendun Rd. ☎ (026 674) 254. Fax (026 57) 62515 (Moyle District Council).

15 🚐 🚥 ⛺ @ £7.25 per night.

Glenariff (or Waterfoot)

GLENARIFF FOREST PARK
98 Glenariff Rd, Ballymena BT44 0QX. ☎ (026 67) 58232.
Forest Service long-stay site.
The forest park's foremost attraction is the spectacular glen walk with three waterfalls. A scenic path runs round the sheer sides of the gorge and there are waymarked walks and trails to mountain viewpoints. In spring and early summer the upper glen is bright with wild flowers. Visitor centre, café. On A43, Waterfoot 4 miles, Cushendall 6 miles.

20 🚐 50 🚥 @ £4/6.50 per night
40 ⛺ @ £4/6.50 per night.
Prices under review.

Camping & Caravanning In Larne Borough
3 excellent sites are available

CARNFUNNOCK COUNTRY PARK

Situated on the Coast Road just outside Larne Town, Carnfunnock Country Park is a paradise for campers and caravanners. The unspoilt backdrop of the park gives a perfect location and access to many tourist attractions, shops, entertainment and restaurants could not be easier!

Full site facilities are now available

CURRAN PARK

Located close to both the harbour and Larne town. A host of facilities are available, including bowling, putting, picnic areas, walks and children's playground. It is also close to an indoor heated pool, a sandy beach, local shops and restaurants.

BROWN'S BAY, ISLANDMAGEE

This site is situated close to an excellent long sandy beach and is an ideal location for a family holiday. Many local attractions and facilities are within easy reach and includes horse riding, an open farm, and many interesting historical features.

For further information on these sites and details of the many attractions in this area contact: Larne Tourist Information Centre, Narrow Gauge Road, Larne. Tel: 0574 260088

RED BAY CARAVAN PARK
50 Main St. ☎ (026 67) 71267.

6 🚐 🚙 8 ⚤ (family) @ £5 per night.

🐕 🏠 ☉ 🚰 ⚡ 📞 🗑 ✛ ⚙ 🅿 ◬

Islandmagee

BROWN'S BAY CARAVAN PARK
At head of Islandmagee peninsula,
overlooking sea. Long sandy beach.
Brown's Bay. ☎ (0574) 260088 or (0960)
382497. Fax 260088 (Larne Borough
Council).

29 🚐 🚙 @ £5.30 per night ⚤ @ £3.20
per night.

🐕 🏠 ☉ ⚓ ⚡ 📞 ⚑ ⚒ 🅿 ∪ ◬ ✓✓✓✓

RANCH CARAVAN PARK
93 Mullaghboy Rd. ☎ (0960) 382441.

5 🚐 🚙 @ £4 per night.

🐕 🏠 ☉ 🚰 ⚓ 📞 🗑 ⚙ ⚒ ∪ ◬

Larne

BALLYBOLEY FOREST
Convenient for cross-channel ferries,
camping. On unclassified road south of
A36. Larne 8 miles.
Contact Forest Service for details.
☎ (0232) 524456.

6 🚐 🚙 @ £3.50 per night.
Prices under review.

CARNFUNNOCK COUNTRY PARK
Coast Rd. ☎ (0574) 260088/270541.
Fax 260088 (Larne Borough Council).
Maze, walled garden, walks, picnicking,
coffee shop, gift shop. Children's
adventure playground. Superpitches
available. Nine-hole golf course and
putting from summer 1994.

28 🚐 🚙 @ £5.30 per night ⚤ @ £3.20
per night.

🐕 🏠 ☉ ⚓ ⚡ ✕ 📞 ⚙ ⚒ ⚑ ⚒ 🅿 ∪ ◬
✓✓✓✓

CURRAN CARAVAN PARK
131 Curran Rd. ☎ (0574) 260088/273797.
Fax 260088 (Larne Borough Council).
Convenient for cross-channel ferries.
Leisure centre and bowling nearby.

29 🚐 🚙 @ £5.30 per night ⚤ @ £3.20
per night.

🐕 🏠 ☉ ⚓ ⚡ ⚡ 📞 🗑 ⚙ ⚒ ⚑ ⚒ 🅿 ∪ ◬
✓✓✓✓

Portballintrae

PORTBALLINTRAE CARAVAN PARK
On B145, 2 miles north-west of Bushmills.
60 Ballaghmore Rd. ☎ (026 57) 31478.

36 🚐 5 🚙 from £8 per night, hook-up
£1 per night, awning £1 per night
11 ⚤ @ £4.50 per night. 1993 prices.

🐕 🏠 ☉ ⚓ 🚰 ⚡ 📞 🗑 ⚒ ⚑ ⚒ 🅿 ∪ ⚲

Portglenone

KINGFISHER ANGLING CENTRE
On banks of Bann river, coarse fishing, convenient for forest walks.
54 Gortgole Rd. ☎ (0266) 821301/ 821630.

20 🚐 🚍 @ £6 per night   10 ⚑ @ £4 per night.

⚑ ⛺ ☉ 🚐 ⚓ ⛰ ⚓

Portrush

BLAIR'S CARAVAN PARK
29 Dhu Varren, Portstewart Rd.
☎ (0265) 822760.

25 🚐 🚍 @ £7/8 per night, awning £1 per night.

⚑ ⛺ ☉ 🚐 ⌂ ⚓ ⚡ 📺 ⛰ ⚓ ⚓ ⚐ ∪ ⚓

CARRICK DHU CARAVAN PARK
12 Ballyreagh Rd. ☎ (0265) 823712.
Fax 53489 (Coleraine Borough Council).

45 🚐 🚍   20 ⚑ @ £7/8 per night.

⚑ ⛺ ☉ 🚐 ⌂ ⚓ ⚡ ⚐ 📺 🔲 ⊕ ⛰ ⚓ ⚓ ⚐ ∪ ⚓ ⚓

GOLF LINKS HOTEL CARAVAN PARK
140 Dunluce Rd. ☎ (0265) 823539/ 822539/822288.

🚐 🚍 ⚑ @ £7 per night.

⚑ ⛺ ☉ 🚐 ⌂ ⚓ ✕ ⚡ ⚐ ⊕ ⚓ ⚓ ⚐ ∪ ⚓ ⚓

MARGOTH CARAVAN PARK
126 Dunluce Rd.
☎ (0265) 822531/822853.

70 🚐   20 🚍   30 ⚑ from £7 per night, electric hook-up £1 per night.

⚑ ⛺ ☉ 🚐 ⌂ ⚓ ⚡ ⚐ ⊕ ⛰ ⚓ ⚓ ⚐ ∪ ⚓ ⚓

PORTRUSH CARAVAN PARK
60 Loguestown Rd. ☎ (0265) 823537.

70 🚐   20 🚍   30 ⚑ from £7 per night, electric hook-up £1 per night.

⚑ ⛺ ☉ 🚐 ⌂ ⚓ ⚡ ⚐ 🔲 ⊕ ⛰ ⚓ ⚓ ⚐ ∪ ⚓ ⚓

Rathlin Island

⚑ free at east side of Church Bay.

County Armagh

Lurgan

KINNEGO CARAVAN PARK
At Oxford Island Nature Reserve. Five miles of walks, bird-watching. Lough Neagh Discovery Centre features history and geography of Lough Neagh. Kinnego Marina, Oxford Island. ☎ (0762) 327573. Fax 345514 (Craigavon Borough Council).

10 ⛺ 🚐 @ £4.50 per night   50 ⛺ @ £3 per night.
Prices under review.

🐕 🏠 ☉ 🚰 ⚓ 🔌 🗑 🔧 ⚡ 🚰 🔍 🛒 🚿

Markethill

GOSFORD FOREST PARK
54 Gosford Rd, Markethill BT60 1UG.
☎ (0861) 551277.
Forest Service long-stay site.
Some of the broadleaved and coniferous trees in the forest park are over 200 years old. Gosford Castle belongs to a rare architectural style – Norman revival. Estate has associations with Dean Swift. Walled garden, deerpark, poultry collection, ornamental pigeons in dovecote. Nature trail, barbecue site, café. Off A28, near Markethill. Armagh 7 miles, Newry 12 miles.

80 ⛺ 🚐   50 ⛺ @ £4/6.50 per night.
Prices under review.

🐕 🏠 ☉ 🚰 ❌ 🔧 ⚡ 🔌 ⚡ 🔍 🛒 🚿

County Down

Annalong

ANNALONG CARAVAN PARK
38 Kilkeel Rd. ☎ (039 67) 68248.

18 🚐 @ £7 per night (includes hook-up). 1993 prices.

🐕 🏠 ☉ 🚐 🚰 ⚓ 🔌 🗑 🔧 ⚡ 🚿 ✓✓✓✓

ANNALONG MARINE PARK
Main St. ☎ (039 67) 68736 or (0693) 67226 (Newry & Mourne District Council).

15 🚐 🚐   10 ⛺   Prices not provided.

🐕 🏠 ☉ ❌ 🔧 ⚡ 🔌 🔍 🛒 🚿 ⚡

Ardglass

CONEY ISLAND CARAVAN PARK
74 Killough Rd. ☎ (0396) 841448/ 841210.

30 🚐 🚐 @ £6 per night   50 ⛺ @ £5 per night.

🐕 🏠 🚰 ⚓ ⚡ 🔧 ⚡ 🔌 🛒 🚿 ⚡ 🐾

Ballyhalbert

BALLYHALBERT CARAVAN PARK
96 Shore Rd. ☎ (024 77) 58426.

50 🚐 🚐 @ £5 per night.

🐕 🏠 ☉ 🚐 🚰 ❌ 🔧 ⚡ 🔌 🗑 🔧 ⚡ 🔍 🛒 🚿 ✓✓✓

Lisburn Borough Council
Moira Demesne Public Park and Transit Caravan Site

LOCATION: Within Moira Demesne Park
Off A3 (approximately half mile from Junction 9 on M1)
SITE: 2 acres, level and sheltered - No. of Pitches: 15
FACILITIES: Car parking beside caravan, Toilet Block, including Showers,
Hot Water, Chemical Disposal Points, Play Area, Shops nearby

COST: Caravans £3.00 per night
Tents £1.50 per night

*Special rates available for
caravan club rallies*

OPERATION: All Year Round
BOOKINGS: Contact Mr. G. Bassett, 35 Rawdon Place, Moira. Tel: (0846) 619974
Lisburn Borough Council, Leisure Services Department,
The Square, Hillsborough. Tel (0846) 682477

MOIRA - WINNER 'BRITAIN IN BLOOM'
Hillsborough and Lisburn - Shopping & Sightseeing

KINNEGO MARINA
TOURING CARAVAN SITE

A very attractive select site situated at Oxford Island National Nature
Reserve on the South Shore of Lough Neagh, Britain's largest freshwater
lake.

The site is landscaped, has all facilities and is the ideal location for the
watersports enthusiast, nature lovers or as a base from which to explore
the South of the Province.

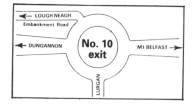

Facilities:
★ 10 sites ★ laundry facilities
★ showers ★ rubbish disposal
★ water supply ★ children's playground
★ gas.

For further information:
Phone (0762) 327573
Price:
£4.50 per night - includes boat launch fees.

Ballywalter

BALLYFERRIS CARAVAN PARK
211 Whitechurch Rd. ☎ (024 77) 58244.

30 🚐 🚎 @ £5.50/6 per night.

🐕 🎒 ☉ 🚐 🚽 🛒 🔌 📦 🏵 ♨ ⚲ 🅿 ∪ ✓✓✓✓✓

GANAWAY CARAVAN PARK
10 Ganaway Rd.
☎ (024 77) 58707/58422.

12 🚐 🚎 @ £5/6 per night (includes hook-up).

🐕 🎒 ☉ 🚐 🛒 🏵 ♨ ⚲ 🅿 ∪

ROCKMORE CARAVAN PARK
69 Whitechurch Rd. ☎ (0247) 861428, or write to: H J Warnock, 6 Ballydoonan Rd, Carrowdore, Newtownards BT22 2HE.

6 🚐   4 🚎 @ £4.50 per night.

🐕 ☉ 🚐 🛒 🏕 🔌 ♨ ⚲ 🅿 ∪ 🔺

ROCKMORE CARAVAN PARK
150 Whitechurch Rd (shore side).
☎ (024 77) 58342.
Note: caravans must be equipped with a chemical toilet.

6 🚐 🚎 @ £6 per night.

🐕 ☉ 🚐 🛒 🏕 🔌 🛒 🏵 ♨ ⚲ 🅿 ∪

ROSEBANK CARAVAN PARK
199 Whitechurch Rd. ☎ (024 77) 58211.

8 🚐 🚎 @ £5.50 per night.

🐕 ☉ 🛒 🏕 🔌 🏵 ♨ ⚲ 🅿 ∪

SANDYCOVE CARAVAN PARK
194 Whitechurch Rd. ☎ (024 77) 58062/58293.

16 🚐   2 🚎 @ £5.50/6 per night.

🐕 🎒 ☉ 🚐 🛒 🏕 🔌 🛒 🏵 ♨ ⚲ 🅿 ∪ ✓✓✓✓✓

Banbridge

OLD MILL CARAVAN PARK
Ballydown Rd. ☎ (082 06) 22842.

28 🚐 🚎 @ £3/4 per night   🔺 @ £2 per night.

🐕 🎒 ☉ 🚐 🔌 🏵 🎣 ♨ 🅿 ∪

BANBRIDGE GATEWAY AMENITY AREA
Newry Road. ☎ (082 06) 23322. Fax 23114 (Banbridge District Council).

8 🚐 🚎 @ £6/7 per night   6 🔺 @ £3.50 per night.

🐕 🎒 ☉ 🚐 ✗ 🛒 🏵 🎣 ♨ 🅿 ∪

Castlewellan

CASTLEWELLAN FOREST PARK
The Grange, Castlewellan BT31 9BU.
☎ (039 67) 78664.
Forest Service long-stay site.
Outstanding feature of the forest park is
the national arboretum, begun about 1740
with trees, shrubs and exotic plants from
all over the world. The Scottish Baronial
style castle is now a conference centre.
The lake is stocked with trout (fishing
permit required). The early 18th-century
farmstead is a fine example of Queen
Anne style courtyards. Tropical birds in
glasshouse. Sculpture trail, barbecue site.
Visitor centre has café. Entrance Main St.

80 🚐 🚛 30 ▲ @ £4/7 per night.
Prices under review.

Cloughey

KIRKISTOWN CARAVAN PARK
55 Main Rd. ☎ (024 77) 71183.
Fax 72053.

50 🚐 🚛 30 ▲ @ £5.50/£6 per night.

RINGBUOY CARAVAN PARK
73 Main Rd. ☎ (024 77) 71418.

6 🚐 🚛 Prices not provided.

SILVER BAY CARAVAN PARK
15 Ardminnan Rd, Portaferry. ☎ (024 77)
71321.

24 🚐 🚛 @ £5.50 per night (includes
hook-up) 20 ▲ @ £3.50 per night.

Donaghadee

BALLYVESTER CARAVAN PARK
Millisle Rd. ☎ (0247) 883781 or (0232)
763171/763038. Fax (0232) 760376.

30 🚐 @ £5 per night.

DONAGHADEE CARAVAN PARK
Edgewater, 183 Millisle Rd. ☎ (0247)
882369.

10 🚐 🚛 10 ▲ @ £4 per night.

Groomsport

BIRCHES CARAVAN PARK
Donaghadee Rd. ☎ (0247) 270723 or
(0232) 763171/763038. Fax (0232)
760376.

30 🚐 5 🚛 @ £5 per night.

WINDSOR CARAVAN PARK
Donaghadee Rd. ☎ (0247) 464323.
Fax 464323.

50 🚐 🚛 @ £6 per night.

✓✓✓

Kilkeel

CHESTNUTT CARAVAN PARK
3 Grange Rd, Cranfield West.
☎ (069 37) 62653.

25 🚐 🚚 🛖 @ £7 per night (includes hook-up). 1993 prices.

🐕 ☎ ⊙ 🛖 🔌 ✕ 🔋 📞 🔵 ⚙ ♨ 🔍 🚩 U ✓✓✓✓✓

CRANFIELD CARAVAN PARK
123 Cranfield Rd. ☎ (069 37) 62572.

50 🚐 🚚 @ £8.50 per night.

🐕 ☎ ⊙ 🛖 🔌 🔋 📞 🔵 ⚙ ♨ 🔍 🚩 U ✓✓✓✓✓

LEESTONE CARAVAN PARK
62 Leestone Rd. ☎ (069 37) 62567.

10 🚐 🚚   6 🛖 (family) @ £5/6 per night.

🐕 ☎ ⊙ 🛖 🔌 🔋 📞 🔵 ⚙ ♨ 🔍 🚩 U

SANDILANDS CARAVAN PARK
30 Cranfield Rd, Cranfield East.
☎ (069 37) 63634.

22 🚐 🚚 @ £7 per night.

🐕 ☎ ⊙ 🛖 🔌 🔋 📞 🔵 ⚙ ♨ 🔍 🚩 U ✓✓✓✓✓

SHANLIEVE CARAVAN PARK
69a Cranfield Rd. ☎ (069 37) 64344.

20 🚐 🚚 @ £6 per night   10 🛖 @ £5 per night.

🐕 ☎ ⊙ 🛖 🔌 🔋 📞 🔵 ⚙ ♨ 🔍 🚩 U

SILVERCOVE CARAVAN PARK
98 Leestone Rd. ☎ (069 37) 63136.

5 🚐 🚚 @ £6.50/7.50 per night (includes hook-up).

🐕 ☎ ⊙ 🛖 🔌 🔋 📞 🔵 ⚙ ♨ 🔍 🚩 U

Killough

MINERSTOWN CARAVAN PARK
50 Minerstown Rd, Downpatrick.
On A2, 3 miles west of Ardglass.
☎ (0396) 851527.

16 🚐 🚚 @ £6/8 per night.

🐕 ☎ ⊙ 🛖 🔌 🔋 🔵 ⚙ ♨ 🚩 U 🔺 ✓✓✓

Millisle

BALLYWHISKIN CARAVAN & CAMPING PARK
216 Ballywalter Rd. ☎ (0247) 862262/862304.

20 🚐 🚚 @ £3.50/£4.50 per night
20 🛖 @ £2.50 per night.

🐕 ☎ ⊙ 🛖 🔌 🔋 📞 🔵 🔲 ⚙ ♨ 🔍 🚩 U 🔺

HAPPYVALE CARAVAN PARK
112 Ballywalter Rd. ☎ (0247) 861457.

6 🚐 🚚 @ £2.50 per night.

🐕 🔌 ⚙ 🔍 🚩 U 🔺

RATHLIN CARAVAN PARK
45 Moss Rd. ☎ (0247) 861386/861314.

4 🚐   4 🚚 @ £2/5 per night.

🐕 ⊙ 🛖 🔌 📞 🔍 🚩 U 🔺 ✓✓✓

WHEREVER
YOU ARE

CALOR
That's Life

For further information contact:
Customer Services Department, Calor Gas (NI) Ltd., Airport Road West, Sydenham, Belfast BT3 9EE. Tel: (0232) 458466

• All cylinders remain the property of and are to be filled only by Calor Gas Northern Ireland •

SEAVIEW CARAVAN PARK
1 Donaghadee Rd. ☎ (0247) 861248.

30 🚐 @ £7 per night (includes hook-up).

🐕 🅿 ☉ 🔌 🎚 📞 🔲 🍴 📶 🔍 🅿 ∪ 🔺

WALKER'S CARAVAN PARK
Ballywalter Rd. ☎ (0247) 861672.

5 🚐 🚎 @ £6 per night.

🐕 🅿 ☉ 🔌 🎚 🍴 🔲 📶 🔍 🅿 ∪ 🔺

WOBURN CARAVAN PARK
Ballywalter Rd. ☎ (0247) 861620
or (0232) 763171/763038.
Fax (0232) 760376.

10 🚐 🚎 @ £5 per night.

🐕 🅿 ☉ 🎚 📞 🍴 🔍 🅿 ∪ 🔺

WOODLANDS CARAVAN PARK
24 Drumfad Rd. ☎ (0247) 861309.

6 🚐 🚎 @ £5 or £5.50 (hook-up) per night
6 ▲ @ £5 per night.

🐕 ☉ 🔌 🎚 🍴 📶 🔍 🅿 ∪ 🔺

MOIRA DEMESNE
Main St. ☎ (0846) 619974/682477. Fax
689984 (Lisburn Borough Council).

15 🚐 🚎 @ £3 per night   25 ▲ @ £1.50
per night.

🐕 🅿 ☉ 🔲 📶 🍴 ∪ ✓✓✓✓✓

BONNY'S TRAILER PARK
82 Tullybrannigan Rd. ☎ (039 67) 22351.
Fax 26593.

15 🚐 🚎 @ £5 per night, electric hook-up
£1 per night. 1993 prices.

🐕 🅿 ☉ 🔌 🎚 📞 🍴 🔲 📶 🔍 🅿 ∪ 🔺

BOULEVARD CARAVAN PARK
114 Dundrum Rd. ☎ (039 67) 22130 or
(0846) 638336.

10 🚐 @ £4/5 per night (includes hook-up).

🐕 🅿 ☉ 🔌 🎚 📞 🍴 🔲 📶 🔍 🅿 ∪ 🔺

BRYANSFORD CARAVAN PARK
1 Bryansford Village. ☎ (039 67) 24017.

5 🚐   4 🚎 @ £5 per night.

🐕 🅿 ☉ 🎚 🎚 📞 🍴 🔲 📶 🔍 🅿 ∪ 🔺

GLEN RIVER YMCA CENTRE
Greenhill (follow signs from Donard Park).
☎ (039 67) 23172 (office hours only).
Fax 26230.
Note: parking beside tents not possible.

35 ▲ (family) @ £5.50
per night (4-person tent).

🅿 ☉ 🎚 📞 📶 🔍 🅿 ∪ 🔺 🐎

LAZY BJ CARAVAN & CAMPING PARK
Twelve Arches, Dundrum Rd.
☎ (039 67) 23533.

25 🚐   10 🚎   25 ▲   from £4 per night.

🐕 🅿 ☉ 🔌 🎚 🍴 🔲 📶 🔍 🅿 ∪ 🔺 🐎

MOURNE VIEW CARAVAN PARK

195 Dundrum Rd. ☎ (039 67) 23327 or (0232) 763171/763038. Fax (0232) 760376.

50 ⊞ ⊞ @ £10 per night.

🐎 🏠 ☉ 🍳 🗘 🛆 ✕ 🛒 📞 🔄 ⊙ ♏ ☂ ⚲ 🏴 ∪ ♨

MURLOUGH COTTAGE FARM CARAVAN PARK

180 Dundrum Rd. ☎ (039 67) 23184/22288.

40 ⊞   10 ⊞ @ £8 per night.

🐎 🏠 ☉ 🍳 🗘 🛆 🛒 🔄 ⊙ ♏ ☂ ⚲ 🏴 ∪ ♨

SUNNYHOLME CARAVAN PARK

33 Castlewellan Rd. ☎ (039 67) 22739. Fax 26579.

14 ⊞ ⊞ @ £5 per night, electric hook-up £1 per night. 1993 prices.

🐎 🏠 ☉ 🍳 🗘 🛆 📞 🔄 ⊡ ⊙ ♏ ☂ ⚲ 🏴 ∪ ♨

TOLLYMORE FOREST PARK

176 Tullybrannigan Rd, BT33 OPW. ☎ (039 67) 22428.

Forest Service long-stay site.
At the foot of the Mournes, the 2,000-acre forest park has some magnificent Himalayan cedars and, in the arboretum, a sequoia tree over 100 ft tall. An 18th-century barn contains exhibits, lecture theatre and a café. Pony trekking, game fishing (permit required), wildfowl collection, hill climbs and walks. Nearby (on the Hilltown road) is the Northern Ireland Centre for Outdoor Activities.

70 ⊞ ⊞   35 ⚓ @ £4/7 per night. Prices under review.

🐎 🏠 ☉ 🍳 🗘 🛆 ✕ 🛒 📞 🔄 ⊙ ☂ ⚲ 🏴 ∪ ♨ 🐕

WINDSOR CARAVAN PARK

138 Dundrum Rd. ☎ (039 67) 23367 or (0960) 340200.

60 ⊞   40 ⊞ ⚓ from £6 per night.

🐎 🏠 ☉ 🍳 🗘 🛆 📞 🔄 ⊡ ⊙ ♏ ☂ ⚲ 🏴 ∪ ♨ ✓✓✓✓ 🐕

WOODCROFT CARAVAN PARK

104 Dundrum Rd. ☎ (039 67) 22284.

30 ⊞ ⊞ @ £6.50/£7.50 per night (includes hook-up).

🐎 🏠 ☉ 🍳 🗘 🛆 📞 🔄 ⊙ ♏ ☂ ⚲ 🏴 ∪ ♨

Portaferry

AQUARIUM TOURING CARAVAN PARK

Ropewalk, Castle St. ☎ (024 77) 28062. Fax (0247) 819628 (Ards Borough Council).

12 ⊞ ⊞ @ £5.75 per night.

🐎 🏠 ☉ 🛆 ✕ 🔄 ♏ ⚲ ∪ ♨ ✓✓✓✓

TARA CARAVAN PARK

4 Ballyquintin Rd, Tara. ☎ (024 77) 28459.

10 ⊞ ⊞ @ £4 per night   10 ⚓ @ £2 per night.

🏠 ☉ 🗘 ♏ ⚲ ∪ ♨

Rostrevor

KILBRONEY CARAVAN PARK
In parkland overlooking Carlingford
Lough. Forest walks, barbecue site.
Kilbroney Park, Shore Rd. ☎ (069 37)
38134 (Newry & Mourne District
Council).

36 ⊕ 🚐 @ £7 per night, electric hook-up
£1.50 per night.   25 ▲ @ £4.50 per night.

🛏 🅿 ☉ 🄌 ⚠ ✕ 📞 🗐 ⊕ ⛰ ☂ 🔍 ⌐ ∪ △
✓✓✓✓✓ ☖

ROSTREVOR FOREST
Sheltered site, forest drive, viewpoints,
picnicking, camping. On A2, access
signposted via main forest entrance.
Rostrevor ½ mile.
Contact Forest Service for details
☎ (0232) 524456.

14 ⊕ 🚐 @ £3.50 per night.
Prices under review.

☖

Strangford

CASTLE WARD CARAVAN PARK
Castle Ward Estate (1½ miles west of
village). ☎ (0396) 881680/881204
(National Trust).
The mansion is open to the public.
Restaurant, shop. Victorian laundry,
Victorian pastimes for children, many
acres of wood and lake, walks, formal
gardens and a wildfowl collection.
Restored corn mill. A bird hide, 250 yards
from the park, overlooks the wildfowl
reserve on Strangford Lough. Exhibition in
Strangford Lough Wildlife Centre.

17 ⊕ 🚐   15 ▲ @ £6 per night.

🛏 🅿 ☉ 🄌 ⌐ ∪ △ ☖

Warrenpoint

MOYGANNON CARAVAN PARK
Moygannon Rd. ☎ (069 37) 72589.

4 ⊕ 🚐 @ £6/7 per night   4 ▲ @ £5 per
night.

🛏 🅿 ☉ 🄌 ⚠ 📞 🗐 ⊕ ☂ 🔍 ⌐ ∪ △

County Fermanagh

Blaney

BLANEY CARAVAN PARK
8 miles north of Enniskillen on A46.
☎ (036 564) 634.

24 🚐 🚛   5 🛆 Prices not provided.

🐕 🐾 ☉ 🍴 🗘 🛆 🛒 📞 🗑 🏛 🏳 🛆

Enniskillen

CASTLE ISLAND CAMP SITE
Castle Island. ☎ (0365) 324250.
Fax 323319.

30 🛆 @ £4 per person per night.

Tents, water sports equipment and bikes
for hire. Free ferry service to Castle Island
operates daily 9 am-midnight from jetty
beside Fermanagh Lakeland Forum.

🐕 🐾 ☉ 🗘 🛆 ✕ 🛒 📞 🗑 🖵 🏳 🎣 🎿 🏳 🛆

Florencecourt

FLORENCECOURT FOREST PARK
The forest park lies on the north-east
shoulder of Cuilcagh Mountain. The
restored walled garden dates from the
1780s. Restored waterwheel. National
Trust stately home and Marble Arch Caves
are nearby. Trails. Off A32, Enniskillen 8
miles.
Contact Forest Service for details.
☎ (0232) 524456.

10 🚐 🚛 @ £3.50 per night.
Prices under review.   🚶

Garrison

LOUGH MELVIN HOLIDAY CENTRE
Main St. ☎ (036 56) 58142/58143.
Fax 58719 (Fermanagh District Council).

27 🚐 🚛 @ £7.50/8.50 per night   60 🛆 @
£5.50/6.50 per night.

🐕 🐾 ☉ 🍴 🗘 🛆 ✕ 📞 🗑 🖵 🏳 🏛 🛆

Irvinestown

CASTLE ARCHDALE CARAVAN PARK
In Castle Archdale Country Park, off B82
Enniskillen/Kesh road. Irvinestown 3
miles. ☎ (036 56) 21333 or 32159.
Good centre for visitors to Lower Lough
Erne. The marina, in the country park, has
full servicing for cruisers and water-based
sports and ferry to White Island. Once an
RAF base, the outhouses contain a WWII
exhibition on the Battle of the Atlantic.
Pony-trekking through park.

80 🚐 🚛 @ £8 per night, electric hook-
up £1 per night.   60 🛆 @ £5 per night.
1993 prices.

🐕 🐾 ☉ 🍴 🗘 🛆 🛒 📞 🗑 🖵 🏛 🛆

Kesh

CLONELLY FOREST
On A35, Kesh 3 miles. Castle Archdale
Country Park 5 miles.
Contact Forest Service for details.
☎ (0232) 524456.
Camping (tents) information:
☎ (036 56) 31253.

12 🚐 🚛 6 🛆 @ £3.50 per night.
Prices under review.

LAKELAND CARAVAN PARK
Boa Island Rd, Drumrush.
☎ (036 56) 31578/31025.

50 � 60 ▲ Prices not provided.

♓ ⌂ ☉ ☻ ☝ ♨ ✕ ⚓ ☎ 🗑 ☐ ⊕ ⚠ ⌐ ∪ ⚓
✓✓✓✓

LOANE EDEN CARAVAN PARK
Near shores of Lough Erne. 5 minutes'
walk to beach, jetty, marina and Kesh
village. Highgrove, Muckross Bay.
☎ (036 56) 31603.

24 ⊕ @ £7/£8 per night, awning £1
per night.   20 ▲ @ £6 per night.

♓ ⌂ ☉ ☻ ☝ ♨ ⚓ ☎ 🗑 ☐ ⊕ ⚠ ⚲ ⌐ ∪ ⚓

Lisnaskea

MULLYNASCARTHY CARAVAN PARK
On B514, 1½ miles north-west of
Lisnaskea. ☎ (036 57) 21040. Fax (0365)
322024 (Fermanagh District Council).

33 ⊕ @ £7/8 per night   23 ▲ @ £6 per
night.

♓ ⌂ ☉ ☻ ♨ ☎ ⊕ ⚠ ⚓ ✓✓✓✓✓

SHARE CENTRE
Smith's Strand, Shanaghy.
☎ (036 57) 22122/21892. Fax 21893.

29 ⊕ @ £7.50 per night, electric hook-
up £1 per night   50 ▲ @ £5 per night.

♓ ⌂ ☉ ♨ ✕ ☎ 🗑 ☐ ⊕ ⚠ ⚲ ⚓ ☥

County Londonderry

Ballyronan

BALLYRONAN CARAVAN PARK
Ballyronan Marina. ☎ (064 87) 62205
(office hours) (Cookstown District
Council).

12 🚐 🚚 @ £6 per night   20 ⛺ @ £3 per
night.
Opens Easter 1994.

🐕 🏕 ☉ 🚐 🛒 🍴 🔋 🛒 🔌 🏪 🎣 🔍 🏹 ⚓ ◈

Castlerock

CASTLEROCK HOLIDAY PARK
24 Sea Rd. ☎ (0265) 848381.

20 🚐   5 🚚   10 ⛺ @ £4/5 per night,
electric hook-up £1.50 per night.

🐕 🏕 ☉ 🚐 🛒 🍴 ✕ 🔌 🏪 🎣 🔍 🏹 ⚓ 🏃

DOWNHILL CAMPSITE
On A2, 1 mile west of Castlerock.
☎ (0265) 848728 or (026 57) 31159
(National Trust).

⛺ one night only (dusk to 10 am).
Donation to National Trust. Minimal
facilities.

🐕 🔍 🏹 ⚓ 🏃

Hayes Caravan Park

HAYES CARAVAN PARK
1 Solitude Park. ☎ (0265) 848296.

🚐 🚚 @ £5 per night.

🐕 🏕 ☉ 🚐 🛒 🍴 🔋 🔌 🏪 🎣 🔍 🏹 ⚓ ◈

Claudy

LOUGHERMORE FOREST
Wild mountain scenery, trails. On B69 at
Loughermore Bridge. Claudy 4 miles,
Limavady 8 miles.
Contact Forest Service for details.
☎ (0232) 524456.

6 🚐 🚚 @ £3.50 per night.
Prices under review.

Coleraine

MARINA CARAVAN PARK
Overlooks Coleraine Marina. Bann river
cruises. 64 Portstewart Rd. ☎ (0265)
44768. Fax 53489 (Coleraine Borough
Council).

6 🚐 🚚 @ £7 per night   6 ⛺ @ £3.50/7
per night.

🐕 🏕 ☉ 🚐 🍴 🏪 🎣 🔍 🏹 ⚓ ◈ 🏃

SPRINGWELL FOREST
Close to Causeway Coast seaside resorts.
On A37, Coleraine 7 miles, Limavady 7
miles.
Contact Forest Service for details.
☎ (0232) 524456.
Camping (tents) information ☎ (050 47)
62547.

12 🚐 🚚   5 ⛺ @ £3.50 per night.
Prices under review.

🏃

TULLANS FARM CARAVAN PARK
46 Newmills Rd. ☎ (0265) 42309.

30 🚐 🚍 @ £7 per night   6 ▲ @ £3 per night.

🐕 🏠 ☉ 🚐 🔦 🗑 🕃 🏛 🍴 🔍 🏳 ∪ 🔻 🕴

Limavady

BENONE COMPLEX
Adjacent to Benone beach. Binevenagh Mountain 1 mile. Roe Valley Country Park 12 miles. 53 Benone Ave. ☎ (050 47) 50555. Fax 22010 (Limavady Borough Council).

71 🚐 🚍 @ £6/7 per night, awning £1 per night 30 ▲ @ £4 per night.

🐕 🏠 ☉ 🚐 🔻 ✕ 🔦 🗑 🏛 🍴 🔍 🏳 ∪ ✓✓✓✓✓

GOLDEN SANDS CARAVAN PARKS
26a Benone Ave. ☎ (050 47) 50324.

60 🚐 🚍 @ £5.50/6.50 per night   40 ▲ @ £5.50 per night.

🐕 🏠 ☉ 🚐 🚽 🔻 ⚖ 🔦 🗑 🕃 🏛 🍴 🔍 🏳 ∪ ✓✓✓✓✓

ROE VALLEY COUNTRY PARK
41 Leap Rd. ☎ (050 47) 22074 (Department of the Environment).
The park caters for the naturalist, walker, angler, canoeist and rock climber. Visitors can see Ulster's first hydro-electric domestic power station (opened 1896) with much of the original equipment. Old water mills for grinding, scutching, weaving and beetling. Small museums. Off B192 a mile south of Limavady.

10 🚐 🚍 @ £7.44 per night.   5 ▲ @ £4 per night. 1993 prices.

🐕 🏠 ☉ ✕ 🔦 🕃 🍴 🔍 ∪

Moneymore

SPRINGHILL CARAVAN PARK
20 Springhill Rd. ☎ (064 87) 48210 (National Trust).
The caravan park is in the farmyard of Springhill, a 17th-century whitewashed manor house in National Trust care. There are splendid woodland walks, a formal garden and a costume museum.

35 🚐 🚍 @ £2 per night.

🐕 🔻 ✕ 🏛 ∪

Portstewart

JUNIPER HILL CARAVAN PARK
70 Ballyreagh Rd. ☎ (0265) 832023. Fax 53489 (Coleraine Borough Council).

80 🚐 @ £7/8 per night   12 ▲ @ £3.50/4 per night.

🐕 🏠 ☉ 🚐 🚽 🔻 ⚖ 🔦 🗑 ☐ 🕃 🏛 🍴 🔍 🏳 ∪ 🕴

PORTSTEWART HOLIDAY PARK
80 Mill Rd. ☎ (0265) 833308/833092.

36 🚐 🚍 ▲ @ £8/9 per night, awning £1 per night.

🐕 🏠 ☉ 🚐 🚽 🔻 ⚖ 🔦 🗑 🕃 🍴 🔍 🏳 ∪ 🔻 🕴

County Tyrone

Clogher

CLOGHER VALLEY COUNTRY
CARAVAN PARK
Fardross Forest (signpost 1 mile west of
Clogher on A4).
☎ (066 25) 48932 or (066 252) 631.

20 🚐 🚍 @ £6 per night   15 ▲ @ £3 per
night.

🐕 🏕 🚗 🏕 🏕 🏕 🏕 🚻 🐾 ⛲ 🚾 U

Cookstown

DRUM MANOR FOREST PARK
Oaklands. ☎ (064 87) 62774 or (086 87)
59664.
The pretty little forest park has two lakes
and a walled butterfly garden. The
demonstration shrub garden is well worth
a visit. Nature trail, interpretive centre and
lecture theatre. On A505, 4 miles west of
Cookstown.

30 🚐 🚍 @ £5 per night   26 ▲ @ £3.50
per night. Prices under review.

🐕 🏕 ⛲ 🐾 ⛳ U

Dungannon

KILLYMADDY CENTRE
Ballygawley Rd. On A4, 2 miles west of
Parkanaur Forest Park. ☎ (086 87)
67259/25311. Fax 22541 (Dungannon
District Council).

6 🚐 🚍 @ £6/8 per night   12 ▲ @ £4/6
per night.

🐕 🏕 ⊙ 🏕 ✕ 🚾 🚻 🚾 ⛲ 🐾 ⛳ U

PARKANAUR FOREST PARK
Castlecaulfield. ☎ (086 87) 59664/67432
(office hours).
This small forest park has a herd of white
fallow deer, and is colourful in spring with
daffodils and rhododendrons. A nature
trail runs through oak and beech trees,
passing a Victorian garden, wishing well
and old archway. Exhibition and lecture
halls. Off A4, 4 miles west of Dungannon
(signposted).

10 🚐 🚍   12 ▲ @ £3.50 per night.
Prices under review.

🐕 🏕 ⛲ 🐾 ⛳ U

Fivemiletown

ROUND LAKE CARAVAN PARK
Murley Rd. ☎ (086 87) 25311.
Fax 22541 (Dungannon District Council).

12 🚐 🚍 @ £6/8 per night   6 ▲ @ £4/6
per night.

🐕 🏕 ⊙ 🏕 🏕 🚾 🚾 🚻 ⛲ 🏕 🐾

Gortin

GORTIN GLEN CARAVAN, CAMPING & CHALET PARK

Lisnaharney Rd, Lislap, Omagh. Opposite Gortin Glen Forest Park and adjacent to Ulster History Park. Ulster American Folk Park 5 miles. Omagh 7 miles.
☎ (066 26) 48108. Fax 243888 (Omagh District Council).

24 🚐 @ £7 per night, electric hook-up £1.30 per night   50 ▲ @ £3/6 per night.

🐕 🏕 ☉ 🚐 🅿 ♨ 🚾 🔌 📷 🏧 ♨ 🏔 ☏ 🔍 🏌 ∪ 🏕

Newtownstewart

HARRIGAN CARAVAN PARK

Old Bridge, Gortin Rd. ☎ (066 26) 61560. Fax (0504) 382264 (Strabane District Council).
Note: arrival on site before 5 pm please.

6 🚐 🚛 @ £3 per night   3 ▲ @ £1.50 per night.

🐕 🏕 ☉ ♨ ⊕ 🏔 ☏ 🔍 🏌 ∪

MILLBROOK FISHING & LEISURE PARK

Millbrook, Newtownstewart.
☎ (066 26) 62048.

20 🚐 🚛 @ £7.50 per night, electric hook-up £1 per night.

🐕 🏕 ☉ 🚐 🅿 ♨ 🚾 🔌 📷 🏔 ☏ 🔍 🏌 ∪

Pomeroy

ALTMORE OPEN FARM & FISHERIES

32 Altmore Rd. ☎ (0868) 758977 or 758992 after 6pm.

20 🚐 🚛 @ £5 per night
50 ▲ @ £4 per night.

🐕 🏕 ☉ 🚐 🅿 ♨ 🚾 🔌 📷 🏔 ☏ 🔍 🏌 ∪

Activity holidays

Many of the hotels, guesthouses and other accommodation listed in this guide are ideally suited to those whose idea of a good holiday is to 'get away from it all' in the tranquillity of the Ulster countryside. On the other hand, Northern Ireland has much to offer the more active holidaymaker and you are never more than a few miles away from splendid golf courses, well stocked angling waters and other sporting and leisure facilities. Any office of the Northern Ireland Tourist Board will supply you with information on your kind of activity holiday or write to the head office in Belfast (address on page 16). Once you arrive, there is a network of tourist information centres to help you.

Golf

There are whole series of golf links along Northern Ireland's coast, a dozen excellent courses within five miles of Belfast City Hall - and, of course, the famous fairways of Royal Portrush and Royal County Down. Green fees are modest, and it is often possible to get a round without booking, particularly midweek. The tourist board's information guide 17 has details.

Pony-trekking and riding

Some 40 centres around Northern Ireland provide expert riding tuition, pony-trekking or beach riding for children and adults, including complete beginners. Some have residential summer camps and most charge as little as £6 or £8 per hour (information guide 19).

Coarse fishing

In Northern Ireland there is coarse fishing - that is, everything except salmon and trout - all year round. Permits and licences are needed and tackle can be hired locally. See information guide 28.

Game fishing

You can fish for salmon or trout throughout the country; information guide 23 lists scores of lakes and rivers, all easily accessible by car, controlled and stocked by angling clubs or in public ownership. Permits and rod licences are needed. These are inexpensive and can be obtained from the tourist board in Belfast and from tackle shops.

Sea fishing

Northern Ireland has 300 miles of coast and its beaches, rocks and offshore waters provide excellent angling. No licence or permit is needed, whether fishing from the shore or from one of the dozens of boats available for day hire from coastal towns and villages. Ask for information guide 9.

Cruising

Visitors who want to get off dry land can spend, say, a week of their holiday exploring the Fermanagh Lakeland. The 50-mile-long waterway of Lough Erne is dotted with wooded islands, many with traces of early Christian settlements. There is excellent fishing in the area and other attractions include the Marble Arch Caves and stately homes in National Trust care. For details of luxury cruisers for hire, send for *Holidays Afloat* (see page 16).

Other activity holidays

The tourist board can advise you on organised or tailor-made activity holidays for individuals or groups. Popular options include cycling holidays - bicycles and tandems can be hired easily - rambling, walking the challenging Ulster Way, visiting ancient monuments and historic buildings, and 'heritage' holidays devoted to tracing family connections with Ulster. In most cases the tourist board will be able to provide information and will put you in touch with the right organisation.

Index to hotels and guesthouses

Index to hotels and guesthouses

Index to hotels and guesthouses

Getting around in Northern Ireland

Driving

Throughout Britain and Ireland the rule is 'drive on the left and overtake on the right'. The speed limits are 30 mph (48 kph) in towns unless signs indicate otherwise; 60 mph (97 kph) on ordinary roads, and 70 mph (113 kph) on dual carriageways and motorways. Drivers and all passengers must wear seatbelts. Roads in Northern Ireland are well surfaced and signposted, and traffic volume is markedly lower than in Britain.

Driving licence

Your own driving licence is sufficient for short stays in Northern Ireland. Remember to carry it with you.

Parking

The universal blue 'P' sign shows a carpark or a layby at the roadside where you can park. You can usually park on the street if there is no yellow line at the kerb. On a single yellow line you may park except at the times shown on the small yellow signs on nearby posts. It is important not to leave your car in control zones, which are usually in town centres and are indicated by pink or yellow signs 'control zone, no parking'. Do not park near pedestrian crossings.

Car rentals

Main international car rental firms are represented at the airports and can offer fly-drive deals: consult your travel agent. There are also many local firms: see the tourist board's information guide 13 or consult the Yellow Pages.

The total cost of hiring a standard family car for a week, including insurance, unlimited mileage and tax, is £140-220. A weekend rate (Fri-Mon) would be between £50-£80. Insurance and VAT may be added to the quoted price, so check what the total cost will be when you

book. Most cars have manual gearshift, so ask in advance if you need automatic transmission. If you hire a car in the Irish Republic, you will find it cheaper to do a round trip and return the vehicle to the pick-up point.

If you break down

If the car is rented, contact the hire company. If you are a member of the Automobile Association, the Royal Automobile Club, or an affiliated organisation, you can use their 24-hour breakdown services. There are also plenty of commercial breakdown services to call on - unless a friendly Ulster driver stops to help you first.

Petrol (gas)

Prices fluctuate. At the time of going to press the approximate cost of unleaded petrol per litre was 51p and leaded fuel 56p.

Rail

There are three main rail routes from Belfast Central Station ☎ (0232) 230310 - north to Londonderry city via Ballymena and Coleraine, east to Bangor, and south to Dublin via Lisburn, Portadown and Newry. The Larne boat train (for Scotland) leaves from Yorkgate Station, Belfast (0232) 235282.

Bus

Northern Ireland has an excellent bus network with regular services to towns not served by a rail link. Ulsterbus operates express buses from Belfast to Ulster's main towns and an express coach service to Dublin four times daily (three times on Sunday) ☎ (0232) 333000.

Index to towns and villages

Index to towns and villages

Index to towns and villages

Index to towns and villages

Index to towns and villages

Distances between towns

	BELFAST	DUBLIN	ARMAGH	CORK	ENNISKILLEN	LARNE	L'DERRY	NEWCASTLE	NEWRY	OMAGH	PORTRUSH	ROSSLARE	SHANNON	SLIGO
BELFAST	BELFAST	165	65	405	133	37	117	49	61	109	98	323	338	200
DUBLIN	103	DUBLIN	128	253	173	202	230	138	106	176	256	157	211	213
ARMAGH	40	80	ARMAGH	374	83	102	112	64	29	58	106	288	301	149
CORK	262	158	234	CORK	342	454	440	390	358	386	470	205	123	333
ENNISKILLEN	83	108	52	214	ENNISKILLEN	170	98	147	112	43	155	330	269	67
LARNE	23	126	64	284	106	LARNE	115	86	98	117	86	360	374	237
L'DERRY	73	144	70	275	61	72	L'DERRY	158	141	54	62	387	354	134
NEWCASTLE	31	86	40	244	92	54	99	NEWCASTLE	43	125	147	306	330	178
NEWRY	38	66	18	224	70	61	88	27	NEWRY	86	158	261	285	109
OMAGH	68	110	36	241	27	73	34	78	54	OMAGH	112	341	325	192
PORTRUSH	61	160	66	294	97	54	39	92	99	70	PORTRUSH	413	389	317
ROSSLARE	202	98	180	128	206	225	242	191	163	213	258	ROSSLARE	224	218
SHANNON	211	132	188	77	168	234	221	206	178	203	243	140	SHANNON	218
SLIGO	125	133	93	208	42	148	84	133	111	68	120	198	136	SLIGO

KILOMETRES (upper-right of diagonal) — MILES (lower-left of diagonal)

Reminder

This book is intended only as a convenient reference guide to accommodation in the province. Care has been taken to ensure the information is correct at the time of going to press, but the Northern Ireland Tourist Board does not accept responsibility for errors or omissions. While every effort is made to visit regularly each establishment listed, except camping/caravan parks, changes will inevitably occur after this book goes to press. In addition, before confirming your booking you should make your own enquiries.